CONCEPTUAL FOUNDATIONS OF ANTITRUST

This is a philosophical study of concepts that lie at the foundation of antitrust – a body of law and policy designed to promote or protect economic competition. Topics covered are: the nature of competition; the relation between competition and welfare; the distinction between per se rules and rules of reason; agreements; concerted practices; and the spectrum from independent action to collusion. Although there are many legal and economic books on antitrust, this is the only book devoted to the philosophical scrutiny of the concepts that underpin it. No prior knowledge of philosophy is presupposed. The book is primarily directed at students, theorists and practitioners of antitrust, but will also interest lawyers, economists, philosophers, political scientists and others who have no special concern with the discipline.

OLIVER BLACK is Senior Visiting Research Fellow in Law and Philosophy at King's College London and is a practising solicitor, working as a consultant in antitrust and regulatory law at international law firm Linklaters. He has been at King's since 2000 and at Linklaters since 1989. He read philosophy at Cambridge and received his PhD from the University of London. He has taught at Cambridge and been a fellow at the University of California, Berkeley. He has published articles on a variety of topics in philosophy and law and has also published a novel.

CONCEPTUAL FOUNDATIONS OF ANTITRUST

OLIVER BLACK

CAMBRIDGE
UNIVERSITY PRESS

CAMBRIDGE UNIVERSITY PRESS
Cambridge, New York, Melbourne, Madrid, Cape Town, Singapore,
São Paulo, Delhi, Dubai, Tokyo

Cambridge University Press
The Edinburgh Building, Cambridge CB2 8RU, UK

Published in the United States of America by Cambridge University Press, New York

www.cambridge.org
Information on this title: www.cambridge.org/9780521142076

First published 2005
This digitally printed version 2010

A catalogue record for this publication is available from the British Library

Library of Congress Cataloguing in Publication data
Black, Oliver, 1957–
Conceptual foundations of antitrust / Oliver Black.
p. cm.
Includes bibliographical references and index.
ISBN 0-521-84795-8
1. Antitrust law – England. 2. Antitrust law – Philosophy. I. Title.
KD2218.B53 2005
343.42′0721 – dc22 2005045726

ISBN 978-0-521-84795-7 Hardback
ISBN 978-0-521-14207-6 Paperback

CONTENTS

PREFACE

That slim and dispiriting publication *Jobs for Philosophers* made particularly brief and dismal reading in 1987, when I got my philosophy doctorate. The ratio of available posts in university philosophy departments to the people applying for them was said to be about one to 300. Assuming therefore that, even if I found such a post, it would be temporary and in the sticks, I proposed to myself a choice of non-academic jobs: an easy one that would leave me the time and energy to pursue philosophy in my free time or a challenging one that would absorb the energy I would otherwise have spent on philosophy. Partly because challenging jobs tend to be better paid, I chose the latter. As philosophers often do, I picked the law, and I now practise antitrust law and regulatory law. (A colleague tried to persuade me to go into tax law on the ground that it is 'metaphysics with fees'.) The work is often challenging, but the philosophical itch persisted, so I have come to divide my time between law and philosophy. This book, a philosophical study of antitrust, thus connects my two halves.

The book is a mixture of new work and a reworking and expansion of earlier material: ancestors of the text are cited in the bibliography at the end. I am grateful to the friends and colleagues who have helped me form my thoughts: particular thanks go to David Papineau and Richard Whish (both at King's College London); to Bill Allan, David Bailey, Juliet Lazarus, Melat Negash, Carole Thomas and the late Dan Goyder (all now or formerly at Linklaters); and to Simon Evnine, Edmund Fawcett, Donald Franklin, Michael Grenfell, Donald Peterson and Jo Wolff.

I always groan when an author thanks his wife, children, dogs and goldfish for lovingly tolerating his reclusion. But I can't resist thanking Jenny, because she is such a new wife. There are no children or pets to thank.

INTRODUCTION

Antitrust is a body of law and policy designed to promote, or at least to protect, economic competition. There are many legal books and many economic books on the subject, but so far as I know there is no other book devoted to the philosophical scrutiny of the concepts that underpin it. The idea of a philosophy of antitrust may seem abstruse, but there is nothing puzzling about it. Philosophy may be conceived as a set of meta-studies associated with first-order disciplines: for psychology there is philosophy of mind, for mathematics there is philosophy of mathematics, for moral thinking there is philosophical ethics, and so on. (This is not to say that the boundary between a discipline and its philosophy is, or should be, sharp; for example, some of the most interesting work in ethics in recent decades has been by philosophers who have engaged with practical moral issues.) For law there is philosophy of law, and different parts of the law are associated with different branches of its philosophy: one such branch is the philosophy of antitrust.

The concepts studied in this book lie at the foundation of antitrust, but they are not peculiar to antitrust. Those of competition, agreement and joint action, for example, arise in various areas of theory and practice. I hope therefore that the book will interest people – economists, philosophers, political scientists and others – who have no special concern with antitrust. As to those who do have such a concern, the book is directed not only at academic readers but also at practitioners, in government, law firms, economic consultancies and elsewhere, who seek a deeper understanding of their discipline. Although the book's primary aim is theoretical, it may also be useful in practice: specifically, the models it proposes give guidance as to when a crucial concept can and cannot properly be applied. If, say, a situation diverges widely from the models of a concerted practice given in chapter 5, that is reason to think that it is not a concerted practice and to act accordingly.

Given the breadth of the intended readership, a word is in order about the style of presentation. I write in a manner that comes naturally to those trained in analytic philosophy: there are numbered propositions, attention is paid to their logical relations, and various schematic abbreviations are used, the most common being 'X', 'Y' . . . for people, firms or groups; 'Ax', 'Ay' . . . for their respective actions; 'Gx', 'Gy' . . . for their respective goals; and 'P', 'Q' . . . for sentences and propositions. The manner is not a mannerism: the alternative would be unbearable longwindedness, as if a book of mathematics were written exclusively in prose. But this book contains no mathematics and no one should be frightened by its symbols. Nor does it presuppose any knowledge of philosophy: on the few occasions when I use a philosophical term of art, I explain its meaning. If you find some passages too dense, you can skip them without losing your bearings, as each chapter starts with an extensive overview of the argument.

Here is a brief overview of the book. The concepts discussed appear, with variations, in all systems of antitrust, but because I practise English and European law I refer most frequently to legislation and cases in those jurisdictions (chapter 3 is the exception). The book can, in fact, be viewed as a meditation on Article 81 of the Treaty of Rome (hereafter 'Article 81 EC'), paragraph 1 of which says:

> The following shall be prohibited as incompatible with the common market: all agreements between undertakings, decisions by associations of undertakings and concerted practices which may have as their object or effect the prevention, restriction or distortion of competition within the common market . . .

Thus chapters 1 and 2 concern competition; chapter 3 concerns its prevention, restriction or distortion; chapter 4 concerns agreements; chapter 5, concerted practices; and chapter 6, various forms of conduct that approximate more or less closely to a concerted practice.

Chapter 1 answers a question which theorists and practitioners of antitrust should consider more often: What is competition? The answer takes the form of a model of competition, the central idea being that X and Y compete where X achieves X's goal only if Y does not achieve Y's. The model allows a distinction to be drawn between competition and rivalry. I show how the model applies to economic competition and then use it to illuminate the relation between competition and two forms of cooperation: joint action and agreement. The discussion reveals some truth and some falsity in the claim that competition and cooperation are inherently opposed.

From competition's nature I move to its justification. The current orthodoxy is that competition is desirable because it maximises welfare.

Chapter 2, which differs from the other chapters in having a purely negative purpose, attacks the orthodox view. The argument is that 'welfare' has either a meaning in which welfare is valuable but competition does not maximise welfare, or a meaning in which competition does maximise welfare but the fact that it does so is no *justification* for competition, because welfare in this sense is not worth maximising.

Antitrust is hostile to restrictions on competition, but to be workable it must be selective in the restrictions it prohibits. In the United States, principles of selection are embodied in the doctrine of per se rules and rules of reason. There is a debate whether antitrust in the European Community does, or should, have a similar doctrine, and in the US itself there is a debate as to the proper scope of per se rules and rules of reason. Chapter 3 aims to clarify these debates by analysing the two kinds of rule and identifying the relations between them.

The rest of the book is concerned with various forms of bilateral conduct. Chapter 4 presents two models of agreement which develop the idea that an agreement exists where one party gives a conditional undertaking and the other responds with an unconditional undertaking. The models accommodate plausible justifications for making and complying with agreements. I then examine the distinction drawn in Article 81 between the object and the effect of an agreement, assessing different views of this distinction by comparing them with what I call the Intuitive View: this is that the object limb of Article 81 catches agreements which the effect limb does not catch (and vice versa) but that, often at least, object is evidence for effect (but not vice versa). The final part of the chapter discusses the concept of a dishonest agreement, introduced into UK antitrust by the Enterprise Act's 'cartel offence'. The account of dishonesty in the leading case, *Ghosh*, falls to objections of circularity. I conclude that the concept of dishonesty would be best deleted from the cartel offence.

To be effective, antitrust must apply not only to formal contracts but also to looser understandings: that is why Article 81 mentions not only agreements but also concerted practices. Chapter 5 presents two models of a concerted practice, one applying ideas from the philosophy of language, the other based on the concept of reliance, which is modelled in turn. The claim is that reliance is the core, and concerted practices are instances, of joint action. I show that joint action and agreement are distinct phenomena and hence that it is misleading to conceive of concerted practices as a pale kind of agreement. The two models converge in two respects: both imply that concerted practices involve communication between the parties and neither implies that they involve obligations. In the first respect the models are consistent, and in the latter inconsistent, with legal authority, but I maintain that the authority for the thesis about obligation is confused and misleading. The argument that concerted practices on the second model do not involve obligations is based on the proposition that there is no interesting relation of conditionality connecting reliance and moral obligation. This proposition, which is important to many areas of law, is defended in the appendix to the chapter.

Antitrust must deal with a spectrum of situations running from independent action to collusion. Different types of intervention are appropriate to different points on the spectrum. In the middle are cases that create the 'oligopoly problem' – the fact that oligopolists may display parallel behaviour that is anticompetitive but results from individual decisions by the parties. One question is whether the types of intervention, such as application of Article 81, that are fitted to the collusive end of the spectrum can be extended to such cases. To reach a principled answer, an understanding is needed of the spectrum itself. Chapter 6 models the spectrum in a way that shows where various kinds of conduct fall on it and how they are related to each other. The results are applied to introduce some terminological order and to illuminate the oligopoly problem and the related concept of 'coordinated effects' as that concept is used in the European Commission's Guidelines on horizontal mergers.

It is obvious from this summary that the book does not purport to cover all the important concepts that underpin antitrust: I have selected those that interest me most. Some readers may regret the lack of attention given to unilateral conduct: the methods of dealing with such conduct are currently much discussed, as theorists and practitioners try to reconcile the complexities of economic reality with the often crude jurisprudence. (The recent judgments of the Court of First Instance in the *British Airways* and *Michelin II* cases show how much the Court has to learn about the economics of incentive arrangements.) But, although the antitrust of unilateral conduct is interesting, its interest does not strike me as distinctly philosophical: hence its omission from this book.

It is worth making some methodological remarks about the various models that are presented. These models – of competition, agreements, concerted practices and so forth – are intended only to represent central cases of central concepts: for example there may be other concepts of competition (and the boundaries between them may be hard to draw). Moreover, for any given concept, a model of this kind need not purport to specify necessary and sufficient conditions for every application of the concept; accordingly it should not be rejected merely if a case can be found that either does not fit certain clauses of the model or has certain features, relevant to the concept's application, that the model fails to capture. It is debatable whether illuminating necessary and sufficient conditions can be given for any concept, but the aspiration to specify them is quixotic in the case of concepts, such as the ones at issue here, which have been described and applied in obscure, confused and arguably contradictory ways. For such concepts a model may be treated as prescriptive, regimenting our intuitive judgments. Nevertheless it is a virtue of a model that it should fit those judgments, and it must be rejected if it diverges from them too often or too widely. The aim should be, in Rawls's phrase, a reflective equilibrium of intuition and theory.

1

What is competition?

Overview

It is a scandal of antitrust that neither its practitioners nor its theorists agree – in so far as they consider the question at all – on what competition is. Opportunistically, insouciantly or ignorantly, we still lurch among the five definitions that Bork identified decades ago: the process of rivalry; the absence of restraint over one firm's economic activities by another firm; the state of the market in which the individual buyer or seller does not influence the price by his purchases or sales; the existence of fragmented industries and markets; and – Bork's preferred definition – a state of affairs in which consumer welfare cannot be increased by moving to an alternative state of affairs through judicial decree.[1] One response is to say that the plurality of definitions does not matter, because actions promoting or protecting one kind of competition promote or protect all the others. But there is no reason to believe that that is so. Another response is to say that we need different definitions in different contexts – say, cartels and mergers. But that by itself is unsatisfactory, for it fails to identify significant connections between the definitions. We must hope that there are such connections; otherwise antitrust is as incoherent as would be a body of law and policy that concerned banks and covered both financial banks and river banks.

The first of Bork's definitions differs from the others in that, broadly, it describes a form of behaviour whereas they describe economic structures. In this respect the first definition captures one of antitrust's concerns: although, as a result of Bork's work and that of other members of the Chicago school, it is now widely accepted that the main aim of antitrust should be to maximise welfare,[2] it is also believed that this aim is to

[1] Bork (1978), 58 ff. 'Competition' is used in the sense of 'rivalry' in Bork (1966), 377, fn. 5. The variety of meanings of 'competition' in the economic context is also discussed in Bishop and Walker (2002), ch. 2.

[2] Other aims that have been pursued in the name of antitrust are reviewed in chapter 3.

be achieved, at least in part, by encouraging competitive behaviour.[3] Means and end, thus described, are taken not to be trivially connected by definition: 'competitive behaviour' is understood not to mean whatever behaviour conduces to welfare,[4] but to identify a type of behaviour that can be identified otherwise than by its effect on welfare. An illustration of this approach is the UK Office of Fair Trading's introduction to the 'substantial lessening of competition' test under the Enterprise Act 2002:

> The OFT views competition as a process of rivalry between firms seeking to win customers' business. This process of rivalry, where it is effective, impels firms to deliver benefits to customers in terms of prices, quality and choice.[5]

The purpose of this chapter is to identify the behaviour in question. I propose a model of competition, in the sense of competitive behaviour, which applies both to economic and to other kinds of competition. The central idea is that X and Y compete where X achieves X's goal only if Y does not achieve Y's. The model shows that distinctions are blurred by identifying competition with rivalry, as Bork and the OFT do. After setting out the model and comparing it with another account, I consider factors that other authors have associated with competition, and for each factor I show that the model already incorporates it or can be expanded, or does not need, to incorporate it. The factors are simultaneity; scarcity; chance, uncertainty, or lack of knowledge, as to the outcome; a distinction between 'title' and 'possession', or between 'prize' and 'jungle', competition; a distinction between those goals that are constitutive of and those that are

[3] In Fielding's terms, welfare is a social ideal (possibly only an intermediate one) and competitive behaviour a procedural device: Fielding (1976), 137. See also Simmel (1955), 72, on competition as a technique, and Prvulovich (1982), 81, on competition as a device for distribution and selection. Fielding distinguishes competition as a procedural device from the act of competing: the former might be conceived as consisting of widespread cases of the latter. Compare Wolff (unpublished), where it is argued that the only plausible justification for the harm caused by competitive behaviour in the economic sphere is consequentialist in form and that this poses a problem for those who defend competition from a standpoint of deontological libertarianism. Wolff's consequentialist approach echoes Simmel's: Simmel (1955), 79.

[4] But Bork (1978) appears to understand it to mean this. Bishop and Walker use effect on welfare as a 'benchmark', but not as a 'formal definition', of *effective* competition: Bishop and Walker (2002), para. 2.51. 'Whether a market is characterised by effective competition or not . . . depends on the outcomes it produces': para. 2.10.

[5] Office of Fair Trading (2003b), 15. A similar view of competition as a form of behaviour is expressed in Competition Commission (2003a), para. 1.20, (2003b), para. 1.16. Feltkamp (2003) takes the same approach in relation to the EC state aid rules.

external to the competitive situation (I argue that in economic competition the goals are mainly external); the various attitudes that competitors may have; and a distinction between willing and unwilling competition. Then I show the model's suitability for the purposes of antitrust, by explaining how it applies to various forms of economic competition.

The final section discusses the relation between competition and certain forms of cooperation, namely joint action and agreement: this discussion reveals some truth and some falsity in the claim, used by certain writers to attack competition, that competition and cooperation are inherently opposed. I shall argue that, on certain conditions, competition and joint action are incompatible and that competition is compatible with making an agreement but not with complying with one. Here I touch on the justification of competition, but this chapter is primarily concerned with what competition is, not with the reasons for promoting it. Justification will be the subject of chapter 2.

The model

The Introduction's general remarks about models – in particular, that they are intended only to represent central cases of central concepts, not to specify necessary and sufficient conditions, and that they should aspire to fit our intuitive judgments – apply to the present model.[6] In the case of competition the standard of fit with intuition may justifiably be set fairly low, to accommodate the fact that the concept's application in economics has a theoretical dimension absent from its everyday uses: this is preferable to the despairing conclusion that 'competition' in economics has become a term of art that has broken away from ordinary usage (compare the point above on the connections between Bork's definitions).

For simplicity the discussion will be restricted to competition between two parties (it can be easily extended to cases where they number more than two), who may be individuals, firms or groups: X and Y compete

[6] The model is thus invulnerable to Fielding's strictures on 'essentialism': Fielding (1976), 125–8; see also K. Kim (1991), 300. Fielding might object to the model on other grounds he discusses, that it ignores the normativity, the historical dimension and the essentially contested nature of the concept of competition. The only reason he offers for the view that the concept is normative is that people have held normative beliefs about competition (133–4) – which is a non-sequitur. I do not deny that the concept has developed over time and I am agnostic as to whether it is essentially contested: these questions do not affect the utility of the model. As to the concept's historicity, McMurtry (1984), 45, notes that the etymological sense of 'competition' is 'seek together', a sense which associates competition and cooperation (see further below).

with each other *tout court* if and only if there are actions Ax and Ay by which, and goals Gx and Gy in respect of which, they compete with each other. This formulation accommodates the obvious point that they may compete with each other in some respects but not others. The actions and the goals are connected in that, standardly, each person performs his action with the intention of achieving his goal.[7] 'Action' should be read broadly, to cover courses of conduct and other forms of *durée* that may or may not be readily parcelled into discrete actions.[8] 'Goal' also has a broad sense, in which the achievement of an action's goal need not be distinct from, and specifically need not be an effect of, the action itself: for example, I give you a present with the goal of showing my affection for you. In such cases I achieve the goal *in* performing the action; I achieve it *by* performing the action where the action causes the achievement of the goal. Goals and intentions are distinct from results[9] and motives:[10] from the motive of hatred, I reprimand you with the intention of achieving the goal of humiliating you, which I fail to achieve. In some cases it is unclear what the agent's intention and goal are: the obvious course is to ask him, but he may be unable to give an articulate reply.

I shall take 'X and Y are in competition with each other' to be another way of saying that X and Y compete with each other.[11] But X and Y may be in competition without being in *a* competition:[12] the two examples to be given shortly are cases in point. Certain branches of antitrust – specifically the rules on procurement by public bodies and utilities – concern competitions, rather than just competition; but competitions are not the concern of antitrust generally, so I shall not distinguish them further. MacCallum's 'title' model of competition, discussed below, gives a fair characterisation of a competition.[13]

[7] See Harman (1986), 97. [8] See Giddens (1984), 3.

[9] Simmel (1955), 57–60, stresses the distinction between the goal and the result of competition. Compare the distinction between object and effect in Article 81 EC, discussed in chapter 4 below.

[10] Mead (2003), 16, blurs the distinction between goal and motive. On competition as a motive, see the discussion of Fielding at the end of the next section.

[11] Dearden's account, discussed later, uses the former locution where mine uses the latter: Dearden (1972), 120.

[12] Compare Kleinig (1982), 164–5, where it is said that 'to compete' can mean either 'to take part in a competition' or 'to act competitively'.

[13] The table in MacCallum (1993), 217, lists title competition's indicia. Acton's description of 'jungle' competition includes an additional feature characteristic of competitions, that the winner is determined by an awarding authority: Acton (1993), 69. See also the account in Brownson (1974), 229, of competition in schools.

The core of the model is this:

X competes with Y where there are actions Ax and Ay and goals Gx and Gy such that:
(1) X does Ax with the intention of achieving Gx;
(2) Y does Ay with the intention of achieving Gy; and
(3) X achieves Gx only if Y does not achieve Gy.[14]

(Here and elsewhere in the book I use the timeless present tense to cover a variety of temporal relations: where the timeless present is used in a clause of a model, it is to be read as allowing substitution-instances in different tenses. Here there is no implication that Ax and Ay are simultaneous – a point taken up below.)

For example X proposes to Z with the intention of making Z his wife; Y sends flowers to Z with the intention of making Z his lover; and, because Z is faithful by nature, she will be X's wife only if she will not be Y's lover. An economic example: X runs an advertising campaign with the intention of getting a 70 per cent share of a certain market; Y starts a research programme with the intention of getting 60 per cent of that market; and X will get 70 per cent only if Y will not get 60 per cent. Later I shall consider economic cases that are harder to fit to the model.

Different relations between X's achieving Gx and Y's not achieving Gy will ground (3) in different cases. In the first example the relation is causal: roughly, Z's not being Y's lover is a necessary causal condition of Z's being X's wife. In the second example the relation is entailment: it is arithmetically impossible for market shares to sum to more than 100 per cent. 'Only if' in (3) has a sense stronger than in elementary logic, for in the latter sense (3) makes the uninterestingly weak claim that either X does not achieve Gx or Y does not achieve Gy. Below I shall assume that 'Q if P', and equivalently 'P only if Q', entails 'It is not possible that both P and not-Q'; beyond that I shall rely on an intuitive understanding of conditionality. If (3) is true, so is its converse: Y achieves Gy only if X does not achieve Gx. Competition is thus symmetric.[15] One variant of

[14] (3) expresses the 'mutually exclusive goal attainment' by which Kohn defines what he calls 'structural' competition: Kohn (1992), 4. Compare Berkowitz (1962), 178; Deutsch (1973), 20; May and Doob (1937), 6. Kohn later, and seemingly by a slip, substitutes 'if' for 'only if', describing a competitive situation as one in which 'I succeed if you fail, and vice versa' (136). In a situation of this kind one or other party must succeed; that is not true of competition in general. Compare the discussion below of variants of (3).

[15] To say that a relation is symmetric is to say that, if A bears it to B, B bears it to A. In ecology one organism is said to compete with another where the first limits the second's resources:

(3) replaces 'only if' by 'if and only if': the model then describes a form of competition in which either X or Y succeeds. Another restricts (3) to say that X achieves Gx, *in or by doing Ax*, only if Y does not achieve Gy in or by doing Ay: this incorporates a feature of certain forms of competition governed by rules, Ax and Ay being actions that the rules permit. These variants limit the model to subclasses of competitive situations. A variant that, at the price of vagueness, extends the model's scope substitutes something weaker for 'only if': thus (3) could be revised to say that Y's achieving Gy makes it hard or harder – possibly in specified respects – for X to achieve Gx. On this version competition is not symmetric, unless it is added that X's achieving Gx also makes it hard or harder for Y to achieve Gy.

It is plausible to hold that, at least in many cases of competition, the parties have the same goal:[16] in the first example, although X wants Z to be his wife, and Y wants her to be his lover, each wants her to be his sexual partner; and, in the second, although X wants 70 per cent of the market and Y wants 60 per cent, each wants a majority share of the market. This thought motivates the addition of another clause to the model:

(4) Gx = Gy.

But it is often uncertain whether the parties' goals are the same. Apart from the fact, already noted, that people may be inarticulate as to their goals, the criteria for identifying and individuating goals can be unclear. The fact that each party may have several goals causes no difficulty: if X and Y compete, in the sense of (1)–(3), in respect of various goals, only some of which they share, they meet (4) in the case just of the shared goals. But, even if each party competes in respect of only one goal, it can be hard to tell whether their goals are the same. Suppose that Z requires 100 widgets, that X's goal is to supply Z with 80 per cent of his requirement and that Y's goal is to supply Z with 80 widgets: 80 per cent of the requirement

Cooper (1993), 361. Competition in this sense is non-symmetric: it may be that X limits Y's resources but Y does not limit X's. The sense is an extended and technical one which my model does not purport to capture: ecological competition can exist among inanimate things and thus need not involve actions, intentions or goals. Compare the statement in Ong (1981), 43, that 'competition' suggests interaction between conscious beings. On other logical properties of competition – specifically the questions of transitivity and irreflexivity – see below.

[16] Michelman (1983), 82, says that in the economic context 'competitors seek the same orders, the same resources, the same employees'. Simmel (1955), 57, speaks of competition as consisting of parallel efforts by the parties 'concerning the same prize'.

equals 80 widgets, so do X and Y have the same goal? The question can be important in antitrust, for the authorities are more likely to prohibit an agreement to supply a certain proportion of a party's requirement than to prohibit one to supply a specified volume:[17] the reason – not a strong one – is that the former is exclusionary on its face whereas the latter is only contingently so.

The answer to the question is no. If the goals are the same, then, if X has the goal of supplying 80 per cent, he has the goal of supplying 80 widgets. In that case – assuming, as mentioned, that 'Q if P' entails 'It is not possible that both P and not-Q' – it cannot be that he has the first goal but not the second. But this statement of impossibility is false, so the goals are not the same. It is false because 'X has the goal of . . .', and similar phrases such as 'X's goal is to . . .', are intensional contexts. What that means is this: suppose that the dots are filled in to make a complete sentence and that among the added words is an expression with a certain denotation: substitution of another expression with the same denotation may change the truth-value of the sentence. The phrases '80 per cent of Z's requirement for widgets' and '80 widgets' do not mean the same but they have the same denotation,[18] so substitution of the latter for the former in 'X has the goal of supplying 80 per cent of Z's requirement for widgets' may change the sentence from true to false (assuming there are no other factors to preclude the change). Thus it is possible that X has the goal of supplying 80 per cent but does not have the goal of supplying 80 widgets. That these contexts are intensional can be seen from an analogous case: Oedipus's goal was to kill the offensive traveller, 'the offensive traveller' has the same denotation as 'Oedipus's father', but Oedipus did not have the goal of killing his own father. A weak sense of 'goal' might be admitted in which the contexts are not intensional, but that sense is not the one in the model.

Suppose now that both X and Y have the goal of supplying Z with 80 per cent of his requirement: here it appears clear that they have the same goal. But it may be objected that the appearance is due to an imprecise representation of their goals. The goals are more precisely represented by 'that'-clauses: X's is that he supplies Z with 80 per cent, Y's is that *he* supplies Z with 80 per cent. These, it may be said, are different goals as

[17] Case 85/76, *Hoffmann-La Roche & Co. AG* v. *Commission* [1979] ECR 461; [1979] 3 CMLR 211.

[18] There is a large philosophical literature on the distinction between meaning and denotation; the modern discussion starts from Frege (1952). The denotation of the two phrases in question is all sets of 80 widgets.

they relate to different people. On this approach it seems that (4) (Gx = Gy) is instantiated in no, or almost no, situation in which (1)–(3) are, in which case there is strong reason not to add (4) to the model. One possible reply is that the new representations of the goals are third-person proxies for a first-person thought that X and Y have in common,[19] 'My goal is that I supply Z with 80 per cent': of course 'I' denotes a different person in each case, but that is irrelevant to the identity of the goal. Another possible reply is that goals are the same where they concern the same type of action, even if the agents involved are different. This needs to be refined to cover cases where one person's goal is that another person performs a certain action; for example, if X's goal is that Y supplies Z with 80 per cent, and Y's goal is that X supplies Z with 80 per cent, their goals are clearly different. One response is to say that, strictly, a person's goal can only concern his own performance of an action; but that seems too restrictive.

There is no need to pursue the dialectic further, for enough has been done to show that it is often uncertain whether (4) is met. The best solution is not to build (4) into a general account of competition but to allow that in some cases the goals in respect of which the parties compete may be the same.

For all that (1)–(4) say, X and Y may each be unaware of what the other is doing or even that he exists. This is the case in some instances of competition,[20] for example, sometimes where X and Y are suppliers in a market that approaches perfect competition in the economic sense, or where they send in answers to a crossword set by a newspaper; but often – and more often in the case of rivalry, discussed below – there will be a level of mutual awareness:[21] in the earlier examples, each of the suitors may know what the other is up to and the two firms seeking market shares may be monitoring each other's behaviour. For such cases the model can be supplemented by:

(5) X and Y know (1)–(3).

[19] 'He' in those representations is a 'quasi-indicator' in Castañeda's sense: Castañeda (1999), esp. chs. 1 and 2.

[20] See the remarks on 'impersonal competition' in Acton (1993), 69–72, and on competition that is not 'direct' in Caillois (2001), 17. Acton claims that the parties must know each other where competition involves rivalry. Fielding (1976), 127, distinguishes 'competition as either direct or indirect struggle'. For differing views on the relation between competition and awareness, compare Cooley (1899), 79, and Beals and Siegel (1966), 18.

[21] Scherer and Ross write of 'a clear awareness by the parties involved that the positions they seek to attain may be incompatible': Scherer and Ross (1990), 16.

Variants of (5) replace 'know' by 'justifiedly believe' – where justification might be conceived either actionally or statally (roughly, this is the distinction between a case where a person carries out a justification and a case where he merely has one available[22]) – or just 'believe'; or include iterations of these – for example, 'X knows that Y knows' – or common versions of them – for example, 'X and Y have common knowledge of (1)–(3)' (on some accounts of common knowledge, it is the special case of iteration where the iteration continues to infinity[23]); or introduce asymmetry, so that, for example, X knows more than Y does; or limit both parties' knowledge to a subclass of (1)–(3); or extend it to include (4).

Clauses (1)–(5) do not capture the concept of rivalry. Some people – Bork and the OFT among them, as has been seen – think that competition is the same as rivalry,[24] others distinguish them.[25] The essence of rivalry is that X does not merely intend to achieve Gx, he also intends to prevent Y from achieving Gy. Sometimes there is an instrumental connection between X's two goals: he intends to achieve Gx as a means of thwarting

[22] See Black (1987a), 394.

[23] On common knowledge and belief, see Aumann (1976); Bennett (1976), 127; Binmore and Brandenburger (1990); Geanakoplos (1992); Gilbert (1989), ch. 4; Heal (1978); Kemmerling (1986); D. Lewis (1969), 52–60; Loar (1981), 250; Milgrom (1981); Nielsen (1984); Parikh and Krasucki (1990); Schiffer (1972), chs. 2–3; Schiffer (1987), 245–6; H. Smith (1982); and Tuomela (1995), 41–51. The concepts of common knowledge etc. are used further in chapters 4–6 below.

[24] This view also appears in Huizinga (1949), 200; K. Kim (1991), 301, 306–8 (discussed in Houston (1991)); Kohn (1992), 5, 123, 135, 138, in relation to 'intentional' competition; Lyon *et al.* (1939), 249; Michelman (1983), 79, 84; Prvulovich (1982), 78–9; Reeve (1906), 92; and Caillois (2001), 37. Caillois says (29) that *agôn* differs from *ludus* in that the former does but the latter does not involve rivalry. Flew (1983), 271, says that competition 'essentially involves a striving by every competitor in some way to do better than all the rest of the competition': this is related to but different from the claim that it involves rivalry of any of the forms identified below.

[25] Acton (1993), 67–71; Dearden (1972), 127; Knight (1956), 92; Mead (2003), 17; and Simmel (1955), 70–1. Fielding distinguishes competition from rivalry and also object-centred from opponent-centred competition: Fielding (1976), 127. He does not explain what he has in mind, but the distinctions are presumably related, for it is plausible to say that rivalry is normally opponent-centred. It also seems that this need not be the case: in the terms of clauses (1a) and (1b), introduced below to express the concept of rivalry, X's main intention may be to achieve Gx, even though he also intends to prevent Y from achieving Gy. (This is consistent with (1b)'s claim that X intends to achieve Gx as a means of preventing Y from achieving Gy; for X may also intend to achieve Gx as an end, and this intention may dominate his intention to thwart Y.) Here it can be said that X's activity is centred on his object Gx rather than on his opponent Y. The distinction between object- and opponent-centred competition collapses in the case of (1c), for there X's only intention is to thwart Y.

Y's achievement of Gy.[26] In the example of the suitors, X may intend not only to make Z his wife but also, or thereby, to prevent Y from making Z his lover. In a third case X has no intermediate goal: his goal is simply to prevent Y from achieving Gy.[27] In an auction, for instance, X may bid not in order to buy an item but only to prevent Y from buying it. (Arguably the third case is one not of competition but of mere spoiling.) These situations are respectively captured by modifying (1) as follows:

(1a) X does Ax with the intention of achieving Gx and the intention of preventing Y from achieving Gy;
(1b) X does Ax with the intention of achieving Gx and thereby or therein preventing Y from achieving Gy;
(1c) X does Ax with the intention of preventing Y from achieving Gy;

with (3) (X achieves Gx only if Y does not achieve Gy) remaining the same. In the case of (1a) and (1b), (2) (Y does Ay with the intention of achieving Gy) is modified correspondingly, but in the case of (1c) (2) must be left as it stands, to avoid circular indeterminacy: X's goal is to prevent Y from achieving Y's goal, which is to prevent X from achieving X's goal.

Someone who identifies competition with rivalry might claim that (1a) follows from (1) and (3): if X does Ax with the intention of achieving Gx, and X achieves Gx only if Y does not achieve Gy, then X does Ax with the intention that Y does not achieve Gy – which is just another way of saying that X does Ax with the intention of preventing Y from achieving Gy. But that claim is false, for intention is not closed under the conditional, i.e. it is not the case that if (a) X intends that P and (b) if P then Q, then X intends that Q: Oedipus intends to kill the offensive traveller; if he does so, he kills his own father; but he does not intend to kill his own father.[28] Also, unless 'prevent' is used in an abnormally weak sense, the intention that Y does not achieve Gy is distinct from the intention to prevent Y from achieving Gy: I may tell you that Jack will be at the party, with the

[26] Kohn (1992), 4–5, considers the converse situation, where X must make Y fail in order for X to succeed.

[27] Compare Michelman's claim that in economic competition 'the defeat of the opposition becomes a goal in itself': Michelman (1983), 84.

[28] See Black (1995a), 357, where it is also argued that there is a broad sense of 'intention' – 'imputed' intention – that is closed not under the conditional but under the reasonably believed conditional; i.e. if (a) I intend that P, in this sense, and (b) it is reasonable to believe that if P then Q, then I intend that Q. Compare the discussion of the 'principle of the nondivisiveness of intention' in Chisholm (1976), 74. The closure properties of intention are discussed further in chapter 4, in the section on object and effect.

intention that you will not go to the party, but I need not intend to prevent you from going.

It is instructive to compare my account of competition with another one, proposed by Dearden:

> First of all, X and Y must both want [some object] O . . . The second condition is that X's gaining possession of O must exclude Y's gaining possession of it . . . Yet a third condition is that both X and Y should persist in trying to gain exclusive possession of O even when they know that one of them must be excluded.[29]

The two accounts are similar but differ in various ways. First, Dearden is more ambitious than I in that he purports to be not merely giving a model but stating a set of necessary and sufficient conditions.[30] Next, he talks of wanting something and gaining possession of it, where I talk of acting with the intention to achieve a goal. In this respect my formulation is broader, for a person can act to achieve a goal without wanting the goal – he may work for a cause in which he does not believe – and achieving the goal may not involve possessing anything, for example where the goal is to be physically fit. Senses of 'want' and 'possess' can be contrived to accommodate such examples, but those senses are uninterestingly thin or awkward. Since my formulation thus covers more than Dearden's without covering too much, it is to that extent better than his. It might be said that in one way my account is narrower than Dearden's in that the former mentions action where the latter mentions mere desire; but that is not so, for 'trying to gain' in Dearden's third clause signifies action. This is as it should be, for one cannot compete without doing something. Another respect in which Dearden's account is narrower than mine, and unnecessarily so, is in its reference to persistence: people may compete for too brief a time for that concept to apply, as where, in a game on a beach, they simultaneously each throw a stone to knock a tin over.

Dearden's third clause introduces an epistemic concept – 'even when they know' – as does my clause (5) (X and Y know (1)–(3)). The proposition which Dearden's clause contemplates the parties' knowing – that one of them must be excluded – is similar to (but, as already noted, not the same as) my clause (3) (X achieves Gx only if Y does not achieve Gy); but (5) attributes more knowledge to the parties, as it also attributes knowledge

[29] Dearden (1972), 120. For uniformity, 'X', 'Y' and 'O' have been substituted for Dearden's 'A', 'B' and 'X'.

[30] A feature that exposes him to Fielding's objection of essentialism: note 6 above.

of (1) (X does Ax with the intention of achieving Gx) and (2) (Y does Ay with the intention of achieving Gy). In this respect Dearden's clause is broader than mine. It is broader in another respect too, for unlike (5) it does not say that the parties know anything: it only says that they persist 'even when' they know something.[31] Dearden cannot object, however, as I objected to him, that my account is thus unduly restrictive; for I have already allowed that (5) is not instantiated in every case of competition, whereas Dearden's clauses purport to state necessary conditions. Dearden goes on to say, seemingly to clarify the point that his clause does not attribute knowledge that one of the parties must be excluded, that the parties 'may be in competition with each other without yet knowing it'; but in fact this is a different point, for, even if Dearden's analysis of competition were correct, there would be no implication in either direction between 'X and Y know that one of them must be excluded' and 'X and Y know that they are in competition with each other'. The first does not imply the second, because X and Y may lack the concept of competition; and the second does not imply the first, because one can know that a concept applies without knowing that a necessary, even an analytically necessary, condition for its application is met.[32]

Further aspects of competition

Dr Johnson defined competition as 'the action of endeavouring to gain what another endeavours to gain at the same time',[33] a definition followed almost verbatim by Mead and her collaborators.[34] The requirement of simultaneity limits the definition unnecessarily: two people may compete in the long-jump even if their jumps are days apart. It might be replied that the example can be squared with the requirement by distinguishing the case where the first jumper is still in the game when the second one jumps from the case where the first one has withdrawn by that time: in the former case, the first jumper is still competing with the second even though at the time he is not doing anything relevant; in the latter, he is no longer competing. This reply raises further questions. As to the former case, an account is needed of the sense in which the first jumper is still

[31] Kim adopts a categorical version of Dearden's epistemic clause: K. Kim (1991), 301.

[32] To think otherwise is to commit a version of the Socratic fallacy: see Geach (1972), 33–4.

[33] Cited in the *Oxford English Dictionary* under 'competition'.

[34] Mead (2003), 8. See also the passage quoted later from MacCallum (1993), where it is said that the competitors' strivings are 'concomitant'.

competing, that is, in the terms of Johnson's definition, 'endeavouring'. It will not do, for example, to invoke the distinction between jumping and the disposition to jump, for the first jumper need not be disposed to jump when the second one does: he may rather be disposed to comply with rules of the contest that prohibit him from having another jump. As to the latter case, it might be objected that it conflicts with the proposition – implied by the model, as shown earlier – that competition is symmetric: even if the first jumper is not competing with the second at the time, surely the second is competing with the first? To this it might be replied that the second is competing not with the first but with the first's *score*: this is a different and attenuated sense of 'compete with' in which it means something like 'strive to beat'.[35] Whether or not the example and the requirement of simultaneity can be reconciled, the model would lose flexibility if the requirement were added. Thought would also be needed as to how to formulate the requirement in the model's terms: it would not be enough to add a clause saying that X and Y respectively do Ax and Ay at the same time, for that would not encompass the example.

Other authors discuss the relation between competition and scarcity. Simmel writes:

> If there is competition for something not available or accessible to all competitors and accruing only to the winner among them, then competition, clearly, is impossible – either the members of the group do not strive after a good which is equally desirable to all of them, or they do, but the good is equally available to all.[36]

The last words of this obscure passage appear to indicate that competition can only be for something scarce.[37] Acton wavers on the issue: at one point he says that all competition presupposes either scarcity or a belief in scarcity, but earlier he says that what he calls 'jungle' competition can exist where there is enough for all.[38] It is unclear what he has in mind: it

[35] This is, or is similar to, McMurtry's 'inclusive' sense of competition: McMurtry (1984), 45.

[36] Simmel (1955), 67–8.

[37] This reading is reinforced by Simmel's claim, on the following page, that in a religious community there is no competition 'because the attainment of the goal by one member does not exclude the others'.

[38] Acton (1993), 69–71. Competition and scarcity are also explicitly connected in Brownson (1974), 229; Flew (1983), 270; K. Kim (1991), 301, 308; Kohn (1992), 4; and Rich (1988), 185. On MacCallum's 'possession' model (see below), scarcity is a cause of competition: MacCallum (1993), 215–16.

may be a distinction between classes and either subclasses or individuals: for example, two lions may compete for the same zebra even if there are enough zebras for both. The requirement of scarcity is a case of (3): if X and Y compete for food and there is not enough for both, X achieves his goal only if Y does not achieve his. According to the model, the lions compete in respect of the goal of getting the particular zebra, but not the goal of getting some zebra or other.

The next question is how competition relates to uncertainty. The passage from Simmel can be interpreted – particularly in the light of the words 'accruing only to the winner' – to mean that, for competition to exist, the outcome cannot be a foregone conclusion. In similar vein Hayek, following von Wiese, says that competition is a procedure of discovery:

> [C]ompetition is a sensible procedure to employ only if we do not know beforehand who will do best . . . No theory can do justice to it which starts from the assumption that the facts to be discovered are already known.[39]

Others talk in terms of chance: Caillois says that competition and chance are 'parallel and complementary' and that there is a 'basic compatibility' between them,[40] while MacCallum distinguishes the roles of chance in different cases of competition: sometimes – as in a game – it heightens interest or is needed to settle the initial order or position of play, sometimes its role is open.[41] Various concepts are at issue here: chance, uncertainty and lack of knowledge are related but distinct, as are objective and subjective concepts of chance and uncertainty, and uncertainty can be assessed against various standards. In any event, the model imposes no requirement of uncertainty, and this seems right: it may be certain which tennis-player is going to win the match, but the players compete with each other for all that. In those circumstances one might say 'It's not a proper competition', and a sense of 'competition' can be admitted in which this is true; the thought behind the statement motivates the imposition of handicaps in some sports. But such cases are an inadequate ground for building a clause about uncertainty into a general model of competition.

It might be objected that, if one of the players is certain that he will lose, he cannot intend to win: in that case either he does not compete or the model does not apply, since by clause (1) or (2), and the assumption that Gx and Gy are respectively X's and Y's goals of winning, he does have that intention. The objection rests on a general thesis as to the incompatibility

[39] Hayek (1982), vol. 3, 67–8.

[40] Caillois (2001), 74. See also ch. 8.

[41] MacCallum (1993), 217.

of intention and certainty of failure:[42] I believe, but shall not argue, that the thesis artificially constrains the concept of intention. If the thesis can be sustained, the intuition that the player competes can be rejected. There will be no need to add to the model a clause on uncertainty, for if the thesis is true such a clause is already implicit in each of (1) and (2): if X does Ax with the intention of achieving Gx, it follows, by the thesis, that X is not certain that he will not achieve Gx.

MacCallum associates the different roles of chance respectively with a 'title' model and a 'possession' model of competition:

> The title model attaches to competition the notions of entitlement or merit, and award. It emphasises connections between competition and rules, and it encourages us to see competitions as tests or trials of superiority in some respect or other . . . On [the possession model], competition results from scarcities in what is needed or desired, and consists in the (at least roughly) concomitant strivings of two or more creatures for all or some portion of what is scarce.[43]

The former applies to many games, the latter to struggles for survival and to economic competition. A similar, but not identical, distinction is drawn by Acton, who contrasts 'prize' competition with his 'jungle' competition.[44] Clauses (1)–(3) of my model capture most of possession competition: as already noted, the condition of scarcity is a case of (3). They do not incorporate the point that the competitors' strivings are concomitant: this has already been discussed under the heading of simultaneity. In title competition, the superiority at issue will normally be that of one competitor to another: this form of competition is thus akin to rivalry. Its main distinguishing features can be built into the model by rewriting (1) as:

(1d) X does Ax with the intention of achieving Gx and thereby or therein demonstrating his merit in certain respects or his superiority (typically to Y) in those respects;

[42] A parallel thesis asserts the incompatibility of intention and chance: if X's doing Ax merely gives X a chance of achieving Gx, X cannot do Ax with the intention of achieving Gx. On that view some versions of the earlier example of the newspaper crossword do not fit the model, as where the winner is selected by drawing a name from a hat containing the names of those people who sent in correct entries.

[43] MacCallum (1993), 214–15.

[44] Note 38 above. See also Caillois (2001), 15, where *agôn* is described in a way that assimilates it to MacCallum's title model. Ong's view of competition is closer to the possession model: 'it involves acquisition of something in addition to mere victory, generally of something more or less tangible': Ong (1981), 43.

and correspondingly for (2). Further wording can be added to capture MacCallum's point that the competition between X and Y is governed by rules.[45]

A related distinction is that between the case where Gx and Gy are constitutive of and the case where they are external to the competitive situation.[46] The model captures both cases, but could be elaborated to distinguish them. The distinction is hard to analyse, but clear enough from examples. Typically, constitutive goals exist where X and Y act within a framework of constitutive rules, such as a board game: the rules of chess are constitutive of the game in the sense that, if a player breaks them too radically or too often, he is not playing chess. Similarly the goal of checkmating one's opponent is constitutive of the game: leaving aside degenerate cases, such as that of the adult who lets a child win, you are not playing chess if you do not act with that goal.[47] But a person may also play chess with the goal of winning a prize: that goal is external to the game.[48]

In economic competition generally, the rules – and specifically the antitrust laws – that govern the parties' actions are regulative rather than constitutive and the parties' goals are for the most part external to the competitive situation: to take an earlier example, the firm running the

[45] The role of rules in competitive situations is emphasised in Brownson (1974), 229; Caillois (2001), 75; Combs (1979), 19; Kohn (1992), 94; and Lentz and Cornelius (1950). Rich (1988), 185–6, argues that rules are needed to prevent competition from degenerating into conflict. (On the relation between competition and conflict, see note 63 below.) See also Fielding (1976), 126–7, on the related question how competition is connected to regulation.

[46] Compare Flew, who holds that competition may serve as a means of allocating scarce goods that are internal to the competition itself: Flew (1983), 270. Dearden (1972), 128, makes a related but distinct point, that competition itself, rather than certain goals, is intrinsic to certain games. 'Internal to' and 'intrinsic to' seem to mean much the same as 'constitutive of'. See also Wilson (1989), 28.

[47] On constitutive rules, see Searle (1967), 111–12, and compare Rawls (1967), 157–67. On constitutive goals, see Dummett (1978), 2.

[48] See Brownson (1974), 238, and Kohn (1992), 59–61, 206, on extrinsic rewards of competition. (Kohn also describes competition itself as an extrinsic motivator: this perhaps is shorthand.) McMurtry uses a similar idea to reconcile contradictory views about the vices and virtues of competition: McMurtry (1991). He says that in the dominant form of competition (which includes economic competition), but not in the 'submerged, spontaneous' form, payoffs extrinsic to the activity itself are conferred on one party at the expense of others. He argues that the vices – violence, cheating, etc. – are a law-like consequence of the dominant form, but not of competition as such. (For a contrasting view, see Kohn (1992), ch. 7.) McMurtry's distinction is not identical to mine, for payoffs are not the same as goals. For different accounts of the differences between good and bad forms of competition, see Meakin (1986); Nove (1983), 41–2, 181, 203–5; Prvulovich (1982); and Rich (1988), 186–7.

advertising campaign could still be competing with the firm conducting the research programme even if the former did not have the goal of getting a 70 per cent market share and the latter the goal of getting 60 per cent. (Certain very general goals are arguably constitutive of economic competition, such as the goal of improving or sustaining one's economic position.) This is compatible with the distinct point that there is a sense in which firms themselves may have constitutive goals and compete in respect of them: for example the goal of producing widgets of the highest quality and best value may be included in the memoranda of association or mission statements of X and Y.

That a goal is constitutive of a competitive situation does not imply that the person whose goal it is, or any other person, regards it as the most important goal in that situation. Wilson puts the point in terms of a distinction between form and spirit:

> A formally competitive game like tennis may be seen, by the players as well as spectators, as a work of art mutually generated by competitors who are primarily concerned to produce a good game, and concerned with winning only as a means to producing it.[49]

Kew distinguishes three attitudes that competitors in sport may have: the 'Lombardian' attitude treats winning, whereas the 'radical' attitude treats playing well, as the paramount goal, and the 'counter-culture' attitude is primarily concerned with what the individual gains – fun or self-realisation – by taking part.[50] Economic competition is normally Lombardian, but the other attitudes may play a minor role: for example, there is authority in EC law for the principle that a dominant firm has a 'special responsibility not to allow its conduct to impair undistorted competition on the common market':[51] where a firm willingly complies with that principle, or with other laws of fair trading, it may be said to have the goal of playing well. The model as it stands is insensitive to these distinctions, which gives it the advantage of generality. They are akin to the distinction between rivalrous and non-rivalrous competition and could be

[49] Wilson (1989), 28. Compare Dearden (1972), 128.

[50] Kew (1978), 103–8. As to self-realisation, compare the suggestion considered by Dearden, that through competition 'we come to know ourselves better and so form a truer self-concept': Dearden (1972), 130. See also Caillois (2001), 13, on the spectrum from *paidia* to *ludus*, and Brownson (1974), 228, on competition as essential to fulfilment. For a denial that competition is either enjoyable or character-building, see Kohn (1992), chs. 4–5.

[51] Case 322/81, *Michelin* v. *Commission* [1983] ECR 3461; [1985] 1 CMLR 282, para. 57.

incorporated in the model by revisions of (1) and (2) similar to those introduced above to express the concept of rivalry.

Fielding mentions a distinction between voluntary and involuntary competition.[52] 'Involuntary' is an unhappy word, for it suggests reflex jerks rather than intentional actions: the distinction is better expressed as one between willing and unwilling competition. It could most simply be incorporated in the model by adding 'willingly' or 'unwillingly' to (1) and/or (2), but this would not capture the distinctive feature of cases in which (say) X is willing to do the action in question but unwilling to do it in competition. That feature can be included by drawing on the epistemic clause (5) (X and Y know (1)–(3)):

(1e) X does Ax with the intention of achieving Gx, but, in the light of his knowledge that (3) (X achieves Gx only if Y does not achieve Gy), he does so unwillingly.

Fielding's own view appears to be that unwilling competition is not competition properly speaking.[53] He writes:

> [O]ne cannot compete outside a competitive situation, nor can one compete in a competition without a competitive motive. This rules out the notion of competing against one's will; it is, however, possible to take part in a competition without a competitive motive, e.g. we may not wish to take part or to win, or we may not even be aware that there is a competition going on.[54]

Fielding thus infers that unwilling competition is impossible from the claim that one can only compete – at any rate in a competition – with a competitive motive.[55] The inference, which presupposes a fairly tight connection between motive and will, is questionable, but I shall not pursue

[52] Fielding (1976), 127. Compare the distinction between deliberate and involuntary competition in J. Harvey *et al.* (1917), 23.

[53] Compare Flew, who states that 'if someone takes part in some sort of race without trying to win we protest – truly – that he is not, or is not really, competing in that race': Flew (1983), 271. This is a different point, for a person who races unwillingly could still try to win.

[54] Fielding (1976), 139.

[55] Fielding (1976), 138–9, suggests that one's description of the competitive motive will depend on one's account of competition as a process: 'For the individualist a description of the competitive motive might be in terms of striving against others to establish one's meritorious rivalry; for the socialist it might be in terms of the selfish desire to excel at the expense of others, whilst a "neutral" description might merely be in terms of the desire to win.'

that issue. My model does not entail the claim from which the inference is made (or its contrary), which is an advantage, as the claim is implausible: it can surely be said that the schoolboy who, in Fielding's example,[56] reluctantly runs in a cross-country race is not only participating in a competition but also competing.[57] A sense of 'compete' can be allowed that makes the claim true by definition, but that sense is too narrow for use in a general account of competition.

Economic competition

The example of the two firms seeking market shares that sum to more than 100 per cent fits the model particularly easily: the model's application to certain other cases of economic competition needs more explanation. Suppose that X and Y compete in the same relatively atomistic market; for example, they are fruit sellers in a street market. What are their actions and goals for the purposes of the model? We can distinguish (a) the activities, such as purchasing from a wholesaler, that are necessary or desirable to make sales, (b) the sales themselves and (c) the earning of a profit on the capital invested in the business. One approach is to treat the sales as Ax and Ay and the earning of a profit as Gx and Gy, but now it may be objected that (3) is not met, for both parties may earn a profit; in that case, if X competes with Y in respect of that goal, the model fails. An answer is to redescribe the parties' goals: each has the goal of *maximising* his profit, and it can realistically be assumed that X achieves this only if Y does not. Care needs to be taken here in specifying the parameters with respect to which maximisation is measured: X's maximum profit is the most he can earn, absent the assumption that Y does Ay, and conversely for Y; if X's maximum were calculated on the assumption that Y does Ay, and vice versa, the objection would stand. Suppose however that X and Y are concerned not with maximisation but only with making specified rates of return. In that case, whether (3) is met depends on what the rates are: if they are low enough, X and Y may not compete by their sales and in respect of their goals of achieving those rates.

This is not to say that they do not compete at all, for another approach is to treat activities in (a), i.e. those necessary or desirable to make sales, as Ax and Ay and sales as Gx and Gy: for example, and more precisely, X and Y may each have the goal of supplying Z's requirement for peaches. X achieves this only if Y does not, so here (3) is met. But X may compete with Y even if they aim to supply to different customers: if their goals in such

[56] Fielding (1976), 138.

[57] Compare Brownson, who talks of being 'coerced to compete': Brownson (1974), 237.

cases are to be understood in terms of sales of goods, the model needs to be elaborated. An easy elaboration which does the job is to extend the model to indirect competition through a chain of substitution: X competes with A, who competes with B, who competes . . . with Y[58] (competition in this sense is transitive[59]).

A feature of competition emphasised in antitrust is that it influences the terms on which the parties supply to their customers: it is taken to be as important that X's prices are reduced or held to a competitive level as that Y displaces X in supplying to Z. This feature is compatible with the model. Assume that X and Y each have the goal of supplying Z's requirement at £5 and that X achieves the sale, but that the competitive pressure from Y forces X to reduce his price to £4. (Normally Y can only apply pressure by transmitting information – possibly unintentionally and/or indirectly, for example via a shared customer – to X: this motivates the application of the epistemic condition (5) to such cases.) Clause (3) is met because X supplies at £5 only if Y does not: they cannot both supply Z's requirement. This conditional is unaffected by the fact that, in the event, neither party achieves his goal. A variant case is one where Y disciplines X's terms not by competing with X but merely by virtue of the fact that Y *could* supply to Z: this may be the case even if Y is not currently present in the relevant market. Again this is compatible with the model, which neither affirms nor denies that a rational economic actor may take the possible actions of other actors into account in deciding his terms. The model concerns actual competition whereas the contemplated case concerns potential competition: it would be confusing and pointless to build a reference to the latter into an account of the former.[60]

58 See Bishop and Walker (2002), paras. 4.72–4.76, and the authorities cited there.

59 To say that a relation is transitive is to say that, if A bears it to B and B bears it to C, A bears it to C. Dearden does not consider transitivity but does hold that competition is irreflexive: 'Taken literally, competition with oneself would involve a contradiction': Dearden (1972), 122. Kohn (1972), 6, and Rich (1988), 185, share this view. According to the core of my model, competition is not irreflexive but is non-reflexive: if I perform one action with one goal and another action with another goal, it may or may not be the case that I achieve the first goal only if I do not achieve the second. To say that a relation is irreflexive is to say that nothing bears the relation to itself; to say that it is non-reflexive is to say that it is not reflexive; and to say that it is reflexive is to say that everything bears the relation to itself.

60 The European Commission has used 'competitor' and 'competing undertaking' to cover both actual and potential competitors: see e.g. Guidelines on the applicability of Article 81 of the EC Treaty to horizontal cooperation agreements 2001/C 3/02, OJ C3, 6.1.2001, 2, para. 9; Notice on agreements of minor importance, 2001/C 368/07, OJ C368, 22.12.01, 13, para. 7; Commission Regulation (EC) 772/2004 on the application of Article 81(3) of the Treaty to categories of technology transfer agreements, OJ L123, 27.4.2004, 11, Article 1(1)(j)(ii).

It might be objected that the model misrepresents economic competition because competitive markets promote economic growth, thereby enabling competitors to achieve goals that they would otherwise be unable to achieve. On this view, (3) is misconceived, for one party does not achieve his goal at the price of another's failure: what is important, rather, is that the parties act with rivalrous intentions, for that is the stimulus to growth. The short answer is that, if the parties have rivalrous intentions in any of the senses given above, they are bound to meet (3). By (1a) and (2a), for example, X has the intention of achieving Gx and Y has the intention of preventing X from achieving Gx: these cannot both be fulfilled. But the objection is still doubtful if its mention of rivalry is omitted. Even if the existence of a competitive market enables competitors to achieve otherwise unattainable goals, it may also prevent them from jointly achieving certain other goals, in which case (3) holds: competition in the market for widgets might enable widget-makers to achieve otherwise unattainable levels of profit, but it will still be true that two manufacturers cannot both supply the requirement of a given buyer. In any event the objection, in making a general claim about competitive markets, is implausibly optimistic: whether competition extends the range of achievable goals will depend on the market in question. (The claim is more plausible if recast in terms of whole economies rather than markets.) Where a market does have this feature, it may still be the case that (1)–(3) are satisfied by individual pairs of competitors in the market: thus, although competition in the market for widgets may raise profit-levels generally, the activities of one manufacturer may curb the profits of another.

Some cases of economic competition fit just the model's core, others also fit one or more of its elaborations, such as clause (4) on identity of goals. Which of the identified forms of competitive behaviour should antitrust promote or protect? On the orthodox assumption that the purpose of antitrust is to maximise welfare (as to which, see the next chapter) the relevant form of competition is the one that produces the most welfare. Which form that is is an empirical question: to my knowledge, no research has been done that answers it. In particular, there is no evidence to indicate that stronger forms, such as rivalry, produce more welfare than does competition that instantiates only the core of the model. The OFT's identification of competition with rivalry is therefore unmotivated. The OFT might reply that by 'rivalry' it merely means competition,[61]

[61] Compare the weak sense of 'rivalry' in Scherer and Ross (1990), 16.

but in that case its definition of competition in terms of rivalry is circular.[62]

Competition and cooperation

Some people – especially those opposed to competition – hold that competition is incompatible with cooperation,[63] others that it is compatible,[64] and of the latter some even say that competition requires or exemplifies cooperation.[65] Here the issue of compatibility will be limited to two forms of cooperation which are prominent in antitrust: joint action and agreement. I shall use models of agreement and joint action that are proposed respectively in chapters 4 and 5: you may therefore prefer to read this section after reading those chapters.

It is uncontroversial that competition is compatible with either of these forms of cooperation in that people may compete by certain actions and in respect of certain goals while acting jointly or agreeing by certain different actions and with different goals: the question, rather, is whether competition and cooperation of either of these forms are compatible where the

62 The presence of rivalry can determine whether a form of behaviour is prohibited by competition law, notably in the test for predatory pricing laid down in Case C-62/86, *AKZO Chemie BV* v. *Commission* [1991] ECR I-3359, [1993] 5 CMLR 215, para. 72. But that is no reason to define competition as rivalry.

63 Fielding (1976), 131, cites Dahlke (1964) and Luschen (1970). Hobbes comes close to asserting this view when he says that competition is one of the principal causes of quarrel: (1968), Part 1, ch. 13. Kohn seems to assert it, but he allows that '(e)ven in a competitive culture there are aspects of cooperative and independent work': Kohn (1992), 7. Compare Keating (1964), 30, and Russell (1951), ch. 14. On competition as a form of aggression, conflict or strife, see Beals and Siegel (1966), 20–1; Kohn (1992), 143; Nove (1983); and Simmel (1955), 57 ff. For an opposing view, see Boulding (1962), 4–5; Kolnai (1965), 106–9; Mack (1965); and Ong (1981), 43. On competition as selfish, contrast Fielding (1976), 140, and Howerth (1912), 415, with Acton (1993), 36 ff, Meakin (1986), 62–4, and Prvulovich (1982), 79–80; see also McMurtry (1991), 202. G. Thompson (1972) reviews research comparing competitive and cooperative situations in education.

64 Acton (1993), 96–8; Mead (2003), 15–16, 460–1, where it is suggested that the binary competitive/cooperative distinction be replaced by a three-part classification of behaviour into competitive, cooperative and individualistic; Rich (1988), 185–6. Bratman arguably falls into the category of those who hold that competition and cooperation are compatible: he writes, 'A joint activity can be cooperative down to a certain level and yet competitive beyond that': Bratman (1999d), 107. See also Kluge (1991), which discusses a 'competition/cooperation model' for the provision of medical services.

65 Coleman (1987), 84–7; Cooley (1899), 79, 95–6; Dearden (1972), 121–2; Flew (1983), 267, 271–2; Perry (1975); Prvulovich (1982), 79; and Rappoport and Orwant (1964). Mead says that the existence of highly competitive groups implies cooperation within the groups: (2003), 460. Contrast Kohn (1992), 151–5.

parties' actions and goals in competing are the same as those in their acting jointly or agreeing. For example, if each of X and Y sells widgets with a view to maximising his own profits, can they both cooperate and compete by those actions and in respect of those goals? (The existence of joint ventures between competitors might be taken to indicate that they can.)

I first argue that competition and joint action are incompatible where the condition of identity of actions and goals is met. Joint action can be modelled thus (see chapter 5):

X and Y act jointly where:
(i) X, in doing Ax, relies on Y to do Ay;
(ii) Y, in doing Ay, relies on X to do Ax;
(iii) X, in relying on Y to do Ay, has the goal Gx;
(iv) Y, in relying on X to do Ax, has Gy;
(v) Gx = Gy;
(vi) X knows (i)–(v);
(vii) Y knows (i)–(v);
(viii) (vi) is true partly because Y communicates (ii) and (iv) to X;
(ix) (vii) is true partly because X communicates (i) and (iii) to Y.

Reliance, which is mentioned in (i)–(iv), can be modelled as follows (see chapter 5):

X, in doing Ax, relies on Y to do Ay where:
(I) X does Ax;
(II) X has the goal Gx;
(III) If X does Ax, Gx is achieved if and only if Y does Ay;
(IV) X believes (III);
(V) X believes that Y does Ay;
(VI) (I) is true because (II), (III) and (IV) are true.

The argument for incompatibility uses only the core of the model of competition: it applies a fortiori where one or more of the additional clauses discussed are added. The argument is by reductio ad absurdum: it derives a contradiction from the premiss that the parties' actions and goals in competing are the same as those in their acting jointly. More explicitly, the premiss is that the action by which X competes is the same as the action by which he acts jointly with Y, the action by which Y competes is the same as the action by which he acts jointly with X, and the goals in respect of which X and Y compete are the same as their goal in acting jointly.

(α) X and Y compete respectively by Ax and Ay and in respect of Gx and Gy. (β) By (α) and (1) (X does Ax with the intention of achieving Gx), X does Ax. (γ) By (α) and (2) (Y does Ay with the intention of achieving Gy), Y does Ay. (δ) X and Y act jointly respectively by Ax and Ay and with Gx and Gy. (ε) By (δ) and (i), X, in doing Ax, relies on Y to do Ay. (ζ) By (δ) and (ii), Y, in doing Ay, relies on X to do Ax. (η) By (ε) and (III), if X does Ax, Gx is achieved if and only if Y does Ay. (θ) By (ζ) and (III), if Y does Ay, Gy is achieved if and only if X does Ax. (ι) By (β), (γ) and (η), Gx is achieved. (κ) By (β), (γ) and (θ), Gy is achieved. (λ) By (ι) and (κ), Gx is achieved and Gy is achieved. (μ) Assume that Gx is achieved if and only if X achieves Gx, and that Gy is achieved if and only if Y achieves Gy. (ν) By (λ) and (μ), X achieves Gx and Y achieves Gy. (ξ) By (α) and (3), X achieves Gx only if Y does not achieve Gy. (o) By (ξ), it is not the case that both X achieves Gx and Y achieves Gy. (π) By (ν) and (o), it both is and is not the case that both X achieves Gx and Y achieves Gy. (ρ) By (α), (δ) and (π), either it is not the case that X and Y compete respectively by Ax and Ay and in respect of Gx and Gy or it is not the case that X and Y act jointly respectively by Ax and Ay and with Gx and Gy.

So competition and joint action are incompatible provided that the parties' actions and goals in competing are the same as those in their acting jointly. They are compatible where the proviso is false. This argument has implications for Article 81 EC,[66] which prohibits concerted practices that may affect trade between member states and that have as their object or effect the prevention, restriction or distortion of competition within the common market. Granted that, as will be argued in chapter 5, concerted practices are instances of joint action, the argument shows that, where the proviso is met, competition is incompatible with a concerted practice. That is to say (given a reasonably broad reading of 'prevent') that concerted practices as such prevent competition by the same actions and in respect of the same goals. It follows that, where in addition, first, the competition prevented would have been within the common market, second, the concerted practice in question may affect trade between member states and, third, the impact of the concerted practice on competition and on interstate trade is appreciable,[67] the prohibition in Article 81 applies regardless of the concerted practice's subject-matter.

[66] Parallel points apply to national provisions based on Article 81, e.g. section 2 of the UK Competition Act 1998.

[67] See Commission Notice on agreements of minor importance, 2001/C 368/07, OJ C368, 22.12.01, 13.

The next question is whether competition is compatible with agreement, where the parties' actions and goals in competing are the same as those in their agreeing. The question needs to be refined to distinguish the making of an agreement from the actions of complying with it: I shall argue for compatibility in the former case and incompatibility in the latter. Again the arguments use only the core of the model of competition. Agreement can be modelled thus:

X and Y agree that X will do Ax and Y will do Ay where:
(a) X undertakes to Y that, if Y will undertake to X that Y will do Ay, X will do Ax (call X's action of giving this undertaking 'Ux');
(b) Y undertakes to X that Y will do Ay (call Y's action of giving this undertaking 'Uy');
(c) Y's reason for giving Uy is that X gives Ux; and
(d) X has the justified belief that (b).

(This is chapter 4's model (M4). In that chapter I also propose a model (M6) in which X's undertaking is conditional not on Y's undertaking to do Ay, but on Y's doing Ay.) The incompatibility of competition and joint action arose from the fact that both involve the parties' having certain goals: the model of agreement does not mention goals, so at first sight there is no reason to think that competition and agreement are incompatible. The goals of the agreeing parties emerge, however, when one considers the deliberation that leads a rational person to make or comply with an agreement. Take first the actions of making an agreement, Ux and Uy. Chapter 4 will show that X may rationally argue his way to Ux from his desire that Y do Ay and his belief that doing Ux is the best means of getting Y to do Ay, and correspondingly for Y. Normally, where X does Ux having carried out such reasoning, it is the case that:

(1*) X does Ux with the intention of achieving that Y does Ay.

Similarly:

(2*) Y does Uy with the intention of achieving that X does Ax.

(1*) and (2*) are substitution-instances of (1) and (2) in the model of competition. The corresponding instance of (3) is:

(3*) X achieves that Y does Ay only if Y does not achieve that X does Ax.

Assume that the parties' goals in making an agreement are as described by (1*) and (2*). Then competition as modelled by (1)–(3) is compatible with the making of an agreement, where the parties' actions and goals in competing are the same as those in their making the agreement, if (3*) can be true when (1*) and (2*) are. There is nothing in the model of agreement, or elsewhere in this discussion, either to preclude or to ensure the truth of (3*) in those circumstances: whether (3*) is true will depend on facts specific to cases. So, on the assumption that the parties' goals in making an agreement are as described, competition thus modelled and the making of an agreement are compatible even where the condition of identity of actions and goals is met. Of course, where that condition is met, either X or Y will be thwarted in the pursuit of his goal: if, for example, X is thwarted, he will not achieve that Y does Ay, and if he foresees this he may decide not to enter into the agreement. (It might be said that even if X does foresee this he may decide to proceed if he also foresees that Y will do Ay: if Y does Ay independently of anything done by X, and specifically of X's doing Ux, Y does Ay without X's *achieving* that Y does Ay. In that case X's goal is achieved even though X does not achieve it. This claim sits uneasily with the argument that competition is incompatible with joint action, premiss (μ) of which says that Gx is achieved if and only if X achieves Gx; but that argument can be recast without (μ), by adjusting clause (III) of the model of reliance.)

Consider now the actions of complying with an agreement, Ax and Ay. Chapter 4 will also show how, once X and Y have made an agreement by giving their undertakings, they may rationally argue their way to fulfilling them. X's argument uses the premiss that he has an obligation to do Ax – the obligation arises from his undertaking to do Ax – and likewise for Y. Normally, where X does Ax having gone through the argument, it is the case that:

(1**) X does Ax with the intention of achieving the goal that he fulfils his obligation to do Ax.

Correspondingly:

(2**) Y does Ay with the intention of achieving the goal that he fulfils his obligation to do Ay.

(It might be objected that (1**) and (2**) wrongly impose a consequentialist structure on deontological reasoning: if X does Ax purely from an obligation to do so, his action is not goal-directed. This objection is misconceived. The debate between consequentialists and deontologists concerns not the nature of intentional action but normative and evaluative concepts: the main issue is whether, and if so in what sense, the good has primacy over the obligatory, the right, etc. Given that 'goal' is here used in a broad sense (see above), it is harmless to describe the parties as acting with the goals of fulfilling their obligations.)

Assume that the parties' goals in complying with an agreement are as described in (1**) and (2**). As before, these propositions are substitution-instances of (1) and (2). The corresponding instance of (3) is:

(3**) X achieves the goal that he fulfils his obligation to do Ax only if Y does not achieve the goal that he fulfils his obligation to do Ay.

This is equivalent to:

(3***) X does Ax only if Y does not do Ay.

(3***) contradicts the conjunction of (1**) and (2**). Hence competition as modelled by (1)–(3) is incompatible with complying with an agreement, where the parties' actions and goals in competing are the same as those in their complying, and their goals in complying are those described in (1**) and (2**). The implications for Article 81 EC are the same, mutatis mutandis, as in the case of the argument on concerted practices above.

To summarise this section: the original question was whether competition and cooperation are compatible. This was refined into the question whether they are compatible on the condition that the parties' actions and goals in competing are the same as those in their cooperating. This question in turn was limited to two forms of cooperation which are important in antitrust: joint action and agreement. The answer is that on that condition competition and joint action are incompatible and, on plausible assumptions about the goals of the parties in making and complying with an agreement, competition is compatible with making an agreement but not with complying with one.

2

Competition and welfare

Overview

Various arguments have been advanced in favour of economic competition. Some are consequentialist, for example that it encourages the survival of the economically fittest, others are deontological, for example that it embodies certain moral rights or political liberties.[1] The argument usually invoked nowadays by theorists and practitioners of antitrust is a consequentialist one, that competition maximises welfare.[2] (There is a debate, which need not be pursued here, as to whether the welfare in question is consumer welfare, as EC and US antitrust tends to assume, or social welfare, as Bork argues[3] and as economists tend to maintain.[4]) By the same token, antitrust – a body of law and policy designed to promote or protect competition – is defended by invoking its effects on welfare.[5] This chapter has the purely iconoclastic purpose of calling into question the welfare-based argument for competition and antitrust. Crudely, the thesis is that 'welfare' has either a meaning in

[1] The distinction between consequentialist and deontological arguments about competition is central to Wolff (unpublished). For arguments for and against competitive markets, see Buchanan (1985) (which provides a useful survey); Gaus (1998), 29 ff; Hargreaves Heap *et al.* (1992), ch. 4; Lipsey (1989), ch. 23; Samuelson (1970), 204 ff; and Whish (2003), ch. 1. Buchanan (2 f) divides the arguments into those based on efficiency and those based on morality, but acknowledges that the distinction is not sharp. Sen (2002e) proposes a justification of markets on the basis of freedom, contrasting it with welfare-based justifications.

[2] See Whish (2003), 2 f, and the works cited there.

[3] This is obscured by the fact that in Bork's terminology producers are a subclass of consumers: Bork (1978), 110–11. Bork's fifth definition of competition thus talks of consumer welfare: see chapter 1 above.

[4] See Bishop and Walker (2002), paras. 2.22–2.27, where the two standards of welfare are compared and evaluated. See also Crampton (1994) on the differences between consumer surplus, total surplus and total welfare as goals for antitrust.

[5] On the various ends that have been pursued in the name of antitrust, see chapter 3 below.

which welfare is valuable but competition does not maximise welfare, or a meaning in which competition does maximise welfare but the fact that it does so is no *justification* for competition, because welfare in this sense is not worth maximising. In that case competition and antitrust are either ineffective means to a valuable end or effective means to a worthless end.

In more detail, the welfare-based argument raises three questions: (1) What is it to maximise welfare? (2) Does competition maximise welfare? (3) Is it a good thing to maximise welfare? The argument requires the answer yes to (2) and (3). Economics uses a thin sense of 'maximise welfare' which answers (1) in a way that supports the answers yes to (2) but no to (3): it therefore fails to justify competition and antitrust. That problem is perhaps solved by moving to a fuller, philosophical, concept of welfare, but this gives satisfactory answers to (1) and (3) at the cost of supporting the answer no to (2). So again there is a failure of justification. Impaled on this dilemma, we should contemplate alternative justifications for competition and antitrust.

The discussion runs as follows. I start by examining the concept of welfare maximisation used in economics and show that the concept is too thin to provide the answers to (1)–(3) that the welfare-based argument needs. The failure of the economic approach motivates reflection on our intuitive understanding of a person's welfare as what makes his life go well for him. This notion has been amplified in various philosophical theories of welfare, which fall on a spectrum from the subjective/positive to the objective/normative: welfare has been conceived as a mental state; as the satisfaction of actual choice, preference or desire; as the satisfaction of the choices (etc.) that a subject would make in favourable conditions, or that an idealised subject would make; and as participation in various forms of good. I tentatively propose a qualified form of this last, objective, theory. Combined with a definition of maximisation, this gives an answer to (1). I then maintain that the objective theory supports the answer no to (2) and thus undermines the welfare-based argument. A possible defence is to recast the argument more modestly, to state only that competition promotes, not that it maximises, welfare. The defence is problematic, but it is interesting because the statement that competition promotes welfare supports a discriminatory proposal, that – contrary to current practice – antitrust authorities should limit their interventions to markets for products that themselves promote welfare. Assuming arguendo that the statement is true, I defend the proposal in an aside to the main discussion. At the end of the chapter I suggest that the answer yes to (3), if interpreted as a pro-tanto rather than an on-balance claim,[6] is fairly plausible on the objective theory, but implausible on the other philosophical theories reviewed earlier in the chapter. I consider, and reject, the suggestion that, because welfare as conceived by the other theories is a proxy for objective welfare, maximisation of welfare on those theories is good as a means to the maximisation of welfare as the objective theory conceives it.

An economic approach

Answers to questions (1) (What is it to maximise welfare?) and (2) (Does competition maximise welfare?) are supplied by the first theorem of welfare economics, that perfect competition in equilibrium is allocatively efficient.[7] (The second theorem is that, conversely, efficient allocations are competitive equilibria for appropriate distributions of endowments.) This result seems to be the main foundation for the welfare-based argument, as a matter of both justification – it is the main reason *to* believe that competition maximises welfare – and explanation – it is the main reason *why* people believe this. Allocative efficiency is said to exist, first, where an allocation of resources is Pareto optimal, i.e. cannot be changed in such a way that someone is made better off while no one is made worse off, and, second, where the sum of consumer surplus and producer surplus is maximised.[8] Consumer surplus is the difference between consumers' reservation price for a commodity, i.e. the price they are willing to pay for it, and the price they actually pay for it; producer surplus is the difference between the revenue received by the producer of a commodity and the minimum amount he is willing to accept to maintain the same level of supply. The two glosses of allocative efficiency do not mean

[6] To say that something is good pro tanto is to say that it is good so far as it goes; to say that it is good on balance is to say that it is good all things considered. Eating food that you enjoy is good pro tanto, but it is not good on balance if it kills you. In later chapters a parallel distinction is drawn between pro-tanto and on-balance obligations: see chapter 4, note 30.

[7] See Arrow (1951); Boadway and Bruce (1984), 3, 64; and Varian (1978). For the different types of efficiency, see Boadway and Bruce (1984), 12; Buchanan (1985), 4 ff; Leibenstein (1980), chs. 3 (where it is argued (29 ff) that the welfare gains from increasing allocative efficiency are usually very small), 6 and 7; Lipsey (1989), 380 ff; and Whish (2003), 3–4. Vickers (1995) champions competition for its promotion of productive efficiency. Sen recasts the first theorem as one about efficiency of 'opportunity freedom': Sen (2002e), 522.

[8] Since this sum equals social welfare, the first theorem supports an interpretation of the welfare-based argument in terms of social welfare rather than of consumer welfare (see above).

the same, so if one gives a definition, i.e. states the meaning of 'allocative efficiency', the other gives a test[9] (the distinction between definition and test need not be regarded as sharp). Economists are generally uninterested in the question which gloss gives the definition and which the test.

On this approach the answer to (1) is that to maximise welfare is to be allocatively efficient and the answer to (2) is yes. To answer (1) in its intended sense, allocative efficiency must be taken to define, not to be a test of, maximising welfare. In that case 'maximise welfare' has a thin sense. Suppose first that allocative efficiency is defined in terms of Pareto optimality. On a standard view in welfare economics, to say that I am better or worse off is to say that my utility[10] increases or decreases. Utilities are commonly understood to be numerical values of a utility function that represents a person's preferences, and his preferences to be revealed in the choices he makes. As to the first half of this thought, it can be proved that if his preferences conform to certain axioms of rationality – notably that preferences are complete and transitive[11] – they can be represented by a utility function in the sense that, for any pair of options, the function assigns a higher utility to the one that is preferred.[12] As to the second half, talk of revealed preference is entrenched in the literature but is misleading, for the main results of general equilibrium theory can be derived without distinguishing preferences from the acts of choice that 'reveal' them.[13] Thus utility functions can be viewed as

[9] Other possibilities, which can be disregarded here, are that the other gives an analysis of, or specifies conditions for, allocative efficiency: see further chapter 4.

[10] On the various meanings of 'utility', see Broome (1991a), 1 ff; Griffin (1986), 7; Hampton (1998), 93 f; Kahneman and Varey (1993), 127 ff; Kymlicka (2002), 13 ff; Leibenstein (1980), 192; Little (1957), 20; Millgram (2000), 114; Roemer (1996), 13; and Sen (1981), 199 f, (1982j), 344, (1985), 187, (2002d), 27.

[11] To say that preferences are complete is to say that, for any two bundles of commodities A and B, A is preferred to B, B is preferred to A, or they are ranked equally. Transitivity is defined in chapter 1, note 59. For other axioms, see Boadway and Bruce (1984), 34 ff.

[12] Technical accounts are given in Boadway and Bruce (1984), 33 ff; Frank (2003), 91; Johansson (1991), 147 ff; and Roemer (1996), 15 f. For informal accounts see Allingham (2002), 22 ff; Broome (1991a), 3; Hampton (1998), 91 ff; Hargreaves Heap *et al.* (1992), 4 ff, 265 ff; Hausman and McPherson (1993), 680; Sobel (1994), 787; and Weintraub (1998), 308.

[13] 'Thus, the consumer's market behaviour is explained in terms of preferences, which are in turn defined only by behaviour': Samuelson (1970), 91. By contrast, Sen (1982a), 55 ff, argues that economics cannot dispense with a non-behavioural concept of preference. See also Hampton (1998), 91 ff, and Keita (1999), 347.

directly representing acts of rational choice,[14] and utility as that which is maximised in rational choice. On this view utilities are neither states or qualities of mind nor objects of choice – we do not aim to increase or maximise our utility[15] – but are numbers associated with choices by utility functions. 'Maximise welfare' accordingly has a thin sense,[16] for to say that welfare is maximised is to say merely that no one's number can be increased unless someone's number is decreased.

Now suppose that allocative efficiency is defined in terms of consumer surplus and producer surplus. These are defined in terms of sums of money that are identified by reference to consumers' and producers' behaviour (what consumers pay and what producers take) and by their willingness to behave in certain ways (the price consumers are willing to pay, the amount a producer is willing to accept). In line with the behaviourist approach favoured in welfare economics,[17] willingness can in turn be defined in terms of conditional propositions about behaviour: for example, and approximately, 'I am willing to pay £1 for a widget' means 'I shall buy a widget if it costs £1 or less and I shall not buy one if it costs more than £1'. Again, therefore, 'maximise welfare' has a thin sense: to say that welfare is maximised is merely to say something about sums of money identified by reference to certain forms of behaviour by consumers and producers.

If 'maximise welfare' has either of these thin senses, it has little to do with our intuitive understanding of a person's welfare as, roughly, what makes his life go well for him (see below). It is therefore obscure why we should be interested in the maximisation of welfare in these senses. Thus the proposed answer to (1) suggests a negative answer to (3), the question whether it is a good thing to maximise welfare. The obvious way to defend the welfare-based argument against this objection is to reply that allocative efficiency is not a definition of, but a test of or (in a sense to be discussed later) a proxy for, welfare maximisation. But that reopens

[14] See Little (1957), 29. This approach is discussed and criticised in Sen (1985), 187 f.

[15] 'You do not choose to go riding rather than skiing because it gives you more utility; on the contrary, a greater utility is assigned to riding because you choose it': Allingham (2002), 23 f. See also Hausman (1995), 473 f; Hausman and McPherson (1993), 680; Little (1957), 29; and Sumner (1996), 115 ff.

[16] Various authors note that the present sense of 'utility' is purged of the notions of pleasure and satisfaction used by earlier theorists to define the term: Hargreaves Heap *et al.* (1992), 7; Hausman and McPherson (1993), 680; Samuelson (1970), 90–1; and Sumner (1996), 116.

[17] See Sen (1982a), 55 ff, (1982h), 9.

question (1): what is it to maximise welfare? The next section discusses other answers, from philosophy rather than economics.[18]

There are further objections to the economic approach just outlined. First, in the version that defines allocative efficiency as Pareto optimality, it treats 'maximise welfare' as a semantic unit in which 'maximise' and 'welfare' do not have independent meanings. In particular, where Pareto optimality is conceived in terms of utility, 'welfare' cannot mean 'utility', for to say that no one's utility can be increased unless someone's utility is decreased does not imply that utility is maximised in any intuitive sense. If, on the other hand, allocative efficiency is defined to exist where the sum of consumer and producer surplus is maximised, 'welfare' can be independently defined as the sum of consumer and producer surplus; but that leaves the problem of the previous paragraph, why we should be concerned to maximise welfare in this sense.

Second, the construction of utility functions requires that people's choices conform to the axioms of rationality, but they often fail to do so.[19] Third, if rationality is understood for these purposes as, or as including, internal consistency of choice, it can be argued that the concept is confused: Sen has maintained that what counts as consistency can only be determined by reference to the chooser's motivation, which is external to his acts of choice.[20] Fourth, there are objections both to Pareto optimality as a normative criterion[21] – for example, that it is blind to distributive injustice[22] (a state in which one person has everything and everyone else has nothing is Pareto optimal), that it gives no guidance where, as is

[18] In welfare economics the behaviourist approach, embodied in the two senses of 'maximise welfare' just identified, has an older rival according to which choice behaviour is regarded as evidence of welfare, which in turn is taken to consist in a mental state or in the satisfaction of preferences or desires. This approach, which was taken by Pigou (see Pigou (2002), 10 ff), is exemplified in two recent textbooks: Boadway and Bruce (1984), 11, 39, 56, and Johansson (1991), 3 f, 40, 147; see also Sen (1982a). Pigou's theory is lucidly analysed in Sumner (1996), 113 ff. On the differences between 'old' and 'new' welfare economics, see Samuelson (1970), 249. Mental-state and satisfaction theories of welfare are discussed below.

[19] See Hargreaves Heap *et al.* (1992), ch. 3; Hausman (1995), 485; Kahneman and Tversky (1990); Little (1957), ch. 3; and Sen (1981), 206, (1982h), 2, (1985), 188. Leibenstein (1980) and Sen (1982k) offer critiques of conventional microeconomics' model of rationality.

[20] Sen (2002c), (2002d), 19 ff. See also Sen (1982h), 5 ff, (2002j), 225 ff.

[21] For the appeal of the Pareto test, see Boadway and Bruce (1984), 101; Buchanan (1985), 7, 10 f; Hausman and McPherson (1998), 208 f; and Head (1974a), 257.

[22] See Boadway and Bruce (1984), 62, 83, 174, 190; Buchanan (1985), 9 f; Goldman (1995), 709; and Sen (2002e), 504.

usually the case, a change from one state to another makes some people better off and others worse off[23] or where institutional constraints prevent the achievement of Pareto optimality,[24] that it is in tension with certain liberal principles[25] and that a Pareto optimum need not be unique[26] – and to attempts to answer those objections by the use of such devices as compensation principles.[27]

Fifth, the relevant theorems of welfare economics concern competition in the sense of perfect competition in equilibrium, but antitrust uses a broader concept of competition. There are two points here: one is the commonplace that perfect competition rarely if ever exists, the other that perfect competition is a matter of market structure whereas antitrust, as has been seen in chapter 1, is also concerned with competitive behaviour (it can be allowed that the structure/behaviour distinction is not sharp). As to the latter point: competitive behaviour is neither necessary nor sufficient for perfect competition;[28] it is unclear how levels of competitive behaviour are to be measured, either intensively or extensively;[29] there is no clear evidence that perfect competition is approached as competitive behaviour increases (by whatever measure); and, even if it is, there arguably remains the problem of the 'second-best', that a market which comes close to being perfectly competitive may be less efficient than one that comes less close.[30] This last objection reinforces the first point by impugning the claim – which is anyway clearly false in many cases – that actual markets approximate to perfect competition closely enough for them to approach allocative efficiency.[31]

[23] See Boadway and Bruce (1984), 3–4, 16, 62, 135, 138; and Hausman and McPherson (1993), 702.

[24] See Boadway and Bruce (1984), 135. On the implications of this for the second theorem, see Sen (2002e), 505.

[25] Sen (1982e) is the locus classicus for this objection. See also Sen (1982b), 81, (1982i); Barry (1986); Boadway and Bruce (1984), 63; and Hylland (1989), 59 ff.

[26] See Samuelson (1970), 214.

[27] See Boadway and Bruce (1984), 4, 96–7, 102; Hausman and McPherson (1993), 702–3, (1998), 209; and Little (1957), 88 ff.

[28] See Lipsey (1989), 200–1; and Scherer and Ross (1990), 16.

[29] See Vickers (1995), 3, on the various meanings of the claim that there is 'more competition' in some activity.

[30] See Lipsey and Lancaster (1956). The result is generalised in Foster and Sonnenschein (1970).

[31] See Buchanan (1985), 14.

A philosophical approach

Question (1): theories of welfare and maximisation

To identify a sense of 'maximise welfare' that leaves room for an explanation why maximising welfare is a good thing, we need to go behind the apparatus of welfare economics and to reflect on our intuitive understanding of welfare and, separately, on the idea of maximisation. As suggested earlier, our intuitive understanding of a person's welfare is: what makes his life go well for him.[32] This notion is developed by various theories in the philosophical literature, which can be roughly ordered on a spectrum from – in certain senses of those words – the subjective and positive to the objective and normative[33] (a paradoxical description, to those who view the positive as objective and the normative as subjective). The theories can be read as giving either a definition or a test of welfare.[34]

At the subjective/positive end are theories that identify welfare with one or more mental states. Such theories are usually hedonistic, identifying it with happiness, pleasure, comfort,[35] contentment, enjoyment or

[32] Approximate synonyms for 'welfare' in this sense are 'well-being', 'interest' (but see Raz (1986), 295 ff, which conceives of self-interest as narrower than well-being), 'benefit' and 'flourishing'. 'My good' is also close to 'my welfare', 'what is good for me' less so: spinach is good for me but is at best a partial cause, not a component, of my welfare. The present sense of 'welfare' should be distinguished from the one at issue in discussions of the welfare state: these concern, roughly, social programmes designed to secure a fair distribution of basic goods and services or to establish a safety net for the disadvantaged: Sumner (1996), vii. (See Davies (1997), Griffin (2000) and Gaus (1998) for conceptions of welfare in that sense.) Moore and Crisp distinguish the minimal case, in which a life of well-being is a life worth living, from the case of the fortunate, for whom it is a matter of life's going well: Moore and Crisp (1996), 599. Raz regards well-being as comprising not only what makes a person's life go well for him but what makes him a good person: Raz (1994d), 36. Parfit (1984), 493, talks in terms not of what makes a person's life go well for him but of what makes his life go for him as well as possible. On that approach the concept of welfare itself includes maximisation; so the claim that competition maximises welfare involves, rather obscurely and arguably pleonastically, a double maximisation.

[33] For classifications of theories of welfare, see Barry (1973), 38–9; Brock (1993), 96 f; Buchanan and Brock (1990), 31 ff; G. Cohen (1993); Elster and Roemer (1993b), 5; Goldman (1995), 711; Hausman and McPherson (1998), 206 ff; Kagan (1998), 29 ff; Kymlicka (2002), 13 ff; Moore and Crisp (1996), 599–600; Parfit (1984), 493 ff; Qizilbash (1997); Scanlon (1993b), 186 ff; Scoccia (1987), 584; Sen (1982h), 29–30; Skorupski (2000), 250–1; Sumner (1996), chs. 2–6; and Weale (1998).

[34] Compare Buchanan (1985), 11, 26–7, which distinguishes definitional from empirical accounts of well-being. For the requirements on a theory of welfare, see Sumner (1996), ch. 1.

[35] On the importance of the distinction between pleasure and comfort, see Elster and Roemer (1993b), 5; Kahneman and Varey (1993), 145–6; and Scitovsky (1992), ch. 4.

some similar state. (It may be doubted whether contentment and enjoyment are merely mental states, as 'I am contented with / enjoy X' can be read extensionally, i.e. as true only if X exists;[36] in that case contentment and enjoyment involve a possibly extra-mental state of the world.) Hedonistic theories were advanced by the classical utilitarians[37] and still have their defenders,[38] but they face strong objections: (a) There appears to be no set of mental states common and peculiar to all situations that make for a person's welfare, for example a walk in the woods and the receipt of a legacy.[39] (b) The theories give counterintuitive results in cases of adaptive hedonic states – the fox may bring himself to be pleased not to have eaten the grapes, a slave may achieve happiness by adjusting her aspirations to her miserable circumstances – and, conversely, of people who are hard to please or who gain pleasure in antisocial ways.[40] These cases make hedonistic theories hard to combine with theories of distributive justice:[41] the implication is that resources need to be moved from the happy slave to the discontented millionaire until their hedonic levels are the same. (c) It seems that welfare depends not only on one's mental states but on whether they are veridical:[42] if a man happily but falsely believes that his wife loves him, his welfare is lower than it would be if his belief were true. Nozick dramatises this thought with the idea of an 'experience machine' which enables a person to have any experience he likes while floating in a tank with electrodes attached to his brain:[43] according to hedonistic theories, if the machine provides him with blissful experiences, his welfare is high. But that fails to acknowledge that our welfare depends not just on our experiences but on what

[36] See Griffin (1986), 18; and Sumner (1996), 111.

[37] See e.g. Bentham (1948). The utilitarians' theories are reviewed in Sumner (1996), 83 ff. For Epicurean ancestors, see Diogenes Laertius (1980), bk 10, para. 34.

[38] See e.g. Bernstein (1998); Kawall (1999); and Tännsjö (1996).

[39] See Griffin (1986), 8; and Sumner (1996), 92.

[40] See Elster (1985); Elster and Roemer (1993b), 5–7; Rawls (1982), 168 ff; Scoccia (1987), 584 ff; and Sen (1985), 190, (2002h), 82–3. On the 'hedonic treadmill' that can result from adaptation, see Brickman and Campbell (1971); Brickman *et al.* (1978); Kahneman and Varey (1993), 141; and Scitovsky (1981), 72. On 'prospect theory' as a response to the treadmill, see Kahneman and Tversky (1990). See further note 108 and compare the discussion below of the regress of desires.

[41] See Elster and Roemer (1993b), 8.

[42] See Gibbard (1986), 169; Griffin (1986), 28; Kagan (1998), 34 ff; Scanlon (1993a); and Sumner (1996), 94.

[43] Nozick (1974), 42–5. See also Bernstein (1998), 42 ff; Finnis (1980), 95 f; Kane (1974), 67 ff; Kawall (1999); Kymlicka (2002), 14; Larmore (1987), 48 f; and Lomasky (1987), 231 ff. Nozick's machine is anticipated in Smart (1973), 19–20.

we *do*.[44] One way of amplifying this objection is to argue that autonomy is a component of welfare.[45] (d) In so far as welfare is determined by mental states, they are not all readily classed as hedonic: for example, excitement can be an element of welfare.[46] But the preceding objections apply to non-hedonistic, or composite, versions of the mental-state theory. In any event it seems that welfare is not just a matter of mental states: starvation normally diminishes a person's welfare, whatever his mental state.[47]

These objections motivate a shift along the spectrum to theories that identify welfare with satisfaction, of choice, preference or desire: my welfare consists in my getting what I choose, prefer or want. Such theories tend to be favoured by those economists who (in so far as they attend to the distinction) view allocative efficiency as a test, rather than a definition, of the maximisation of welfare:[48] the main reasons are that they appear to allow empirical tests of welfare and to avoid paternalism.[49] Although choice, preference and desire are or involve mental states, satisfaction theories are not pure mental-state theories, for satisfaction is a relation between (say) desire and the world. Satisfaction in this sense is distinct from any *feeling* of satisfaction: if I desire to win the lottery and I do so without knowing, my winning gives me no such feeling.

The discussion can be limited for the moment to the case of desire. Many objections have been raised in the literature to the theory that a person's welfare consists in the satisfaction of his actual desires: (a) Satisfaction of desire is not necessary for welfare: my welfare can be increased when I am pleasantly surprised by something I did not want.[50] (b) Nor is it sufficient: (i) My desire may be disinterested, for example, for the happiness of a stranger whom I encounter once and never expect to see again,[51] or concern something remote, for example that there be life on

44 'What is most disturbing about [such machines] is their living of our lives for us': Nozick (1974), 44.

45 On the relation between autonomy and welfare, see Elster (1985), 132; Elster and Roemer (1993b), 7; Griffin (1986), 11; Scoccia (1987); Seel (1997), 45; Sen (1985), 186; and Sumner (1996), ch. 6. Autonomy and welfare are contrasted in Buchanan and Brock (1990), 40–2, and Sobel (1998). Compare Sen (1985), 201, and (2002d), 14 ff, on the relation between freedom and well-being.

46 See Scitovsky (1981); and Sen (1985), 189.

47 See Sen (1985), 188. 48 See note 18 above.

49 See Boadway and Bruce (1984), 8, 11, 31–2, 39; Goldman (1995), 711; Griffin (1986), 10, 106 (where it is argued that such theories are nevertheless unsuitable for welfare economics), (1993), 48–9; Hausman and McPherson (1998), 207; Scitovsky (1992), 4–5; and Sumner (1996), 114. Paternalism is discussed below.

50 See Sumner (1996), 132.

51 See Griffin (1986), 17; Parfit (1984), 494; and Sumner (1996), 134.

Earth a thousand years after my death: as it is implausible to hold that the satisfaction of such desires increases my welfare, the theory needs to be restricted to, say, desires about one's own life.[52] (ii) People often want things that make their lives go badly for them[53] (cigarettes are an obvious case, certain forms of self-sacrifice are more debatable[54]) – or at any rate that have no effect on their welfare (for example, an idle desire to know how many pebbles there are on Aldeburgh beach[55]) – and fail to want things (for example, education) that help to make their lives go well for them.[56] Economists classify these cases as involving 'merit' or 'demerit' goods, the dubious assumption being that they are rare exceptions.[57] Advertising's ability to distort desires is often mentioned in this context.[58] (iii) Satisfaction of a desire as such, i.e. irrespective of the desire's object, does not constitute an increase in welfare:[59] it merely leads either to boredom or to the formation of a new desire, and so on indefinitely.[60] A radical development of this thought is the idea that welfare requires the abnegation of all desires;[61] a modest one is the idea that the regress of desires is benign and that a person's welfare is compatible with there being, or even requires that there be, a certain proportion of his desires unsatisfied at any time.[62] (iv) The theory produces odd results, which are hard to reconcile with an account of distributive justice, in the case of adaptive, unduly demanding or antisocial desires (this corresponds to objection

52 Such restrictions are discussed in Griffin (1986), 16–17; Parfit (1984), 495; Kagan (1998), 37 f; and Qizilbash (1998), 58 f. Parfit contemplates a further restriction, to 'global' desires: Parfit (1984), 496 f; compare Raz (1986), 293, on the importance of 'pervasive' goals to welfare.

53 See Goldman (1995), 711; Griffin (1986), 10, 106; and Sumner (1996), 129 f.

54 On self-sacrifice, see Brandt (1982); Buchanan and Brock (1990), 32 f; Sobel (1998), 250; Griffin (1986), 316; and Overvold (1980), (1982).

55 On idiosyncratic desires and preferences, see Hausman and McPherson (1993), 690; and Parfit (1984), 499.

56 In antiquity Menedemus made a similar point: 'On hearing someone say that the greatest good was to get all you want, he rejoined, "To want the right things is a far greater good"': Diogenes Laertius (1980), bk 2, para. 136.

57 See for example Boadway and Bruce (1984), 39. On merit and demerit goods generally, see Head (1974a), (1974b); and Musgrave (1959).

58 See Buchanan (1985), 27 ff; G. Cohen (1977); P. Harvey (1990), 53, (2000), 223; Head (1974a), 216; Musgrave (1959); Samuelson (1970), 223; and Scitovsky (1992), 133, 273. For a defence of advertising, see Hicks (1981), 140 f.

59 See Scanlon (1993a), 38; and Scoccia (1987), 588.

60 See Griffin (1986), 12; P. Harvey (2000), 220–1 (distinguishing craving from purpose); Hobbes (1968), 160–1; Millgram (2000), 129–30; Schopenhauer (1951), 21–3; and Scitovsky (1992), chs. 4, 6. Compare Schumacher (1973), 26 ff.

61 See P. Harvey (1990), 60 f, (2000), 196 f.

62 See Elster (1985), 136 ff; Leibniz (1875–90), vol. 5, 152, 175; and Raz (1994c), 111 f.

(b) to hedonistic theories).[63] (v) A desire may be irrational or based on a false belief[64] (this overlaps (ii) above and corresponds to objection (c) to hedonistic theories): if I want to drink the liquid in this glass, mistakenly believing it to be water when in fact it is poison, my welfare will not be improved if I do so. (vi) A person's first-order desires may fail to reflect his values as manifested in his higher-order desires (i.e. desires to desire).[65] (vii) The theory fails to acknowledge that the autonomous formation of a desire is important to welfare[66] (compare the similar point above relating to hedonistic theories). (viii) If today I want something tomorrow, but tomorrow I do not want it, my getting it may not (although in some cases it may) increase my welfare.[67] (ix) Sometimes at least, the satisfaction or thwarting of my desire makes no difference to my welfare if I fail to know, or even to believe, that it has been satisfied or thwarted[68] (compare (i) above). (c) Other objections are that the theory treats desires as brute facts,[69] reverses the proper relation between desires on the one hand and reasons[70] or values[71] on the other – we hold desires for reasons, or because we view their objects as valuable; a desire is not itself a reason or a source

[63] See notes 40 and 41 above; see also Elster (1989), 109; Hausman and McPherson (1993), 690 f; Kymlicka (2002), 15–16; Qizilbash (1998), 58; and Sen (1985), 191.

[64] See Hausman and McPherson (1993), 676; Kagan (1998), 38; Kymlicka (2002), 15; Qizilbash (1998), 58; Sen (1981), 202; and Sobel (1994), 788. Qizilbash argues (52) more generally that desire-satisfaction theories impose excessive demands on knowledge, imagination and fellow-feeling; see also Qizilbash (1997), 228. Hahn and Hollis note that orthodox economic theory cannot admit any serious sense in which preferences may be irrational: Hahn and Hollis (1979) 10. Head (1974a), 251, claims that the notion of irrational beliefs is elitist and authoritarian.

[65] See Qizilbash (1998), 58. On valuing as desiring to desire, see D. Lewis (1989), 114 ff. G. Dworkin (1988), 20, associates values with higher-order preferences. See Goodin (1989), 83 ff, on the censoring of preferences that conflict with higher-order preferences. On the importance of higher-order desires in the informed-desire theory of welfare (discussed below), see Griffin (1986), 13.

[66] See Scoccia (1987). Contrast Goodin (1989), 91 ff.

[67] See Brandt (1979), 251; Griffin (1986), 16; and Sen (1981), 202. On people's poor ability to predict their future tastes, see Kahneman and Snell (1990); Kahneman and Varey (1993), 133; and Weinstein (1982). On the bearing of changes of ideals on personal identity, see Black (2002), 10; and Parfit (1984), 327 ff.

[68] See Sen (1981), 202. Contrast Elster and Roemer (1993b), 7.

[69] See Plant (1991), 140, 168–9; and Raz (1994c), 111–12, (1994d), 37.

[70] See Raz (1986), 300 ff, (1994c), 112; and Scanlon (1975), 660, (1993b), 191 ff. (Scanlon (1993b), 194 f, holds that this objection does not apply where one person acts as agent or representative of another.) See also Scanlon (1993a), 38.

[71] See Sen (1985), 190; Raz (1986), 300 ff. Griffin rejects the 'taste model' (valuable because desired) without committing himself to the 'perception model' (desired because valuable): Griffin (1993), 61. See also Griffin (1986), 26 ff, criticised in Black (1994a), 80 ff.

of value – and makes it impossible to compare different people's welfare in a morally acceptable way.[72]

In the face of these difficulties many philosophers have moved further towards the objective/normative end of the spectrum by refining the theory to state that a person's welfare consists in the satisfaction not of any desires he happens to have, but of the desires he would have under certain favourable conditions (for example, that he is perfectly rational and fully informed) or of the desires that an idealised subject would have in his position.[73] The latter formulation can be subsumed under the former, given that the desires of an idealised subject are the desires that the person would have if he were an idealised subject, but the distinction marks the fact that there may be no remotely likely conditions under which he would be such a subject.

Although the revised theory can avoid some of the objections just rehearsed – for example (v) that desires may be irrational or based on false beliefs – it remains vulnerable to others, for example (ii) that people, no matter how clear-headed and well informed, often want things that make their lives go badly for them.[74] Of course, all objections to the effect that satisfaction of desire is insufficient for welfare can be avoided by gerrymandering the conditions, or the specification of the idealised subject, to ensure that the revised theory applies only to those desires unaffected by the objections; but that risks trivialising the revised theory and still leaves it exposed to the objection (a) that satisfaction of desire is unnecessary for welfare. Other objections, specific to the revised theory, concern the specification of the favourable conditions or the idealised subject and their relation to a person's actual circumstances.[75] An obvious objection is that in the revised theory the concept of desire is idle:[76] roughly, we are interested in the desires that a person would have under favourable conditions, or that an idealised subject would have, because we are inclined to believe that the objects of those desires are worth having.

[72] Hausman (1995) makes this objection to the parallel theory about preferences. For criticism of Hausman's argument, see Weintraub (1996). Hausman replies in Hausman (1997). For an approach to interpersonal welfare comparisons within a satisfied-preference theory, see Arrow (1963).

[73] See Goodin (1989); Griffin (1986), ch. 2; Harsanyi (1982); Kymlicka (2002), 16 ff; and Scoccia (1987); and compare the analysis of 'a man's future good on the whole' in Sidgwick (1907), 111–12.

[74] Sumner (1996), 129 ff, traces the problem to the prospectivity of desire and explains how it cannot be removed by requiring that desires be informed.

[75] See Darwall (2002), 27 f; Kavka (1986), 41; and Overvold (1980), 117 f.

[76] See Griffin (1986), 17; and Kagan (1998), 39.

In that case the objects, rather than the fact that they would satisfy certain desires, constitute welfare.[77]

The revised theory is thus unstable: it tends to tip into the theory that stands at the objective/normative end of the spectrum, according to which a person's welfare consists in his participating in various forms of good, regardless of whether they make him happy etc. or of whether he desires them (or would do so under certain conditions). Call this the objective theory. Various lists have been given of the relevant goods. Griffin suggests: accomplishment; the components of a characteristically human existence (specifically autonomy, minimum material provision and liberty – all of which Griffin claims to be components of agency); understanding, at least of certain basic personal and metaphysical matters; enjoyment; and deep personal relations.[78] In some versions the objective theory is perfectionist, in treating the goods as elements of a life that fully realises the distinctive and essential features of human nature.[79] Each entry on a list such as this must be viewed as a mere outline which can be filled in with any number of detailed specifications of the relevant form of good and which leaves room for qualitative distinctions. To take the last two entries: enjoyment of a walk in the woods is a component of welfare, enjoyment of pulling the wings off flies is not;[80] a loving marriage is a component of welfare, an obsessive and mutually destructive relationship is not.

The theory faces two main objections.[81] One is that it confuses different dimensions of value: welfare is a matter of prudential value, whereas the goods on the list are ethical, aesthetic or perfectionist values.[82] An answer

[77] Darwall (2002), 25 ff, contains further objections to the revised theory.

[78] Griffin (1993), 63, discussed in A. Moore (2000), 75, where a shorter list is proposed, and Qizilbash (1997), 237 ff. Qizilbash (1998), 63 ff, extends Griffin's list. Different lists are given in Finnis (1980), 85 ff; Griffin (1986), 64 ff; Kagan (1998), 39; G. Moore (1959), 188 ff; Rawls (1972), 69, 92, 440, (1993), 180–1 (under the heading 'primary goods'); and Sumner (1996), 180 (but Sumner does not propose an objective theory). Other recent versions of the objective theory are found in Arneson (2002), 322–3; McNaughton and Rawling (2001) (criticising Crisp (2000), who replies in Crisp (2001)); Raz (1986), ch. 12, (1994a), 3 ff, (1994c), 116, (1994d), 36 ff; Scanlon (1975); and probably in Schneider (1995), 27 f.

[79] On perfectionism, see Griffin (1986), ch. 4; Hurka (1993); and Kagan (1998), 40. Hill (2002a), 164–9, describes the transition from objective perfectionist accounts of happiness in ancient philosophy to modern subjectivist accounts.

[80] Compare the distinction between the qualities of pleasures in Mill (1972a), 6 ff. See also the discussion of 'qualitative hedonism' in Kagan (1998), 31 ff.

[81] For objections to Rawls' notion of primary goods, see Elster and Roemer (1993b), 9.

[82] See Griffin (1986), 68 ff (but contrast 161 f); and Sumner (1996), 20 ff, 164 f. Bernstein (1998), 43 ff, distinguishes welfare from the value of a life.

must argue either that the goods are at least partly prudential or that the dimensions are not distinct.[83] The other objection is that the theory fails to recognise the perspectival character of welfare[84] – the fact that a person's welfare is what makes his life go well *for him*: my life does not go well for me if, despite the fact that I participate in all the items on the list, I have no desire for and am unhappy with them.[85] This objection, which is weakened by the fact that the list includes enjoyment, may be answered by adding to the theory a condition as to the subject's experience of the goods in which he participates.[86] But that leads back to a mental-state theory.

It appears, then, that the best account of welfare is likely to combine elements of the different theories in a way that avoids the objections to each.[87] Eclecticism is no embarrassment – it reflects the fact that we have disparate intuitions about welfare – but it is arguable that the intuitions are not only disparate but mutually contradictory, in which case they cannot all be accommodated in a single acceptable theory. The choice would then be between pursuit of a reflective equilibrium between intuition and theory, with some intuitions being rejected in the interest of meeting theoretical constraints, and admission of more than one concept or conception[88] of welfare. It is beyond the scope of this discussion to develop a detailed theory, but my view is that the best one will be a qualified form of the objective theory, emphasising participation in various forms of good.

[83] Raz (1986), 313 ff, argues that welfare and morality are inseparable. See also Raz (1994e), 58 f.

[84] See Griffin (1986), 21; Raz (1986), 289; Scanlon (1993b), 185; and Sumner (1996), 42, 53.

[85] See Kagan (1998), 40.

[86] See Glover (1990), 63–4; Griffin (1986), 23; Seel (1997), 40; and Sumner (1996), 127. Raz (1994a) rejects such a condition. See also Tännsjö (1996) on sub-noticeable changes in well-being.

[87] The eclectic approach is contemplated in Brock (1993), 119 ff; Lane (1994); possibly D. Miller (1976), 144, n. 18, where 'well-being' is said to be 'a blank term to be used indiscriminately for "pleasure", "happiness", "self-realisation", etc., as one chooses'; Parfit (1984), 501 f; and Sen (1981). Sen's 'capability' theory of welfare is perhaps better described as steering a middle course between mental-state and satisfaction theories on the one hand and objective theories on the other: see Sen (1985), 195–6. (For the capability theory generally, see Sen (1982d), 367 ff, (1982h), 29 f, (1993), (2002h), 83; and Franklin (unpublished). The theory is criticised in G. Cohen (1993), 16 ff; Elster and Roemer (1993b), 9; Qizilbash (1997), 229 ff, (1998), 52 ff; and Sumner (1996), 60 ff.) Similarly Sumner says that his own theory of welfare as authentic happiness is 'something in between' hedonism and the desire-satisfaction theory: Sumner (1996), 175.

[88] Conceptions are distinguished from concepts in R. Dworkin (1978), 134–6.

To provide half of the answer to (1) – What is it to maximise welfare? – in the question's intended sense, the theory must be interpreted as defining, rather than providing a test of, welfare. The other half will be a definition of maximisation.[89] Pareto optimality is not a plausible definiens, for to say that no one's welfare can be increased unless someone's is decreased does not imply that welfare is maximised in any intuitive sense. (Compare the objection above to defining welfare as utility.) The obvious sense to give, and the one that will be given here, to the statement that welfare is maximised is that the aggregate level of welfare of people in the relevant group is as high as possible.[90] This raises questions, which can be set aside, about the nature of aggregation,[91] the way to measure an individual's welfare level, the possibility of interpersonal comparisons of welfare,[92] the specification of the reference group and the parameters of the possibility (i.e. what is taken as given when determining whether welfare is as high as possible). Alternative definitions could replace the aggregate level with the mean,[93] median or mode, or could use a maximin standard whereby welfare is maximised if the welfare level of people with the lowest welfare is as high as possible.[94]

Question (2): discriminatory intervention

Question (2) is whether competition maximises welfare. Economics answers yes in the sense of proving that perfect competition in equilibrium is allocatively efficient; but mathematical proof is no longer available once the concept of competition is broadened to cover competitive behaviour and welfare is understood in the fuller terms of a philosophical theory. The question is now an empirical one and the answer is uncertain, as is perhaps inevitable given the limited scope for experiments in social science. The case made by empirical studies for the welfare-maximising effects of

89 For a distinction between maximisation and optimisation, see Sen (2002f), (2002g), 257.

90 Compare the discussion of 'the total view' in Kagan (1998), 41 ff.

91 On the distinction between aggregating and totting up, see Griffin (1986), 34 ff.

92 There is a large literature on this. Some recent contributions are Elster and Roemer (1993a); Goldman (1995); Griffin (1986), ch. 7; Hausman (1995), (1997); Kagan (1998), 44 f; Sen (1982f), (1982g), (2002h), 79 f; Van Praag (1993); and Weintraub (1996), (1998). Hausman and McPherson argue that such comparisons pose no problem for an objective theory of welfare: Hausman and McPherson (1993), 692, (1998), 208.

93 See Kagan (1998), 46 f; Parfit (1984), 420 ff.

94 Rawls (1972), 152 ff, uses a maximin principle. Kagan (1998), 53, notes that maximin is an extreme form of 'weighted benevolence'.

competition[95] is reinforced by the optimistic assertions of theorists such as Hayek[96] and Schumpeter, who famously described competition as a process of 'creative destruction';[97] by the intuitions of common sense (I am likely to be treated better by a supplier who has to compete for my custom than by one who holds me captive); and by broad comparisons between socialist and capitalist economies.[98] The value of such comparisons is limited, however, by the problems of measuring and comparing levels of welfare and competition in different economies and by the fact that pure forms of socialism and capitalism do not exist:[99] as to socialism, it seems that competition can never be wholly eradicated[100] (some societies have adopted regimes of 'socialist competition'[101]); and there are constraints on competition in all capitalist economies, most obviously in the form of state aid. Against all these considerations are arguments that competition impedes rather than improves productivity, for example because it precludes the more efficient use of resources that cooperation allows.[102] (On the relation between competition and cooperation, see the last section of the previous chapter.)

The persuasiveness of an affirmative answer to (2) will vary depending on the theory of welfare adopted. The answer has some plausibility on the actual-desire theory, at least when that theory is artificially restricted to desires that are for products not characterised by externalities[103] and that, in Pigou's phrase, can be brought into relation with the measuring-rod of money;[104] but it has been seen that the theory is overwhelmed by

[95] Much of the empirical literature primarily concerns market structure rather than behaviour. The structure-conduct-performance paradigm pioneered in Mason (1939) treats the causal influence of structure on behaviour as more important than the feedback from the latter to the former. As Faull and Nikpay note, in the paradigm's 'most mechanistic form conduct becomes quite irrelevant to study': Faull and Nikpay (1999), para. 1.10. For overviews of the empirical literature and discussions of its methodological problems, see Scherer and Ross (1990), ch. 11; and Whish (2003), 13 f. See also Bishop and Walker (2002), para. 1.10 f, on the use of empirical techniques in antitrust.

[96] Hayek (1982), vol. 3, 74 f. [97] Schumpeter (1975), ch. 7.

[98] See Kay (2003), part 2. Such comparisons are criticised in Kohn (1992), 241.

[99] Compare Kohn (1992), 1 f, on the different degrees to which cultures use competition to structure their economic system.

[100] See Nove (1983), 203. Wilson (1989), 27, implausibly claims that the ineradicability of competition is a logical rather than a contingent matter. Kohn (1992), 34, by contrast, claims that some cultures appear to be entirely non-competitive.

[101] See Deutscher (1952); Naylor (1975); and Prvulovich (1982), 80.

[102] Kohn (1992), ch. 3. [103] See Lipsey (1989), 400 ff.

[104] Pigou (2002), 11. On non-market goods and services as a source of satisfaction, see Scitovsky (1992), 86.

objections. The answer is implausible on the favoured objective theory, at least if this theory is amplified by a list of goods similar to the one set out earlier. One obstacle to assessment is the fact that each item is a separate maximand, and so some process of balancing is needed where an increase in one brings a decrease in another. Setting that problem aside, consider one item on Griffin's list: deep personal relations. How are these promoted, let alone maximised, by competition? A familiar complaint is that competition erodes social bonds:[105] in that case, or anyway, it is likely to make deep personal relations harder to form and sustain.[106]

A possible reply is that competition promotes economic growth, which in turn promotes the goods described by the objective theory. But, while it can be conceded that extreme poverty makes it hard or impossible to participate in all the goods on the list (which in any case includes minimum material provision), it is doubtful that such participation increases, intensively or extensively, in proportion to a state's or an individual's prosperity.[107] Research indicates that economic growth above a certain threshold does little to improve happiness;[108] it is reasonable to think that a parallel result applies to the good life as described by the objective theory. In that case the reply is irrelevant to rich countries, where antitrust laws are most common.

Another counter-objection to the reply is that it talks of promotion rather than maximisation: the former is presumably weaker than the latter. This prompts the thought that the welfare-based argument for competition might be recast more modestly, to state only that it promotes welfare. Clarification of this vague statement creates a dilemma. One gloss is that aggregate welfare is higher when competition exists than when it does not,[109] which in turn may be construed to say that, however high the aggregate level of welfare that can be reached in a group of people when competition is absent, a higher one can be reached when it is present. But this is just another way of saying that competition *maximises* welfare, in which case promotion is no weaker than maximisation after all. If on the other hand the statement that competition promotes welfare

105 See Buchanan (1985), 95 ff; and Kohn (1992), ch. 6.

106 See Buchanan (1985), 101 ff; Gauthier (1978), 130 ff; Hegel (1952), 105 ff; and Kohn (1992), ch. 6. Compare Singer (1972), 312 ff; and Titmuss (1971).

107 Raz observes that reasonably affluent people can give up quite a lot at no cost to their welfare: Raz (1994a), 28. See also Unger (1996).

108 See Campbell (1981); Diener (1984); Duncan (1975); Easterlin (1974); Inglehart (1996); Kahneman and Varey (1993), 141; Lane (1994), 229; and Scitovsky (1992), ch. 7.

109 Compare Bishop and Walker (2002), para. 2.01.

means only that it enhances some aspect or other of welfare, it is uninterestingly modest, for no one will deny that in some circumstances some instances of some forms of good on the list are enhanced by competition: a trivial example is the enjoyment gained from running a competitive business. The challenge, for a proponent of the revised version of the welfare-based argument, is to specify an intermediate sense for the statement 'Competition promotes welfare' that yields the right answers for the correspondingly revised questions (1)–(3).

Let it be granted arguendo that in some sense competition promotes welfare according to the objective theory (call it objective welfare). Presumably this is true primarily in markets for products that themselves promote welfare. In that case, if competition and antitrust are justified by their effects on welfare, the objective theory motivates discrimination by antitrust authorities: since interventions are costly, they should be limited to protect competition in such markets and not be made in markets for products that reduce or have no effect on welfare levels. That is not the current practice: authorities have intervened in markets for various harmful or trivial goods and services such as cigarettes, betting, perfume, replica football kit, ice cream and video games.[110] It is true that antitrust is generally lenient towards agreements or forms of behaviour that are unimportant, but the criteria of importance do not clearly concern objective welfare; for example 'conduct of minor significance', which is given limited immunity from penalties for abuse of dominance under the UK Competition Act 1998, is defined in terms of the dominant firm's turnover: significance is thus a matter of size, not of effect on objective welfare.[111]

[110] Cigarettes: Cases 209/78 etc., *Van Landewyck* v. *Commission* [1980] ECR 3125, [1981] 3 CMLR 134; and Cases 240/82 etc., *SSI* v. *Commission* [1985] ECR 3831, [1987] 3 CMLR 661. Betting: Competition Commission (1998). Perfume: *Parfums Givenchy*, OJ (1992) L 236/11, [1993] 5 CMLR 579. Replica football kit: Case CP/0871/01, *Price-Fixing of Replica Football Kit*, Decision of the Office of Fair Trading, 1.8.03. Ice cream: Case T-9/93, *Schöller* v. *Commission* [1995] ECR II-1611, [1995] 5 CMLR 659; Case T-65/98, *Van den Bergh Foods Ltd* v. *Commission* (CFI judgment of 23.10.03). Video games: Commission Decision Comp/35.587, *PO Video Games*; Comp/35.706, *PO Nintendo Distribution*; and Comp/36.321, *Omega – Nintendo*, 2003/675/EC, OJ L 255/33, 8.10.2003.

[111] Competition Act 1998, s. 40; Competition Act 1998 (Small Agreements and Conduct of Minor Significance) Regulations 2000, reg. 4. Likewise the European Commission's notice on the handling of complaints emphasises the Commission's discretion whether to take action, depending on the degree of 'Community interest', but the criteria of Community interest that are specified in the notice are not readily construed to concern objective welfare: 2004/C 101/05, OJ C 101/65, 27.4.2004, paras. 41–5. A document that comes closer to invoking objective welfare as a criterion of intervention is Office of Fair

The discriminatory proposal is likely to attract various objections. First it may be said that some of the products mentioned are for children, for whom the standards of objective welfare must be adjusted. But, while this may be true of replica football kit, it does not apply to cigarettes, betting or perfume, and some adults eat ice cream and/or play video games. Next, the proposal may be condemned as snobbish and puritanical.[112] The reply to this is that the proposal does not require agreement on the examples just given: if a case can be made that to smoke cigarettes is to participate in a form of good, so be it: the conclusion does not follow that there is no distinction between products that do and those that do not promote objective welfare.

More seriously, the proposal may be said to amount to paternalism,[113] which is objectionable on epistemic, practical and moral grounds.[114] The epistemic objection is that an antitrust authority is in no better a position than consumers to know what promotes their welfare; the practical objection is that, even if the authority knows about consumers' welfare, it is unable effectively to discriminate in its interventions so as to promote it; and the ethical objection is that, even if it is able to, it ought not to. The epistemic objection concerns the authority's judgments, the pragmatic and ethical objections concern the actions it takes on the basis of its judgments.

The proposal is not paternalistic. A rough definition of paternalism is: interference with a person's liberty in order to prevent harm to, or to benefit,[115] that person.[116] Suppose that there are cartels in the supply of pain-relieving drugs and of cigarettes, that the drugs increase welfare and that cigarettes decrease it, and that on this basis the authority decides to

Trading (2003a), which states that in deciding whether to make a market investigation reference under the UK Enterprise Act 2002 the OFT will consider whether there is 'a significant detrimental effect on customers through higher prices, lower quality, less choice or less innovation' (para. 2.27).

112 Compare Sumner (1996), 166, on the proposal to build a 'value requirement' into the analysis of welfare.

113 Compare Hammond (1995), 97.

114 The locus classicus of anti-paternalism is Mill (1972b).

115 In Feinberg's terminology, 'legal' paternalism is concerned with harms and 'extreme' paternalism with benefits: Feinberg (1973), 33. Lyons (1994), 134–5, draws a similar distinction between 'weak' and 'strong' paternalism.

116 This definition has been refined in the literature: see Archard (1993); Arneson (1998); Barry (1986), 41; Buchanan and Brock (1990), 61–2; Burrows (1993), 558, (1995), 495; G. Dworkin (1972), (1988), ch. 8; Feinberg (1973), 45, (1986), ch. 17; Gert and Culver (1976); Goodin (1993); Hart (1963), 31; S. Kelman (1981); New (1999), 65; Rawls (1972), 249–50; Sartorius (1983); Scanlon (1972), 221; VanDeVeer (1986), 22; and Weale (1978), 163.

intervene in the market for the drugs but not in the market for cigarettes. Now consider separately its decision to intervene, its decision not to intervene and its intervention. The two decisions are not paternalistic by the definition, for they do not interfere with anyone's liberty: arguably the cartellists restrict the liberty of consumers, but it cannot be said that the authority's decision not to intervene in the market for cigarettes thereby indirectly restricts consumers' liberty. The intervention in the drug market avoids paternalism because, although it may interfere with the liberty of the cartellists, it does so in order to prevent harm not to them but to the users of the drugs.

Gerald Dworkin distinguishes pure from impure paternalism:[117] in pure cases the people whose liberty is restricted are, and in impure cases they are not, the same people who are either benefited or prevented from suffering harm. It might therefore be objected that the authority's intervention constitutes impure paternalism. But that is not so, for the feature that distinguishes impure paternalism from other forms of action to prevent harm to others is that in the former case the harm can be avoided by the potential sufferers if they choose. That feature is lacking here: if the cartel raises the price of the drugs, consumers must pay more or forgo the use of the drugs. Either outcome harms them.

Although the accusation of paternalism fails, the three objections underlying it might still be pressed. The epistemic objection, that an antitrust authority is in no better a position than consumers to know what promotes their welfare,[118] may in turn be based on any of three claims, each of which is in tension, but can be made consistent, with the objective theory: that there are no facts about welfare and hence nothing to know about what promotes it (irrealism), or that there are facts about welfare and what promotes it but either no one knows them (scepticism) or a person's life goes well for him just in case he thinks it does (subjectivism). The claims may in turn arise from a concern that, at any rate in pluralistic Western societies, there is a lack of consensus about welfare.[119]

[117] G. Dworkin (1972), 68. Feinberg (1986), 5, draws similar distinctions, between benevolent and non-benevolent forms of 'presumptively blamable paternalism' and within 'presumptively non-blamable paternalism'.

[118] See Buchanan and Brock (1990), 38; Kahneman and Varey (1993), 129; Little (1957), 258; and Mill (1972b), 133. For criticism of anti-paternalistic arguments from the claim that people know their own interests best, see Lyons (1994), 132 f; and New (1999), 71 ff.

[119] Compare the irrealist/sceptical/relativist classification of views on reasonableness and honesty, in the discussion of the cartel offence in chapter 4, where those views are similarly connected to a concern about lack of consensus. The principle which Boadway and Bruce call 'non-paternalism' is subjectivist: 'the household's welfare is identified with its own perception of its utility': Boadway and Bruce (1984), 31.

To discuss these points adequately would require an excursion, beyond the scope of this chapter, into the theory of value. In brief, how plausible the irrealist claim is depends on the sense given to 'facts'; but, even if in some sense there are no facts about welfare, the inference is dubious that we cannot know what promotes it: a defensible view is that, whether or not there is a fact that (say) accomplishment is a component of welfare, we may know that it is and know that education promotes accomplishment. As to the sceptical claim, we surely know, or at any rate have a justified belief or opinion, that operations to remove cataracts generally promote welfare[120] (this proposition is not upset by the story that Brentano, who lost his sight, said that his blindness helped him to concentrate on philosophy). As to the subjectivist claim, it has philosophically respectable forms, but is often no more than a dogma of the half-educated. In this form it encourages inconsistency and complacency – inconsistency in that it is often combined with intrusive views about other people's welfare, complacency in that it is taken to spare one from reflection on how to live.

As to the point about a consensus, it does not entail any of the three claims and thus gives no clear support to the epistemic objection. But it raises a different worry (which could be brought under the ethical objection, discussed below), that democracy will be violated if an antitrust authority acts on judgments which, whether or not they amount to knowledge, diverge widely from those made by substantial sections of society, especially the sections most directly affected by the authority's interventions:[121] if many people think that video-games help to make their lives go well for them, while the authority proceeds on the view that they are a waste of time, its mandate to act is called into question. To pursue this issue it would be necessary to specify the democratic principles in question, to examine their basis and to determine whether indeed they are violated in such cases of divergence.[122] Here it must suffice to observe, first, that governments that pass for democratic usually act against the judgments of much of the electorate and, second, that antitrust authorities do not on the whole

[120] See Raz (1994c), 103, for a denial that value-judgments are especially prone to error.

[121] See Hahn and Hollis (1979), 9; and New (1999), 81 f.

[122] For discussion of the concept of consensus within a liberal framework, see Rawls (1993), lecture 4. On the need for a consensus about welfare in order for considerations of welfare to have the place commonly assigned to them in moral argument, see Scanlon (1975), 655. On the misuse of the concept of democracy in support of toleration, see Raz (1994c), 113 ff.

appear to act on eccentric views as to what makes people's lives go well for them.

To complete the reply to the epistemic objection: an antitrust authority is often in at least as good a position as consumers to know what promotes their welfare. Sometimes it is in a better one, specifically where it has a broader perspective or is more impartial:[123] for example its judgments on the effects of smoking will not, whereas those of a smoker may, be skewed by weakness of will. In any event, even if the authority is generally in a worse epistemic position, its position is strong enough to enable it to draw serviceable distinctions between products that do and those that do not promote welfare. The discriminatory proposal is not undermined by the existence of difficult cases.

The practical objection was that, even if the authority knows about consumers' welfare, it is unable effectively to discriminate in its interventions so as to promote it.[124] This thought springs from the point made earlier, that each entry on the objective theory's list is only an outline which can be filled in with a variety of specifications of the relevant form of good: how, or whether, an individual realises the form in his own life depends on aspects of his abilities, character and circumstances which the tools of antitrust are too crude to influence reliably. The objection misconceives the discriminatory proposal, which is intended only in a modest version: the idea is not that the authority should constantly be trying to make fine adjustments to individual lives, but rather that it may decline to intervene where it is reasonably obvious that a product's positive effects on most people's welfare are negligible.

The ethical objection was that, even if the authority is able to discriminate in a way that promotes welfare, it ought not to.[125] The argument is likely to be that this would infringe people's liberty[126] or autonomy.[127] The analysis of these terms is a vexed issue,[128] but the weakness

[123] See G. Dworkin (1972), 76 ff; and New (1999), 75 ff. For cases in which public authorities are especially liable to error in value-judgment, see Raz (1994c), 103 f.

[124] See Gaus (1998), 31. [125] See Sobel (1994), 789.

[126] For recent discussions of liberty-based objections to paternalism, see Burrows (1993); and Weale (1978), 169 ff.

[127] On autonomy-based objections to paternalism, see G. Dworkin (1972), 70 ff; Feinberg (1986), 23 ff, 57 ff; and Weale (1978), 169 ff.

[128] A sample of the recent literature: On liberty: Feinberg (1984), 206 ff; Lomasky (2000); and Sen (2002a), 585 ff, (2002d), 9 ff, (2002e), 506 ff, (2002h), 92. On autonomy: Arneson (1998), 251 f; Benn (1971); Brock (1993), 97 ff; Buchanan and Brock (1990), 36; Christman (1989); Downie and Telfer (1971); G. Dworkin (1988); Elster (1989), 109–10; Feinberg (1986), chs. 18–19; Frankfurt (1999a); Hill (1991), (2002c), 31–6; Korsgaard (1996),

of the argument can be demonstrated on the basis of an intuitive understanding.[129] In the first place, there is the question what is wrong with infringing liberty or autonomy. If the answer is the consequentialist one that such an infringement reduces welfare[130] – this answer might be based on the thesis that liberty and autonomy are themselves elements of welfare (see above)[131] – the argument loses some of its force, for it then appears to be committed to the view that the reduction is bound to be greater than the increase in welfare that would result from discriminatory interventions by the authority: that view associates an unrealistically high level of welfare with liberty and autonomy. The next question is: whose liberty or autonomy is infringed? Consider again the pain-relieving drugs and the cigarettes. As already mentioned, the authority's two decisions, to intervene in the market for the former and not in the market for the latter, do not infringe anyone's liberty, and the same goes for autonomy. If the intervention in the drug market infringes the cartellists' liberty or autonomy, that is a point only about the intervention itself: it has nothing to do with the fact that the authority's approach is discriminatory. Thus the argument goes too far, implausibly implying that all antitrust interventions, discriminatory or not, are morally objectionable. In any event it is the cartellists, not the consumers, whose liberty/autonomy is arguably infringed: this may be justified in the public interest, and specifically in the interest of promoting welfare. It is uncontroversial that there are circumstances in which the public interest justifies the state in infringing liberty or autonomy: think of the liberty of convicted murderers. If it is replied that 'infringe' has a pejorative sense that makes 'justified infringement' an oxymoron, the point can be rephrased in terms of 'restrictions' and the onus is then on the objector to explain why a restriction on the liberty or autonomy of a cartellist amounts to an infringement.

22 ff; Rawls (1972), 515, (1993), 28, 72–7, 98–9; Raz (1994c), 117 ff; Reath (1998); Scanlon (1972), 215 f; Schneewind (1986); Scoccia (1987), 591 ff; Sumner (1996), 156 ff; VanDeVeer (1986), 129 ff; and Young (1980). On the relation between the two: G. Dworkin (1988), 13 f; Feinberg (1973), 15 ff, (1986), 62 ff (where a distinction is drawn between liberty and freedom); Frankfurt (1999c), 109 f; Griffin (2000), 40 ff; and Hargreaves Heap *et al.* (1992), ch. 6.

[129] See Raz (1994c), 117 ff, for a defence of the view that a government may decide what is good for people, and on that basis promote their welfare, without compromising their autonomy. For discussion of Raz's view, see Morris (1996), 821 ff.

[130] See Buchanan and Brock (1990), 37 f; and Feinberg (1984), 206, (1986), 58 ff, 65. The consequentialist view is criticised in Glover (1990), 81 f.

[131] Contrast Korsgaard (1996), 358, where it is argued that autonomy has no weight if it is defined in terms of utility.

Other objections to the discriminatory proposal are unconnected with the mistaken claim that it is paternalist. One is that parallel reasoning would lead to the repellent conclusion that the state should only protect private property when the thing owned, or the fact of ownership, enhances welfare. The answer to this is that the institution of private property is supported by arguments that do not appeal to welfare.[132] Another objection is that the proposal fails to take account of connections between markets, on both the consumer's and the supplier's side: a consumer who is forced to pay a supra-competitive price for a product that does not enhance his welfare will have less to spend on products that do; a supplier with a dominant position in a market for a product that does not enhance welfare may abuse his dominance so as to increase his power in a market for products that are welfare-enhancing; so the indirect effect of a laissez-faire approach by antitrust authorities to markets for products of the former kind is to reduce welfare. This objection has no force so far as the consumer is concerned. He can raise the amount he has to spend on welfare-enhancing products by declining to buy the product that does not enhance his welfare: by hypothesis this will cause him no welfare loss. On the supplier's side, the objection presupposes that power can be levered from one market to another: although this may sometimes be so, it is not the usual case,[133] and the case in which the products in the respective markets differ as described in their effects on welfare is still less usual.

Finally it may be objected that the discriminatory proposal fails to recognise the fact that a supplier's anti-competitive conduct, whether or not the relevant market is for products that enhance welfare, can reduce the welfare of other *suppliers* – in the extreme, by driving them out of business – and of their employees and shareholders. The existence and seriousness of such adverse effects will depend on the facts of each case: in certain instances, where the products in question reduce welfare, the welfare gain – a reduction in the reduction – caused by the anti-competitive conduct, for example through a raising of price or restriction of supply, may outweigh the loss so caused to other suppliers. So this objection at most restricts, rather than undermines, the discriminatory proposal. In any event, a rejection of the proposal on this ground presupposes the

[132] See Munzer (1998), 759 f.

[133] On tying and bundling of products in the context of abuse of dominance, see Bishop and Walker (2002), para. 6.54 ff; and Whish (2003), 657 ff, 702 f. On leverage and portfolio power in the context of mergers, see Bishop and Walker (2002), para. 7.71 ff; and Whish (2003), 841 f.

view, now widely abandoned, that the business of antitrust is to protect not competition but competitors.[134] (It also presupposes – if competitors are distinguished from consumers[135] – that the welfare with which antitrust is concerned is not only that of consumers: see above.)

The discriminatory proposal thus withstands the objections. But it does not question the assumption, on which the objective theory casts doubt, that competition promotes welfare. That assumption is unclear, as has been seen. If clarification falsifies it, the proposal needs another rationale.

Question (3): welfare proxies

Question (3) is whether it is a good thing to maximise welfare. On our intuitive understanding, according to which a person's welfare is what makes his life go well for him, the answer may seem to be a truistic yes. But even at this level the position is more complicated. Even if maximising welfare is good pro tanto, it may not be good on balance, for it can conflict with other goods, notably fairness of distribution. An attempt might be made to avoid this difficulty by building fairness into the concept of welfare; but that will only preclude the conflict by giving undue – for example, lexical – priority to fairness in determining welfare levels (compare the parallel point above about liberty and autonomy). In any case, it is doubtful whether maximising welfare is good pro tanto, for it may be held that some people – the wicked, who deserve to suffer – should be excluded from the calculation.[136]

The complication increases once one turns to the theories that amplify our intuitive understanding. On the objective theory an affirmative answer to (3) is fairly plausible – how plausible will depend on the theory's list of forms of good – when interpreted as a pro-tanto claim; on the other theories it is implausible. For example one of them says that welfare consists in the satisfaction of desire: in that case to maximise welfare, in the aggregative sense, is to satisfy as many desires as possible, perhaps allowing some to be given greater weight than others. But there is a strong case for the view that satisfaction of a desire as such, and a stronger case for the view that satisfaction of people's desires for things that make their lives go badly for them, is not good even pro tanto[137] (these are analogues to objections (ii) and (iii) above to the actual-desire theory). Likewise

[134] On the decline of this view, see Whish (2003), 19 f.

[135] In Bork's classification, competitors are a subclass of consumers: see note 3 above.

[136] See Kagan (1998), 54 ff.

[137] See Scoccia (1987), 588.

one objection to the economic theory, according to which maximisation of welfare is the same as allocative efficiency, was that it leaves it obscure why we should be interested in maximising welfare.

One response is to suggest that maximisation of welfare as specified by the other theories is good not in itself but as a means to the maximisation of objective welfare. The idea is that welfare as conceived by the other theories is a proxy for objective welfare[138] in the sense that it both correlates reliably with objective welfare and is easier to control through law and policy; indeed there may be a chain in which, say, satisfied choice is a proxy for satisfied preference, which is a proxy for satisfied desire, which is a proxy for objective welfare.[139]

Doubt is cast on this suggestion by the point made earlier, that the persuasiveness of an affirmative answer to question (2) – Does competition maximise welfare? – varies from theory to theory. If the answer is yes on the actual-desire theory but no on the objective theory, it is hard to argue that the maximisation of satisfied actual desires by competition is a means to the maximisation of objective welfare. The suggestion might be saved by contending that some process other than competition can maximise satisfied actual desires in a way that ensures the maximisation of objective welfare; but, apart from the fact that it is obscure what the process might be, the answer is irrelevant to the present topic.

As to the idea of a chain of proxies, it is unclear where the economic theory's conception of welfare would fit, in part because it is unclear what that conception is. As noted earlier, the version that defines allocative efficiency as Pareto optimality does not give separate meanings to 'welfare' and 'maximise'. On the other version welfare can be defined as the sum of consumer and producer surplus: this can perhaps be added at the start of the chain, as a proxy for satisfied choice; for example, as to consumer surplus, it might be said that the larger the difference between a person's reservation price and the price he actually pays, the wider his scope for satisfying his other choices by his purchases or in his leisure time.

The other links of the chain are weak. Suppose I am in bed and am comfortably nodding off for the night when I remember that I have not

138 See Kahneman and Varey (1993), 127. Conversely, objective welfare is sometimes viewed as a proxy for subjective: Elster and Roemer (1993b), 10; Hausman and McPherson (1993), 689; and Scanlon (1975), 657.

139 Pigou (2002), 23 ff, proposes a different chain of proxies: income expenditure as a proxy for intensity of desire, and the latter a proxy for intensity of felt satisfaction. See also Sumner (1996), 114 f. Pigou notes that the chain breaks in the case of attitudes to the future.

brushed my teeth. Wearily I get up and brush them, even though I recognise that it would do no harm to leave them unbrushed for once.[140] Clearly I choose to brush them and my choice is satisfied in the sense that I succeed in doing so. Whether I satisfy a preference to brush them depends on the meaning of 'prefer': if to prefer something is just to choose it – in which case satisfied choice is not a proxy for, but is identical to, satisfied preference – I satisfy my preference to brush my teeth; if to prefer is to desire, the question is whether I desire to brush them.[141] (Elision of these two senses is common among economists and papers over some cracks in revealed-preference theory.[142] There seems little room for a distinct intermediate sense.) Again it depends on the meaning of 'desire': if to desire is to choose, I satisfy my desire to brush my teeth, and likewise if to desire to do something is to do it voluntarily[143] – for I do not brush my teeth by reflex or under coercion. But in a fuller, more natural, sense I surely do not desire to brush them: perversely, I act against my desire to stay in bed. As to the last link in the chain, between satisfied desire and objective welfare, it breaks when people desire things that do not make their lives go well for them (see above).

It might be replied, first, that such counterexamples are unusual enough not to upset the claim of reliable correlation and, second, that the links can be strengthened in the way discussed earlier, by taking account only of the choices that a person would make, and the preferences and desires he would have, under favourable conditions, or of the choices, preferences and desires of an idealised subject in the relevant circumstances. As regards the first reply, the extent of divergence that one finds between people's actual choices, preferences and desires on the one hand and their objective welfare on the other will depend on how stern a view one takes of objective welfare. If the life of *l'homme moyen sensuel* goes well for him, the correlation is perhaps fairly good; it is poor if objective welfare consists in burning always with the hard gemlike flame; and it is unreliable on an attractive intermediate view.

[140] Davidson (1980c), 30, uses this example for another purpose.

[141] On the divergence between choice and preference, see Barry (1986), 32 f; Broome (1979), 324 f; Elster (1989), 106 ff; Elster and Hylland (1989b), 4, 7; Goodin (1989), 81 f; P. Hammond (1995), 89; Hausman and McPherson (1993), 680; Sen (1982a), (1982b), 79, (1982h), 8, (1982k), 94, (2002b); and Tversky (1981). On the conditions under which choice and preference coincide, see Allingham (2002), 17. On the relation between desire and preference, see Pettit (1998), 31 f.

[142] See Hylland (1989), 64; and Sen (2002b), 302; compare Sumner (1996), 115 ff. For other ambiguities of 'prefer', see Buchanan (1985), 11, 26–7; Sen (1982j), (2002a), 587 ff, (2002d), 13 f, (2002e), 513 f, 344; and Sobel (1998), 260.

[143] For a definition of the voluntary, see Feinberg (1973), 48.

The second reply faces two further objections. One is that it is little if at all easier to ascertain what a person would choose, prefer or desire under the specified favourable conditions than to identify his objective welfare[144] (this reflects the earlier point that the revised desire theory tends to tip into the objective theory); so the claim of reliable correlation is secured at the cost of jeopardising the proxy thesis's other component, the claim that the proxy is easier than objective welfare to control through law and policy.

The other objection is that antitrust must take people's choices, preferences and desires as they are, not as they might be. To this it may be replied in turn that antitrust is not the state's only means of promoting welfare: it operates together with other institutions, notably the education system, which help to narrow the gap between actual choices (etc.) and those that would be made under the specified conditions.[145] This view of education is perhaps more cheerful than realistic – how much more so will depend on the stringency of the conditions (compare the point about the sternness of views of objective welfare) – but in any case the reply gives no reason to promote the satisfaction of actual choices until the time – not yet – when the gap has narrowed enough to secure the claim of reliable correlation.

Conclusion

Neither the economic approach nor the philosophical approach to the maximisation of welfare supports the welfare-based argument for competition and antitrust. The current orthodoxy should therefore be abandoned.

[144] Hausman (1995), 486, makes a parallel point about actual preferences.

[145] Compare Bork (1978), 90: 'Antitrust thus has a built-in preference for material prosperity, but it has nothing to say about the ways prosperity is distributed or used. Those are matters for other laws.'

3

Per se rules and rules of reason

Overview

Antitrust opposes restrictions on competition, but would be unworkable if it prohibited every such restriction. Principles are therefore needed to determine the categories of restriction that should be prohibited. In the United States such principles are embodied in the doctrine of per se rules and rules of reason. There is a long-standing debate whether Article 81(1) EC does, or should, be subject to a rule of reason of the kind used by the US courts in applying section 1 of the Sherman Act 1890.[1] In US antitrust itself there is an even older debate as to the appropriate scope of rules of reason and per se rules in the application of section 1. One reason why these debates are unresolved is that the parties lack a shared understanding of the nature of, and relations between, per se rules and rules of reason.[2] The modest purpose of this chapter is to clarify the concepts of the two kinds of rule and to identify, at a fairly abstract level, the relations between them. I shall not be offering substantive proposals as to the kinds of conduct suitable for treatment under one or other type of rule.

People often talk of 'the' rule of reason, which implies that there is only one; but the next section of the chapter identifies three main classes of rule of reason. First there is a rule for interpreting section 1 as applying only to unreasonable restraints. Second, there is a class of rules specifying

[1] The answer no is supported by Case T-112/99, *Métropole Télévision* v. *Commission* [2001] ECR II-2459, [2001] 5 CMLR 1236, but called into question by Case C-309/99, *Wouters* v. *Algemene Raad van de Nederlandsche Orde van Advocaten* [2002] ECR I-1577, [2002] 4 CMLR 913. For commentary, see Whish (2003), 134 ff, and the articles cited there.

[2] Loose formulations abound. Bork (1978) for instance says that '(t)he rule of reason . . . is simply a set of general categories' (21). It is doubtful whether Bork thinks that any rule is literally a set, of categories or anything else. Likewise it may be doubted whether Piraino strictly means what he says when he describes 'the rule of reason' as a 'factual inquiry': Piraino (1991), 689. For complaints about obscurity in this area, see Gellhorn (1986), 427; and Hawk (1994), vol. 2, 96, 110.

criteria of reasonableness and unreasonableness. These fall into two subclasses: one represents what I call the dominant tradition, which judges the unreasonableness of a restraint by its effects on competition; the other represents the 'recessive tradition', which uses a wider range of criteria. Third, there are rules for applying the criterial rules: they are of the form 'An arrangement of kind K must be individually assessed under a criterial rule of reason to determine whether it is illegal under section 1.' Per se rules are of the form 'An arrangement of kind K is illegal under section 1': they are rules for applying section 1. In the course of the discussion I consider the issues arising from the need to weigh factors against each other when applying rules of reason, and I reflect on an analogy between the rule of reason / per se rule distinction and the distinction in ethical theory between direct and indirect consequentialism.

After reviewing the various benefits that people have claimed for the two kinds of rule, I identify two broad views of the relation between rules of reason and per se rules. On the 'simple view', the application of rules of reason and that of per se rules constitute an exhaustive and mutually exclusive pair of methods for assessing arrangements under section 1. On the 'complex view', the two kinds of rule fall on a continuum and there is no sharp boundary between them. Thus stated, the two views are not clear enough for a choice to be made between them. I therefore expand the question, which of them is right, into a set of seven clearer questions:

Does any rule of reason (the questions are restricted to rules of reason of the third class) or per se rule have vague scope? The answer is yes. Does the scope of any rule of reason overlap that of any per se rule? No, with qualifications. Does the union of the scopes of all rules of reason and per se rules – i.e. everything covered by either one or the other – include the scope of section 1? Yes and no. Is there a method of deciding the legality of arrangements under section 1 which involves the application neither of a rule of reason nor of a per se rule, but which has some characteristics of each approach? Three arguments support the answer yes. Do the courts ever change their approach to a kind of arrangement, so that, although first it falls within a per se rule, it later falls within a rule of reason, or vice versa? Yes. Is there a contradiction between the use of rules of reason and the use of per se rules, as some critical legal theorists have held? No. Is it the case that the application of rules of reason, but not of per se rules, involves discretion? I use Ronald Dworkin's distinction between three kinds of discretion to reach a qualified answer no. At the end I note that Dworkin's distinction gives reason to reject the suggestion that, when an arrangement falls within a rule of reason, there is no right answer to the question whether it is illegal under section 1.

Varieties of the two kinds of rule

An interpretative rule of reason

The first sentence of section 1 of the Sherman Act is: 'Every contract, combination in the form of trust or otherwise, or conspiracy, in the restraint of trade or commerce among the several states, or with foreign nations, is hereby declared to be illegal.' It was recognised early on that this prohibition catches too much if 'restraint of trade or commerce' is read as referring to every such restraint, no matter how slight.[3] The US courts therefore adopted towards section 1 the approach taken at common law towards restrictive covenants:[4] they construed the prohibition as applying only to restraints that are unreasonable.[5] This

[3] Justice Brandeis famously remarked that '(e)very agreement concerning trade, every regulation of trade, restrains. To bind, to restrain, is of their very essence': *Board of Trade of the City of Chicago* v. *United States*, 246 US 231, 238 (1918). Compare Bork's point that an agreement to eliminate competition is basic to almost every productive unit consisting of more than one person: Bork (1966), 377. In this connection Bork cites Justice Holmes's dissent in *Northern Securities Co.* v. *United States*, 193 US 197, 404 (1904). Joliet (1967), 22, by contrast, emphasises not the breadth of the concept of restraint of trade, but the fact that Congress left it undefined. Compare Whish (1993), 19.

Justice Peckham's opinion in *United States* v. *Trans-Missouri Freight Association*, 166 US 290 (1897), is authority for the view that section 1 does apply to every such restraint. For an unorthodox reading of Peckham, see Bork (1965), 785 ff. Sullivan (1977), 166, sets out two extreme interpretations of section 1, locating the predominant view between them.

[4] The common law test for restrictive covenants was stated in *Mitchel* v. *Reynolds*, 24 Eng Rep 346 (KB, 1711). Citations for the US courts' use of this test, both before and after the passage of the Sherman Act, are given in Beschle (1987), 471, n. 2. The test is broader than that used in the dominant tradition in the case law of section 1 (see below): *ibid.* 474, n. 15.

[5] The canonical statement of this construal is Chief Justice White's opinion in *Standard Oil Co. of New Jersey* v. *United States*, 221 US 1, 31 S Ct 502, 55 L Ed, 619 (1911), although White preferred the word 'undue' to 'unreasonable'. Bork (1978), 34, maintains that White's opinion contains a 'dynamic principle' which allows the law to change. Compare Chief Justice Hughes's observation that the Sherman Act 'has a generality and adaptability comparable to that found desirable in constitutional provisions': *Appalachian Coals Inc.* v. *United States*, 288 US 344, 359–60 (1933). Wood Hutchinson (1984), 98–9, distinguishes the 'substantive' rule of reason found in *Standard Oil*, and other cases, from a modern use of the phrase 'rule of reason' to connote the lack of a presumption against a practice.

Compare the distinction (a) between reasonable and unreasonable restraints with the distinctions (b) between those provisions that impose and those that do not impose restraints, (c) between direct and indirect restraints and (d) between ancillary and non-ancillary restraints. Bork (1965), 785 ff, finds (b) in Justice Peckham's opinions in *Trans-Missouri* (note 3 above) and *United States* v. *Joint Traffic Association*,

practice conforms to the first rule of reason, which is a rule for interpreting section 1:[6]

(R1) Read 'restraint' in section 1 as 'unreasonable restraint'.

Rules of reason: the dominant tradition

(R1) raises the question, what makes a restraint reasonable or unreasonable?[7] There are two traditions in the case law of section 1,[8] embodying different conceptions of the section's purpose[9] and using correspondingly different criteria of reasonableness and unreasonableness. The dominant tradition has it that the purpose of section 1 is solely to promote competition, and it therefore views the reasonableness or unreasonableness of a restraint, for the purposes of the section, as solely a matter of the restraint's effect on competition.[10] This view is indeterminate because,

171 US 505 (1898), and (c) in Peckham's opinions in *Anderson* v. *United States*, 171 US 604 (1898), and *Hopkins* v. *United States*, 171 US 578 (1898).

As to (d), a prominent line of cases holds that a restraint falls outside section 1 if it is ancillary to a legitimate purpose. On one view, such ancillary restraints form a subclass of reasonable restraints. The principle that they fall outside section 1 was first articulated by Judge Taft, who based it on the common law, in *United States* v. *Addyston Pipe & Steel Co.*, 85 Fed 271 (6th Cir 1898); see also *Whitwell* v. *Continental Tobacco Co.*, 125 F 454, 459 (8th Cir 1903); *National Collegiate Athletic Association (NCAA)* v. *Board of Regents*, 104 S Ct 2948, 2961 (1984). For the doctrine of ancillarity in relation to Article 81 EC, see Whish (2003), 119 ff, and the materials cited there.

6 Compare Gellhorn (1986), 10; Joliet (1967), 61; and Neale and Goyder (1980), 23, 30. Neale and Goyder say that the rule of reason is a rule of construction, whereas per se rules are rules of evidence.

7 For simplicity I shall assume that every restraint is either reasonable or unreasonable. Justice Stone gave rather clumsy expression to the indeterminacy and variability of the concept of reasonableness in *United States* v. *Trenton Potteries Co.*, 273 US 392, 397 (1927). Stone's remarks are echoed in Areeda (1989), 361–2. On the courts' failure to identify clear criteria of reasonableness and unreasonableness, see Piraino (1991), 689; and Wood Hutchinson (1984), 70, 97.

8 Joliet (1967), 5 ff, appears to draw the same distinction. Bork (1965) divides the jurisprudence of section 1 into a different pair of traditions. Bork's 'Brandeis tradition' is the same as my recessive tradition, but his 'main tradition' is defined in terms of the satisfaction of consumers' wants, whereas my dominant tradition is defined in terms of competition. On the relation between competition and want-satisfaction, see chapter 2 above.

9 On the changing political objectives behind antitrust, see Fox (1990), 200–1; Gellhorn (1986), 41–2, 423 ff; Whish (2003), 17 ff; and Whish and Sufrin (1987), 8 ff.

10 This reflects the wording of Senator Sherman's original Bill, which was directed against 'all arrangements [etc.] . . . made with a view, or which tend to prevent free and full competition': see Joliet (1967), 21. The leading case in the dominant tradition is *National Society of Professional Engineers* v. *United States*, 435 US 679 (1978). For criticism of the test in that case, see Wertheimer (1984).

as noted at the start of chapter 1, 'competition' has various meanings. The courts have used different definitions in different cases – an instance of the scandal of antitrust identified in that chapter, that its practitioners do not agree on what competition is.

The cases in the dominant tradition contain, with various degrees of explicitness, various criteria of unreasonableness relating to competition. These criteria can be expressed in further rules of reason, which are subsidiary to (R1) and amplify it in different ways. The first is:

(R2) A restraint is unreasonable if it has significant anti-competitive effects.[11]

(R2) itself can be interpreted in different ways, depending on the measure of significance, the definition of competition and the range of effects. For example the rule may be read as applying to actual effects, or likely effects, or both. If actual effects are in question, the rule may or may not apply to those that are remote, and there are various possible thresholds of remoteness. Similarly, if likely effects are in question, there are various possible thresholds of sufficient probability. (R2) might also be varied by replacing 'significant' with 'material' or 'substantial': 'material' arguably connotes a higher threshold than does 'significant', and 'substantial' than 'material'. The same point applies to the other rules set out below that include the concept of significance.

A second criterial rule of reason is:

(R3) A restraint is unreasonable if its anti-competitive effects significantly outweigh its pro-competitive effects.

Again this rule has various interpretations; for example its measure of significance may be absolute or proportional to the size of the anti-competitive and/or the pro-competitive effects. A restraint that falls within (R2) need not fall within (R3), for it may have significant anti-competitive effects which nevertheless do not significantly outweigh its pro-competitive effects. Likewise, if (R3) is read in terms of a proportional measure of significance, a restraint falling within (R3) need not fall within (R2); for it may have anti-competitive effects which are proportionally

[11] See *Kreuzer* v. *American Academy of Periodontology*, 558 F Supp 683, 685 (DDC 1983), 735 F 2d 1479 (DC Cir 1984); *Pontius* v. *Children's Hospital*, 552 F Supp 1352, 1372 (WD Pa 1981).

much greater than its pro-competitive effects, even though each set of effects is negligible.[12]

A third criterial rule of reason is formed by deleting the reference to significance in (R3):

(R4) A restraint is unreasonable if its anti-competitive effects outweigh its pro-competitive effects;[13]

and further rules are formed by introducing a reference to intention into (R2), (R3) and (R4):[14]

(R5) A restraint is unreasonable if it is intended to have significant anti-competitive effects.
(R6) A restraint is unreasonable if it is intended that its anti-competitive effects should significantly outweigh its pro-competitive effects.
(R7) A restraint is unreasonable if it is intended that its anti-competitive effects should outweigh its pro-competitive effects.

Each of these three rules has various interpretations, depending on the kind of intention at issue,[15] and parallel triads of rules can be formulated by introducing a requirement that the intention in question be predominant,[16] or by substituting for intention various related concepts such as purpose or motive.[17] Further rules are produced by combining the foregoing to yield compound criteria; for example (R2) and (R5) can be combined as:

[12] Compare this distinction between (R2) and (R3) with the distinction in Schechter (1982) between two possible interpretations of Article 81 EC.

[13] (R4) arguably articulates the test in *Professional Engineers* (note 10 above), 650. The European Court of Justice has taken a similar approach to Article 81(1) EC in Case 161/84, *Pronuptia de Paris GmbH* v. *Pronuptia de Paris Irmgaard Schillgalis* [1986] ECR 353. This approach to Article 81 was advocated in Confederation of British Industry (1995), 7–8.

[14] On the role of the concept of intention and kindred concepts in the application of section 1, see *Chicago Board of Trade* (note 3 above), 239; *Appalachian Coals* (note 4 above); Areeda (1989), 389 ff; Neale and Goyder (1980), 447 ff, 470; Oppenheim *et al.* (1981), 14; and the cases in note 18 below. The relation between the object of an agreement, for the purposes of Article 81 EC, and the parties' intentions is discussed in chapter 4 below.

[15] See Areeda (1989), 392; note 28 in chapter 1 above; and the discussion of object and effect in chapter 4 below.

[16] See the reference to 'primary purpose' in *Denison Mattress Factory* v. *Spring-Air Company*, 308 F 2d, 403, 408 (5th Cir 1962); and compare the doctrine of ancillary restraints (note 5 above).

[17] The concepts are often confused with each other in discussions of section 1. See e.g. Joliet (1967), 134. On the distinctions between the concept of intention and similar concepts, see chapter 1 above.

(R8) A restraint is unreasonable if it has or is intended to have significant anti-competitive effects.[18]

Rules of reason: the recessive tradition

Although the dominant tradition regards the purpose of section 1 as being solely to promote competition, the section does not mention competition.[19] The other tradition in the case law, which may be called the recessive tradition,[20] includes the promotion of competition among a broad and open-ended range of purposes which it attributes to section 1.[21] These are reflected by a range of criteria for deciding whether a restraint is reasonable. Criteria that have been invoked are fairness, diversity of choice, protection of consumers and small firms, dispersal of power, access to markets, redistribution of wealth, the spreading of business among a large number of firms, promotion of various industrial and social policies concerning employment, working hours and so forth, dissemination of information on market conditions, diminution of risk, technological innovation and allocation of commercial decisions between firms on the one hand and antitrust authorities on the other.[22] Some but not all of

[18] Compare Chief Justice White's disjunctive test in *United States* v. *American Tobacco*, 221 US 106, 179 (1911). Other cases using disjunctive criteria are *United States* v. *Imperial Chemical Industries*, 100 F Supp 504, 557 (SDNY 1951), and *White Motor Co.* v. *United States*, 372 US 253, 263 (1963).

[19] As Justice Holmes noted in his dissent in *Northern Securities* (note 3 above). Contrast the wording of Senator Sherman's Bill (note 10 above).

[20] In the terminology of Gellhorn and Tatham (1985), 162 ff, this tradition embodies the 'civil rights' approach. This appears to be the same as the 'Interventionist Model' in Piraino (1991), 686.

[21] The main source of the recessive tradition is *Chicago Board of Trade*, anticipated to some extent by *Northern Securities* (both in note 3 above). Other significant cases in the tradition are *Appalachian Coals* (note 5 above); *United States* v. *Associated Press*, 52 F Supp 362 (1943); *United States* v. *Aluminium Company of America*, 148 F 2d 416, 427 (2d Cir 1945); *United States* v. *Paramount Pictures Inc.*, 334 US 131 (1948); *Standard Oil Co.* v. *United States (Standard Stations)*, 337 US 293, 318–19 (1949) (Douglas J dissenting); *Times-Picayune Publishing Co.* v. *United States*, 345 US 594, 614 ff (1953); *Brown Shoe Co.* v. *United States*, 370 US 294, 344 (1962); *United States* v. *Penn-Olin Chemical Co.*, 378 US 158, 176–7 (1964); and *United States* v. *Topco Associates Inc.*, 405 US 596, 610 (1972). The distinction between the dominant and the recessive traditions is comparable to that in UK merger control between the 'substantial lessening of competition' test in the Enterprise Act 2003 and the broader (and now discarded) 'public interest' test in the Fair Trading Act 1973.

[22] EC competition law, and certain other European anti-cartel laws, have also been used to pursue non-competitive aims – most notably, in the case of the former, the integration of the internal market. See Joliet (1967), 24, 60, 71 ff, 113–14; Korah (1986), 85; Scherer and Ross (1990) 328 ff; and Whish (2003), 17 ff.

these criteria can be brought under the rubric of competition:[23] it has been seen that 'competition' has diverse meanings. Just as the courts have vacillated within the dominant tradition among the different definitions of competition, so they have wavered between the dominant and the recessive traditions, now restricting their attention to competition, in one or other sense, now broadening their inquiries to embrace other criteria.[24] This is a second scandal of antitrust, for there is no reason to believe that actions promoting competition will also, say, diminish risk or that the two traditions are appropriate to different situations.

Each criterion in the list can be expressed in a further rule of reason amplifying (R1). Whereas the criterial rules in the dominant tradition are more easily formulated to specify sufficient conditions of *un*reasonableness, those in the recessive tradition are better formulated in terms of reasonableness. A simple example is:

(R9) A restraint is reasonable if it promotes or is intended to promote technological innovation.

However, the decisions within the recessive tradition tend to apply the criteria jointly, so a more realistic rule is:

(R10) A restraint is reasonable if it satisfies or is intended to satisfy a sufficient number of the relevant criteria to a sufficient extent.

(R10) has various interpretations, depending among other things on the measure connoted by each occurrence of 'sufficient'.

Weighing

I shall here use 'arrangement' to cover the extension – whatever exactly it is – of section 1's three words: 'contract', 'combination' and 'conspiracy'.[25] (R10) confronts the courts with the problem of assessing an arrangement against all these criteria at once. In order to apply the criteria jointly, a court must weigh them against each other; for example, is fairness to count for more than diversity of choice? An analogous, if more limited,

[23] See Areeda (1989), 383.

[24] See Bork (1965), (1978); Fox (1990); Gellhorn and Tatham (1985), 164; Wood Hutchinson (1984), 148; and the works cited in note 9 above.

[25] The extension of an expression is the set of things to which it applies. Chapters 4 and 5 discuss arrangements in the different sense or senses used by the UK Enterprise Act 2002 and the UK Restrictive Trade Practices Act 1976.

problem faces a court that espouses the dominant tradition but seeks to apply different definitions of competition simultaneously: is the process of rivalry, for example, more important than the absence of restraint? The need for weighing arises at various points when criterial rules of reason are used. In addition to those just mentioned, a court may have to weigh against each other different forms of the same kind of competition, for instance rivalry between and within brands. Also, the rules refer to matters of degree: if a court applies (R2), it must weigh anti-competitive effects to decide whether they are significant. In the case of rules mentioning predominant intentions, weighing will be necessary to determine which intention predominates.

A theoretical question and a practical question arise here. The theoretical question is: what is weighing? It is not enough to invoke the metaphor of a mental pair of scales. The question needs to be broken into further questions, for example: is there a single mental operation common to these cases and to all others that we are disposed to describe as a matter of weighing? To what extent does the operation, or do the operations, comprise judgments of fact, and to what extent judgments of value? The practical question is: how is a court to reach a decision in any of these cases?[26] Both questions raise the further question whether objective procedures are available, which in turn raises a fourth question, as to the nature of objectivity. Pessimists, including some legal realists, hold that there are no objective procedures in these cases: judges can only dress up their personal preferences. But less gloomy views are defensible. Someone who believes in the subjectivity of evaluation and the objectivity of empirical inquiry[27] may hold that the situation varies, depending on the proportions of evaluation and empirical inquiry involved in the case. He may say, for example, that there are greater objective constraints on a judgment that the anti-competitive effects of a restraint are significant than on a judgment that fairness is more important than diversity of choice. All these questions lead into general legal philosophy; I shall not pursue them here.

[26] Replies to the theoretical and the practical questions tend to be sketchy. On the theoretical question, see Broome (1991b); R. Dworkin (1978), 26–7; Greenawalt (1992), 205–6; Stocker (1992); and B. Williams (1985), 97. On the practical question, see Areeda (1989), 362, 394, 398; and Sullivan (1977), 188. On the question whether weighing requires a common ingredient among the things weighed, contrast Bork (1965), 832, with Griffin (1986), 90–1, and Shafer-Landau (1995), 89 ff.

[27] Contrast the association of the subjective with the positive and of the objective with the normative in chapter 2 above.

Per se rules

Per se rules developed inductively through experience gained in applying rules of reason.[28] The courts recognised that, when arrangements of certain kinds were assessed under a rule of reason, they were almost always found to fall within section 1. Once these kinds were identified, it was a waste of resources to continue to apply a rule of reason to each individual arrangement of such a kind that came to trial: the additional information produced by the application of a rule of reason would not be worth the cost of acquiring it.[29] The courts therefore adopted rules to the effect that arrangements of those kinds are illegal per se under section 1.[30] Once such rules were in place, a court only had to satisfy itself that the arrangement before it was of one of the specified kinds in order to condemn it under section 1. (The benefits of per se rules will be considered in greater detail below.)

Per se rules are thus rules for applying section 1,[31] and they have the form:

(P1) An arrangement of kind K is illegal under section 1.

There is a different per se rule for each kind K.[32] Examples are:

(P2) Naked horizontal price fixing is illegal under section 1.
(P3) Group boycotts are illegal under section 1.

[28] See *Arizona* v. *Maricopa County Medical Society*, 457 US 322, 344 (1982); *Jefferson Parish Hospital District No. 2* v. *Hyde*, 466 US 2, 16 (1984); *Northwest Wholesale Stationers* v. *Pacific Stationery & Printing Co.*, 472 US 284, 289 (1985); *Federal Trade Commission* v. *Superior Court Trial Lawyers Association*, 493 US 411 (1990); Joliet (1967), 103; Neale and Goyder (1980), 449; Piraino (1994), 1770; and Sullivan (1977), 193.

[29] See Ehrlich and Posner (1974), 266.

[30] The language of per se illegality was first used in the context of section 1 in *Socony-Vacuum Oil Co.* v. *United States*, 310 US 150 (1940) (see below), but the idea can be traced back to *Trans-Missouri Freight* (note 3 above): see Scherer and Ross (1990), 317–18. On the purpose of per se rules, see *Northern Pacific Railway Co.* v. *United States*, 356 US 1, 5 (1958); *United States* v. *Container Corp. of America*, 393 US 333, 341 (1969) (Justice Marshall dissenting); *Professional Engineers* (note 10 above), 692; *Broadcast Music Inc.* v. *Columbia Broadcasting System Inc.*, 441 US 1, 19–20 (1979); and *NCAA* (note 5 above). In *Trial Lawyers* (note 28 above), 422–3, Justice Stevens asserted that per se rules are statutory commands, not rules of administrative convenience; contrast Areeda (1989), 396–7, and Wertheimer (1984), 1300, n. 24. Bork (1966), 377, attributes much of the Sherman Act's 'doctrinal chaos' to 'judicial and scholarly fondness for impossibly broad statements of the per se rule'; Bork sets out his own view of the proper scope of per se rules at 383–4. For a different analysis of per se rules, see note 36 below.

[31] Compare Neale and Goyder (1980), 30.

[32] Lists of such kinds are given in Hawk (1994), vol. 1, 276; and Oppenheim *et al.* (1981), 19.

Such rules cannot be combined as a single disjunctive rule, for, as will be made clear below, the class of relevant kinds is open in the sense that kinds are added and removed as judicial attitudes change.

An ethical analogy

There is an interesting analogy between the rule of reason / per se rule distinction in the jurisprudence of section 1 and the distinction in ethical theory between direct and indirect consequentialism. Roughly, direct consequentialism is the view that the rightness or wrongness of an individual action depends on the consequences of that action, whereas indirect consequentialism holds that judgments of right and wrong are made at two levels: whether an individual action is right or wrong depends on its conforming or failing to conform to the relevant moral rules, but the rules themselves are assessed in terms of the consequences of their obtaining. An assessment of an individual arrangement under a rule of reason is analogous to the direct consequentialist approach in that the legality of the arrangement is taken to depend on the arrangement's actual or intended consequences for competition. The per se approach is analogous to that of indirect consequentialism in comprising two levels of assessment: an individual arrangement is judged to be illegal if it falls within an applicable per se rule, and the rule itself is justified by its consequences for competition, judicial efficiency and other matters discussed below.

In ethics there is a continuing debate whether direct or indirect consequentialism is the better theory.[33] It would be instructive to consider the extent to which the arguments on either side of that debate can be adapted to support the use of rules of reason or per se rules in connection with section 1. For example, a standard objection to indirect consequentialism is that it is extensionally equivalent to direct consequentialism, since it must require every rule to have enough riders to prevent any individual action that conforms to the rule from having sub-optimal consequences.[34] Correspondingly it might be argued that the per se approach is no improvement on rules of reason, since a court should either abandon or modify a per se rule whenever the rule turns out to forbid an individual pro-competitive arrangement. Such an inquiry, which cannot be pursued

[33] Useful points of entry into the literature are Hooker (1995) and McNaughton (1998). For an application of the debate to law, see Alexander (1985), 320.

[34] See Lyons (1965).

here, might confirm the plausible view that the two distinctions are in fact instances of a single broader distinction that can be characterised within the theory of bounded rationality.[35]

Rules of reason for the application of criterial rules

There is a large residue of arrangements, not falling within a per se rule, which the courts regard as needing individual assessment under a criterial rule of reason. The courts' position is embodied in a further rule of reason:

(R11) An arrangement which is not of a kind specified by a per se rule must be individually assessed under a criterial rule of reason to determine whether it is illegal under section 1.

(R11) is thus a rule for the application of criterial rules. For example, if (R2) is the selected criterial rule, (R11) requires a court to decide whether the individual arrangement before it includes a restraint with significant anti-competitive effects.

(R11) can be broken into a set of more specific rules which identify kinds of arrangement whose instances require individual assessment. Such rules have the form:

(R12) An arrangement of kind K must be individually assessed under a criterial rule of reason to determine whether it is illegal under section 1.[36]

As with per se rules, there is a different rule for each kind K, for example:

(R13) A non-price vertical arrangement must be individually assessed [etc.];

and, again as with per se rules, such rules cannot be combined in a single disjunctive formulation, as the class of relevant kinds is open.

[35] Compare Heiner (1986), which explains the evolution of legal rules in terms of a theory of behaviour under uncertainty. On bounded rationality generally, see Simon (1982).

[36] Areeda (1989), 414 ff, describes per se rules as precluding inquiry into exculpation, power in the market or reasonableness of prices. In terms of the present discussion, this view represents per se rules as qualifying (R12)-type rules and as having the form: 'In assessing an arrangement of kind K under a criterial rule of reason, no account is to be taken of . . .'. Compare Joliet (1967), 7.

A plurality of rules

To summarise, there are three main classes of rule of reason. First, there is (R1), a rule for interpreting section 1 as applying only to unreasonable restraints. Second, there is the class of rules specifying criteria of reasonableness and unreasonableness. These fall into two subclasses. One represents the dominant tradition, which judges the unreasonableness of a restraint by its effects on competition; (R2)–(R8) are examples of rules in this subclass. The other represents the recessive tradition, which uses a broader range of criteria; (R9) and (R10) fall into this subclass. Third, there are rules for the application of the criterial rules: examples are (R11) and (R13), which satisfies the schema (R12). Per se rules are rules for applying section 1 and satisfy the schema (P1); examples are (P2) and (P3).

There is, then, a plurality of rules of reason and per se rules. People often talk, however, of 'the' rule of reason, which suggests that there is only one.[37] (The literature also contains less frequent mentions of 'the' per se rule.[38]) One explanation may be that they have in mind not a proposition, such as those set out above, but a state of affairs. In this usage 'the rule of reason' is like 'the rule of law': just as the latter signifies a state of affairs in which the law prevails, so the former signifies a state of affairs in which the courts apply section 1 according to criteria of reasonableness and unreasonableness. Another explanation may be that they have in mind just one of the rules of reason listed above. If so, it is probably (R1) (Read 'restraint' in section 1 as 'unreasonable restraint'), for this is, as it were, the rule of reason from which the others grow.

Benefits of per se rules and rules of reason

Something has been said already about the point of per se rules and rules of reason, but it will be useful to set out the overlapping benefits that people have advanced on behalf of either type of rule. Some of these alleged benefits are controversial, but I shall list them without extended comment.

[37] See Bork (1965), (1966), (1978); Easterbrook (1984a), 10; Gellhorn and Tatham (1985), 155; Joliet (1967); and Piraino (1991), 685, (1994), 1755.

[38] See the quotation in note 30 above from Bork. Contrast Joliet (1967), 54; and Sullivan (1977), 194 and 197.

Per se rules in the first place make for efficiency of administration, litigation and adjudication;[39] in particular, they reduce the need for continuous supervision of business practices[40] and the need for courts to make economic judgments, which they are ill-equipped to do.[41] In the second place, per se rules bring the interrelated benefits of certainty,[42] clarity[43] and simplicity.[44] Third, they promote predictability, both as to the legal consequences of arrangements which fall within them[45] and as to the outcome of litigation.[46] The former type of predictability can be invoked to justify strict enforcement, which in turn brings the benefit of deterrence.[47] The latter type increases the likelihood that parties in dispute will settle out of court, thereby saving judicial resources.[48] Fourth, if per se rules are in place, enforcement of section 1 is less likely to be arbitrary, irrational, erroneous, prejudiced or unfair;[49] per se rules thus promote the rule of law.[50] Fifth, they prevent any bias towards defendants in judgments under section 1.[51] Sixth, they are dynamically stabilising in the sense that, even if at first their application produces some undesirable decisions in borderline cases, people learn to adjust their behaviour to avoid such results.[52]

The use of rules of reason has been claimed to have the following advantages. First, as it involves individual assessment, it reduces the risk

[39] See *Northern Pacific Railway* (note 30 above), 5; *Container Corp.* (note 30 above), 341; Bork (1978), 18–19; Easterbrook (1984a), 9–10; Ehrlich and Posner (1974), 264 ff; Gellhorn (1986), 199; Piraino (1991), 691, (1994), 1756; Posner (1986), 513; Schauer (1991b), 145 ff; Sullivan (1977), 193; and anonymous (1983).

[40] See Areeda (1989), 412–13.

[41] See *Topco* (note 21 above), 609, 612; Fox and Sullivan (1989), 282; Neale and Goyder (1980), 449; and Scherer and Ross (1990), 336–7.

[42] See *Trans-Missouri Freight* (note 3 above), 331–2; Areeda (1989), 396–7; Bock (1990), 52; Bright (1995), 515; Gellhorn (1986), 427; Joliet (1967), 84, 189–90; Kennedy (1973), 364, (1976), 1688; Neale and Goyder (1980), 447; Sullivan (1977), 193; and Whish and Sufrin (1987), 37.

[43] See Gellhorn (1986), 197; and Piraino (1991), 691, (1994), 1754.

[44] See Piraino (1994), 1754; and Hare (1973).

[45] See M. Kelman (1987), 43; Schauer (1991b), 137 ff; and anonymous (1983), 710.

[46] See Ehrlich and Posner (1974), 265; M. Kelman (1987), 44; and anonymous (1983), 710.

[47] See Areeda (1989), 412–13; Beschle (1987), 475; Gellhorn (1986), 198–9; Piraino (1991), 691–2, (1994), 1754; and Posner (1986), 513–14.

[48] See Ehrlich and Posner (1974), 265; and M. Kelman (1987), 44.

[49] See Ehrlich and Posner (1974), 264; M. Kelman (1987), 41; Schauer (1991b), 135–7; and Scherer and Ross (1990), 336.

[50] See Katz and Teitelbaum (1978), 4 ff.

[51] See Piraino (1991), 702 ff; and Wood Hutchinson (1984), 110.

[52] See M. Kelman (1987), 44.

that a court will find against an individual arrangement which section 1 is not intended to prohibit.[53] That risk is greater when a per se rule is used, for such rules determine decisions solely by classification: if a court finds that the individual arrangement before it is of the kind specified by the rule, it will make a judgment of illegality. The arrangement may, however, be harmless, for the rule is unlikely to have delineated the kind so accurately that all arrangements of that kind are within the mischief of section 1. Rules of reason thus encourage the courts to respond flexibly to the facts of individual cases and to respect economic reality.[54] A second and closely related advantage is that they avoid the costs of formulating per se rules that are tolerably accurate, and of revising them to maintain the level of accuracy as economic conditions change.[55]

Third, rules of reason promote economic efficiency.[56] Fourth, they are fair;[57] in particular, they ensure a fair hearing for defendants.[58] Fifth, they discourage conduct on the borderline of legality.[59] Sixth, conflicts and gaps are less likely between rules of reason than between per se rules.[60]

Finally, the use of rules of reason is supported by objections to certain of the claims advanced in favour of per se rules. It may be said that the alleged certainty, clarity and simplicity of per se rules are largely illusive, as they are often cancelled by the difficulty of deciding whether the individual arrangement at issue is of the kind specified by the relevant rule.[61] (The characterisation problem will be discussed further below.) As to the claim that per se rules are dynamically stabilising, it may be retorted that in another respect they are *de*stabilising: in order to accommodate exceptions, they tend to grow more complicated, and may become so unwieldy that people start to ignore them.[62]

[53] See Beschle (1987), 475–6; Ehrlich and Posner (1974), 268 ff; Gellhorn (1986), 198; M. Kelman (1987), 40–1; Kennedy (1976), 1689; Piraino (1991), 692, 711; Posner (1986), 514; and Schauer (1991b), 31 ff.

[54] See Bock (1990), 52; Easterbrook (1984a), 10; and Joliet (1967), 189–90.

[55] See Ehrlich and Posner (1974), 267–8; and Posner (1986), 513.

[56] See Bork (1978), 267–8; and Piraino (1994), 1754.

[57] See Bork (1978), 268; and Gellhorn (1986), 199.

[58] See Piraino (1991), 695.

[59] See Gellhorn (1986), 198; M. Kelman (1987), 41 ff; and Kennedy (1976), 1695–6.

[60] See M. Kelman (1987), 44; Kennedy (1976), 1700; and Posner (1986), 514.

[61] See Beschle (1987), 472–3; Ehrlich and Posner (1974), 267; and Gellhorn (1986), 198.

[62] See M. Kelman (1987), 44. Compare the objection above to indirect consequentialism.

Relations between rules of reason and per se rules

The simple view and the complex view

There are two broad and opposing views of the relation between rules of reason and per se rules. The simple view has it that the application of rules of reason and the application of per se rules constitute an exhaustive and mutually exclusive pair of methods for the assessment of arrangements under section 1.[63] The complex view takes various forms in the literature and can be expressed by saying that there is no sharp boundary between the two kinds of rule: rather, they fall on a continuum.[64] Herbert Feigl once asked whether the difference between a difference in kind and a difference in degree was a difference in kind or in degree:[65] if it is granted that per se rules make the difference between arrangements inside and arrangements outside section 1 a difference in kind, whereas rules of reason make it a difference in degree, then the simple view treats the difference between these two differences as a difference in kind, while the complex view treats it as a difference in degree.

The two views as stated are too cloudy for a choice to be made between them. The question which of them is right needs to be replaced by a set of clearer questions. The following cover the ground:

(1) Does any rule of reason or per se rule have vague scope?
(2) Does the scope of any rule of reason overlap that of any per se rule?
(3) Does the union of the scopes of all rules of reason and per se rules include the scope of section 1?
(4) Is there a method of deciding the legality of arrangements under section 1 which involves the application neither of a rule of reason nor of a per se rule, but which has some characteristics of each approach?

[63] See *Professional Engineers* (note 10 above), 692; Easterbrook (1984a), 9–10; Fox and Sullivan (1989), 282–3; and Piraino (1991), 685, (1994), 1753.

[64] See *Topco* (note 21 above), 621 (Burger CJ dissenting); *Professional Engineers* (note 10 above); *NCAA* (note 5 above), 2962; *Massachusetts Board of Registration in Optometry*, 5 Trade Reg Rep 22, 555 (FTC, 1988); *Detroit Auto Dealers*, 111 FTC 417, 493–4 (1989); Antitrust Guidelines for the Licensing and Acquisition of Intellectual Property, 59 Fed Reg 41, 339, para. 4.5 (1994); Areeda (1989), 361, 408–9, 413–14, 427 ff, and Supplement (1995), 923–4; Beschle (1987), 475, Bock (1990), 57, Bork (1966), 388, (1978), 18–19; Brunet (1984), 22; Flynn (1982), 1612–13; Gellhorn (1986), 186 ff; Gellhorn and Tatham (1985), 156; Hawk (1994), vol. 1, 276; Joliet (1967), 54, 65; Neale and Goyder (1980), 25; Piraino (1991), 692, 710, (1994), 1769–70; Sullivan (1977), 193, 196–7, (1987), 838; Whish (1993), 19–20; and Whish and Sufrin (1987), 7.

[65] Quoted in Putnam (1994), 262.

(5) Do the courts ever change their approach to a kind of arrangement, so that, although it first falls within a per se rule, it later falls within a rule of reason, or vice versa?
(6) Is there a contradiction between the use of rules of reason and the use of per se rules?
(7) Is it the case that the application of rules of reason, but not of per se rules, involves discretion?

These questions are still unmanageable if all the varieties of rules are taken into account, so I shall focus the discussion on per se rules and those rules of reason whose function is most similar to theirs, namely rules of the form (R12), which identify kinds of arrangement whose instances need individual assessment under criterial rules.

Question (1): vagueness

Some people hold that 'vague' is itself a vague expression.[66] At any rate it is ambiguous, for it can mean 'ambiguous', 'rough', 'imprecise', 'general' or 'inaccurate', among other things. Question (1) can accordingly be broken into a set of questions, one for each of these concepts. In philosophy, 'vague' has come to be a term of art connoting the phenomenon of blurred boundaries, which give rise to difficult borderline cases.[67] In this sense every (R12)-type rule and every per se rule has vague scope.[68] Consider the expressions used in such rules to identify kinds of arrangement: 'naked horizontal price fixing', 'group boycott', 'non-price vertical arrangement' and so on. All these have extensions whose blurred boundaries are susceptible to difficult borderline cases.[69] Moreover (R12)-type rules refer

66 See Austin (1962), 125–6.

67 See Williamson (1994), 36, 71, and contrast Sainsbury's view that vague concepts do not have boundaries: Sainsbury (1990).

68 On the vagueness of rules of reason, see Hawk (1994), vol. 1, 280. *Nash* v. *United States*, 229 US 373 (1913), involved a challenge to the Sherman Act for unconstitutional vagueness; see the discussion in Bork (1978), 73 ff, where *Nash* is compared with other cases concerning the vagueness of statutes.

69 As to the blurred boundaries of price fixing, see *Chicago Board of Trade* (note 3 above); *United States* v. *Gasoline Retailers' Association*, 285 F 2d 688 (7th Cir 1961); *National Macaroni Manufacturers' Association* v. *Federal Trade Commission*, 345 F 2d 421 (7th Cir 1965); *Broadcast Music* (note 30 above); *United States* v. *Nu-Phonics Inc.*, 1979 Trade Cas (CCH) P62, 652 (ED Mich 1979); *Monsanto Co.* v. *Spray-Rite Service Corp.*, 104 S Ct 1464 (1984); Bork (1966), 391 ff; Fox and Sullivan (1989), 282; Neale and Goyder (1980), 31; Piraino (1994), 1800; Sullivan (1977), 226, 266 ff; Wood Hutchinson (1984), 118 ff; and the discussion of question (5) below.

to criterial rules of reason, which themselves have vague scope. This is obvious in the case of those criterial rules, such as (R2), which contain the paradigmatically vague word 'significant'. It might be contended that the vagueness of the scope of (R12)-type rules and per se rules follows from the fact that they are expressed in natural language, the assumption being that all, or almost all, words in natural language are vague. Whether or not that assumption is true, the answer to question (1) is clearly yes.

Question (2): overlap

Question (2), restricted as explained above, asks whether the scope of any (R12)-type rule overlaps that of any per se rule. There are four possible views, grounding opposing answers:

First, it may be said that the answer of course is yes, for many arrangements contain some elements that fall within an (R12)-type rule and others that fall within a per se rule. Two businesses may, for example, enter into an arrangement that involves both a non-price vertical restraint and naked horizontal price fixing. This, however, is to adopt implicitly a coarse-grained principle for the individuation of arrangements. The second view adopts a fine-grained principle which ensures that (R12)-type rules and per se rules never overlap. On such a principle the example just described involves two arrangements, one comprising the vertical restraint, the other the fixing of prices. The answer to (2) in that case is no.

Assume, however, that a coarse-grained principle is adopted: then an arrangement may instantiate both a kind specified by an (R12)-type rule – say (R13) (a non-price vertical arrangement must be individually assessed under a criterial rule of reason to determine whether it is illegal under section 1) – and a kind specified by a per se rule – say (P2) (naked horizontal price fixing is illegal under section 1). If the arrangement comes before a court, the court must decide which of the two rules to apply. It cannot apply both. For suppose it first applies (P2). Then it finds the arrangement illegal under section 1 without more. In that case, application of (R13) is superfluous. Suppose alternatively that the court first applies (R13). (R13) requires the court to apply in turn a criterial rule of reason. Suppose, for example, that the court uses the criterial rule (R3), which says that a restraint is unreasonable if its anti-competitive effects significantly outweigh its pro-competitive effects. Suppose further that the court finds that the arrangement includes a restraint whose anti-competitive effects do significantly outweigh its pro-competitive effects. Then, by (R13), the court decides that the arrangement is illegal under section 1. In that case, application of (P2) is pointless, first, because it would give the same result and, second, because the court has already expended the resources which it is the purpose of per se rules to save. Now suppose that the court finds the arrangement not to include a restraint whose anti-competitive effects significantly outweigh its pro-competitive effects. Then, by (R13), the court decides that the arrangement is permitted under section 1. If the court now applies (P2), it will find the arrangement illegal under section 1 and will thus be landed with a contradiction.

The court cannot, therefore, apply both (P2) and (R13). This is a manifestation of the characterisation problem – the problem of deciding how to characterise an arrangement in order to apply to it a per se rule or rule of reason.[70] The solution in the present case is for the court to apply a meta-rule:

(M1) Where an arrangement instantiates both a kind specified by a per se rule and a kind specified by an (R12)-type rule, it is deemed to fall within only one of the two rules.

Given (M1), which together with its grounds constitutes the third of the four views of question (2), it may be said either that the answer to (2) is no, or that it is yes but deemed to be no.

As the discussion of question (1) showed, per se rules and (R12)-type rules have vague scope. The scope of such a rule therefore has a core, comprising cases definitely instantiating the kind specified by the rule, and a penumbra of doubtful cases. (The boundary between core and penumbra is itself vague – an instance of the phenomenon of higher-order vagueness.) It might be held – this is the fourth view – that, although a court cannot apply both a per se rule and an (R12)-type rule to an arrangement that falls within the core of both, it can apply them to an arrangement falling within their penumbra.[71] This claim might be developed by saying that the very fact that an arrangement instantiates the kinds specified by

[70] The importance of characterisation was recognised by the court in *Broadcast Music* (note 30 above), 19–20. *Barry* v. *Blue Cross of California*, 805 F 2d 866 (9th Cir 1986) raises the problem in relation to boycotts. (As to boycotts, see also notes 72 and 90 below.) The characterisation problem is discussed in Areeda (1989), 414, 421 ff, and Supplement (1995), 898–9; Schechter (1982), 11–12; and Wood Hutchinson (1984), 100–1. More generally, the issue of conflicting rules was a central theme of legal realism; M. Kelman (1987), 48–9, describes the development of that theme in critical legal studies.

[71] Scherer and Ross discuss the use of rules of reason in borderline cases: Scherer and Ross (1990), 321 ff.

rules of these two sorts is reason to think that it falls within the rules' penumbra. The fourth view does not look promising, for the argument just given against the application of both (P2) and (R13) seems equally persuasive in penumbral situations. If, however, the view can be sustained, (M1) can be restricted to the cores of rules. The meta-rule will then read: 'Where an arrangement definitely instantiates [etc.]'. In that case the answer to (2) is yes, provided that at least one arrangement falls within the penumbra of both a per se rule and an (R12)-type rule.

The answer given to (2) depends, then, on the view selected from these four. I shall not try to establish a conclusive ranking, but the second and third positions appear stronger than the first and fourth. This fact favours a negative, or at most an affirmative-but-deemed-negative, answer.

Question (3): scope

Question (3) asks whether the union of the scopes of all rules of reason and per se rules includes the scope of section 1. Given that only (R12)-type rules are in question, it might be suggested that (3) can be rephrased to ask whether every arrangement which is illegal under section 1 is illegal under either a per se rule or an (R12)-type rule. But the suggestion rests on a mistake, for (R12)-type rules do not state that certain arrangements are illegal: they only specify a method for determining illegality, namely to apply a criterial rule of reason. A more accurate revision of (3) is:

(3′) Is every arrangement that is illegal under section 1 either:
- (a) illegal under a per se rule; or
- (b) such that it both:
  - (i) falls within an (R12)-type rule; and
  - (ii) includes a restraint that is unreasonable according to a criterial rule of reason?

To answer (3′) fully, it would be necessary to deal with various issues, for example to distinguish between actual and merely possible arrangements and between, on the one hand, arrangements and rules at a given time and, on the other, arrangements and rules at any time; and to take account of the fact that the class of per se rules and the class of (R12)-type rules are, like the kinds specified by such rules, open, and the fact that such rules are often not stated explicitly but must be extracted as *rationes* from the cases. I shall not pursue these issues, but shall propose a short, provisional and equivocal answer to (3′):

It is plausible to suppose that an arrangement could be made such that, first, a competent court would judge it illegal under section 1 but, second, it is neither (a) illegal under a per se rule established at the time nor (b) such that it both (i) falls within an (R12)-type rule established at the time and (ii) includes a restraint which is unreasonable according to a criterial rule established at the time. Indeed, there may well exist, or have existed, such arrangements. In that sense the answer to (3′) is no. However, for any such arrangement, it would be possible to formulate either a new per se rule or a new rule of reason that fitted it. In that sense the answer to (3′) is yes.

Question (4): hybrids

Question (4), in its restricted form, asks whether there is a method of deciding the legality of arrangements under section 1 which involves the application neither of an (R12)-type rule nor of a per se rule, but which has some characteristics of each approach. The answer yes is supported by three arguments:

The argument from the problem of characterisation

It was explained in the statement of the third view of question (2) that, if a coarse-grained principle is adopted for the individuation of arrangements, an arrangement may instantiate both a kind specified by an (R12)-type rule and a kind specified by a per se rule, and that in that case a court must apply the meta-rule (M1) deeming the arrangement to fall within only one of the two rules. (M1) however does not itself tell the court which rule to apply. Assume as before that the choice is between (R13) and (P2) and that the court's favoured criterial rule is (R3), which says that a restraint is unreasonable if its anti-competitive effects significantly outweigh its pro-competitive effects. To decide whether to apply (R13) or (P2), the court may make a preliminary and cursory application of (R3), taking into account only the most salient pro- and anti-competitive effects of any restraint included in the arrangement. If, having made this cursory assessment, the court finds that the arrangement appears to include a restraint that is on balance significantly anti-competitive, it will apply (P2) and judge the arrangement illegal under section 1, taking the risk that a more thorough application of the criterion might have established the opposite conclusion. If on the other hand the court, having made the cursory assessment, does not find that the arrangement appears to include any such restraint, it will apply (R13). Assume that (R12)-type rules are to be interpreted as requiring a full assessment to be made under a criterial rule of reason. Since the favoured criterial rule is (R3), the court will apply (R3) again, this time assessing the arrangement fully.[72]

This procedure conforms to a second meta-rule, which supplements (M1):

(M2) Where an arrangement instantiates both a kind specified by a per se rule and a kind specified by an (R12)-type rule, make a preliminary assessment of the arrangement under a criterial rule of reason. If, in the light of that assessment, the arrangement appears to include an unreasonable restraint, deem the arrangement to fall only within the per se rule. If not, deem it to fall only within the (R12)-type rule.

(M2) is a basis for the answer yes to question (4). Given that (R12)-type rules require a full assessment to be made under a criterial rule, the preliminary assessment just described involves the application neither of an (R12)-type rule nor of a per se rule. However, it is like the application of an (R12)-type rule in that it involves the application – albeit in a cursory way – of a criterial rule, and it is like the application of a per se rule in that it does not take account of all the matters that would need to be considered in an application of an (R12)-type rule.

The argument from the breadth of the criteria in criterial rules of reason

The second of the three arguments for the answer yes to (4) is based again on the assumption that (R12)-type rules require a full assessment to be made under a criterial rule, and also on the fact that some criterial rules, on some interpretations, require a very broad range of factors to be considered. For example (R3), read literally, requires all a restraint's pro- and anti-competitive effects, no matter how remote, to be taken into account. A court cannot do this. Some commentators have concluded that rules of reason are empty,[73] but that wrongly suggests that they say

[72] Gellhorn and Tatham refer to the courts' use of 'a rule of reason type of analysis to determine whether the per se test should be applied': Gellhorn and Tatham (1985), 156. Sullivan (1977), 209, talks of 'a rule of reason analysis in truncated form'. See also Sullivan's discussion of the characterisation problem in relation to boycotts: *ibid.*, 247 ff. Compare *Northwest Wholesale Stationers* (note 28 above) and *Universal Amusements Co.* v. *General Cinema Corp.*, 635 F Supp 1505 (SD Tex 1985) on the investigation of market power as a preliminary to the application of a per se rule.

[73] See Easterbrook (1984a), 12, (1984b), 153, 155; and Piraino (1994), 1754.

nothing. The rules in question, on these interpretations, say something clear enough; the point is that they cannot be applied.

The response of the courts is to take only a limited range of factors into account.[74] This practice is similar to the preliminary assessment, described above, that is made when the characterisation problem arises, except that there the range of factors is typically narrower. The present practice likewise is a basis for an affirmative answer to (4): the argument again is that it involves the application neither of an (R12)-type rule nor of a per se rule but that it is like the former, in that it involves the application – albeit incomplete – of a criterial rule, and like the latter in that it does not take account of all the factors that would need to be considered in an application of an (R12)-type rule.

This argument is weaker than the previous one, for it is exposed to the objection that criterial rules of reason should be identified on the basis of the practice of the courts. If, for example, the courts disregard remote effects when applying (R3), then (R3) should be interpreted as not referring to such effects, or, better, it should be rewritten to make this clear. But, if appropriately restricted criterial rules are the rules mentioned in (R12)-type rules, the fact that the courts use them does nothing to establish the existence of a third way between (R12)-type rules and per se rules.

The objection has some force but is not conclusive, for the courts sometimes say one thing and do another: a criterial rule is stated broadly but applied narrowly.[75] In such a case the rule might reasonably be characterised in terms either of the court's statement or of its practice. If the statement is taken to determine the rule, the practice may be taken to instantiate a third way, provided that it does not fall within a criterial rule determined by some other statement.

[74] See *Standard Stations* (note 21 above), 309–10; *Professional Engineers* (note 10 above), 692 ff; *United States* v. *United States Gypsum Co.*, 438 US 422 (1978); *NCAA* (note 5 above), 2965; *Federal Trade Commission* v. *Indiana Federation of Dentists*, 476 US 447, 460–1 (1986); Areeda (1985), 30, (1989), 403 ff, 428, 436; Easterbrook (1984b), 158–9; Hawk (1994), vol. 2, 112 (Hawk, like Sullivan (1977), talks of a 'truncated' rule of reason); and Schechter (1982), 10. See also Wood Hutchinson (1984), 101, on the burden borne by juries in weighing the various factors, and Areeda (1989), 394–5, 405–8, 414, 427 ff, Flynn (1982) and M. Scherer (1987) on the use of presumptions and rules of thumb. As to presumptions, see also note 76 below.

[75] Examples of impracticably broad statements are found in *Chicago Board of Trade* (note 3 above), 238; *Times-Picayune* (note 21 above), 614 ff; and *Penn-Olin* (note 21 above), 176–7. See also *United States* v. *Columbia Steel Co.*, 334 US 495, 527–8 (1948). Compare Bork on 'impossibly broad statements of the per se rule' (note 31 above).

The argument from alternative proposals

The last of the arguments for an affirmative answer to (4) appeals to the variety of methods that commentators have proposed for deciding the legality of arrangements under section 1. For example, Piraino has at different times proposed a fourfold and a threefold scheme for classifying arrangements, the different categories carrying different evidential presumptions;[76] Beschle has proposed the replacement of per se rules by 'strict antitrust scrutiny';[77] Easterbrook has proposed five filters to identify arrangements needing assessment under a rule of reason;[78] and Scherer and Ross have proposed a threefold classification.[79] Each of these methods is similar in some respects to, and different in others from, the application of per se rules and (R12)-type rules of reason.

It may be objected that these methods are irrelevant to question (4), as they are merely the subject of recommendations, whereas (4) is naturally taken to ask about the methods actually used by the courts. But (4) can also be construed more broadly, as encompassing methods that the courts might usefully adopt. In any event, the boundary between recommendations of new practices and descriptions of current ones is not always clear in the literature, and certain cases indicate that the courts and the Federal Trade Commission have already used intermediate methods.[80]

The result is that these three arguments together make a strong case for the answer yes to question (4).

Question (5): changes of judicial approach

Question (5), in its restricted form, asks whether the courts ever change their approach to a kind of arrangement, so that, although it first falls within a per se rule, it later falls within an (R12)-type rule, or vice versa.

[76] Piraino (1991), (1994). [77] Beschle (1987).

[78] Easterbrook (1984a). [79] Scherer and Ross (1990), 323–4.

[80] See *Klor's Inc.* v. *Broadway-Hale Stores Inc.*, 359 US 207 (1959); *Silver* v. *New York Stock Exchange*, 373 US 341, 348–9 (1963); *White Motor* (note 18 above); *Broadcast Music* (note 28 above), 19–20; *Columbia Broadcasting System Inc.* v. *ASCAP et al.*, 620 F 2d 930 (1980), 450 US 970 (1981); *United States* v. *Realty Multi-List Inc.*, 629 F 2d 1351 (5th Cir 1980); *Ball Memorial Hospital Inc.* v. *Mutual Hospital Insurance Inc.*, 784 F 2d 1325 (7th Cir 1986); *Massachusetts Board of Optometry* (note 64 above); *Detroit Auto Dealers* (note 64 above), 493–4; Antitrust Guidelines (note 64 above), para. 4.5; Areeda (1989), Supplement (1995), 923–4; Beschle (1987), 502 ff; Fox (1990), 204–5; Gellhorn (1986), 220 ff, 329 ff; Hawk (1994), vol. 2, 112; Joliet (1967), 55; Whish (1993), 19–20; and the references in notes 72 and 74 above.

The answer is yes.[81] A court may change its approach overtly or covertly. The Supreme Court made an overt change in relation to vertical market division, which it had held in *Schwinn*[82] to be illegal per se. In *Sylvania*[83] the Court explicitly reversed *Schwinn*, holding that such arrangements fall within a rule of reason.

Sylvania was the most striking manifestation of a change of direction by the US courts in the late 1970s. This story has been often told,[84] and a crude summary will suffice here. From the 1940s to the late 70s the courts brought an increasing number of kinds of arrangement within per se rules. Since then, influenced in part by the Chicago school of antitrust and in part by broader and less easily defined political trends,[85] the courts have reduced the scope of per se rules and correspondingly expanded the scope of rules of reason.

The change is seen in judgments about five other kinds of arrangement. The Supreme Court ruled horizontal price fixing illegal per se in *Socony-Vacuum* (1940), the first case to use the language of per se illegality in the context of section 1. Although such arrangements are still said to be illegal per se, the Court narrowed its interpretation of 'horizontal price fixing' in *Broadcast Music* (1979).[86] Vertical price fixing was ruled

[81] Some commentators represent the courts as oscillating between per se rules and rules of reason: see e.g. Bock (1990), 57; and Gellhorn (1986), 164. This is a plausible picture of the courts' approach to certain types of arrangement, e.g. price fixing: see note 86 below. According to certain critical legal theorists, such oscillation is the consequence of mutually inconsistent commitments to rules and standards: see M. Kelman (1987), 15 ff, and the discussion of question (6) below.

[82] *United States* v. *Arnold Schwinn & Co.*, 388 US 365 (1967).

[83] *Continental TV Inc.* v. *GTE Sylvania Inc.*, 433 US 36 (1977). For references to later cases which have developed the approach in *Sylvania*, see Gellhorn and Tatham (1985), 170 ff.

[84] See Beschle (1987), 477 ff; Bock (1990); Fox (1990); Gellhorn (1986), 24 ff, 164 ff; Hawk (1994), vol. 1, 276–7, vol. 2, 110 ff; Malina and Steuer (1991), 773–4; Piraino (1991), 692 ff, (1994), 1755 ff; Whish and Sufrin (1987), 7–8; and Wood Hutchinson (1984), 99–100.

[85] See note 9 above.

[86] See note 30 above. The Court has wavered in its treatment of horizontal price fixing. *Trans-Missouri Freight* (note 3 above) anticipated the per se approach of *Socony-Vacuum*, but the Court used a rule of reason in *Chicago Board of Trade* (note 3 above). In *Trenton Potteries* (note 7 above) the Court returned to the per se approach, but it applied a rule of reason again in *Appalachian Coals* (note 5 above). *Socony-Vacuum* then established the per se rule, but, as noted, the interpretation of 'horizontal price fixing' was narrowed in *Broadcast Music*. The uncertainty has continued: the Court appeared to broaden the interpretation again in *Catalano Inc.* v. *Target Sales Inc.*, 446 US 643 (1980) and *Maricopa*

illegal per se at an early stage, in *Dr Miles* (1911),[87] but again the Court narrowed its interpretation, in *Monsanto* (1984).[88] It ruled horizontal market division illegal per se in *Topco* (1972), and the lower courts then narrowed the interpretation of 'horizontal market division'.[89] In *Klor's* (1959) the Supreme Court ruled that group boycotts are illegal per se, but it narrowed its interpretation of 'group boycott' in *Northwest Wholesale Stationers* (1985).[90] In *Northern Pacific Railway* (1958) the Court ruled tying by a firm with market power to be illegal per se, but it narrowed its interpretation of 'tying' in *Hyde* (1984).[91]

These are all examples of a covert change from per se rules to rules of reason: that is, the court retains the form of the per se rule but narrows the interpretation of the expression substituting for (P1)'s 'kind K'. It continues to treat as per se illegal those arrangements instantiating the narrowed kind, but it now subjects to one or more rules of reason those arrangements that instantiate the original broad kind but not the narrowed kind.

(note 28 above), and then again to narrow it in *NCAA* (note 5 above). (A similarly narrow interpretation was given by the Eleventh Circuit in *National Bancard Corp. (NaBanco)* v. *Visa USA*, 779 F 2d (11th Cir), 479 US 923 (1986).) The Court reverted to a broad interpretation in *Trial Lawyers* (note 28 above), which is criticised in Malina and Steuer (1991) for inconsistency with another decision made by the Court in the same term. For a summary of price fixing agreements granted statutory exemption, see Scherer and Ross (1990), 324–5.

87 *Dr Miles Medical Co.* v. *John D. Park and Sons Co.*, 220 US 373 (1911).

88 See note 69 above.

89 The rule in *Topco* (note 21 above) was anticipated to some extent in *Timken Roller Bearing Co.* v. *United States*, 341 US 593 (1951) and *United States* v. *Sealy Inc.*, 388 US 350 (1967). Subsequent cases in the lower courts are *Dreiling Motor Co.* v. *Peugeot Motors of America Inc.*, 605 F Supp 597 (D Colo 1985) and *Los Angeles Memorial Coliseum Commission* v. *NFL*, 726 F 2d 1381 (9th Cir), 469 US 990 (1984). See also the FTC's split decision in *General Motors – Toyota*, 48 Fed Reg 57, 314 (1983).

90 See notes 28 and 80 above. The course of the jurisprudence on boycotts has been anfractuous. For reviews of the cases, see Areeda (1989), Supplement (1995), 899, n. 12, 918 ff; Beschle (1987), 481–2, 494–5; Gellhorn (1986), 212 ff; Hawk (1994), vol. 1, 313 ff; and Sullivan (1977), 229 ff.

91 See notes 27 and 29 above. *Northern Pacific Railway* took over a per se rule from *International Salt Co.* v. *United States*, 332 US 392 (1947), which had applied section 3 of the Clayton Act 1914 to a tying arrangement. In this area too the law has not developed in a straight line. Other significant cases are *Times-Picayune* (note 21 above); *United States* v. *Loew's Inc.*, 371 US 38 (1962); *Fortner Enterprises Inc.* v. *United States Steel Corp. (Fortner I)*, 394 US 495 (1969); *United States Steel Corp.* v. *Fortner Enterprises Inc. (Fortner II)*, 429 US 610 (1977). Lower courts have had difficulty applying the rule in *Hyde*: see *Digidyne Corp.* v. *Data General Corp.*, 734 F 2d 1336 (9th Cir 1984); 105 S Ct 3534 (1985). On the weakness of the per se rule against tying, see *White Motor* (note 18 above); Beschle (1987), 483; Joliet (1967), 54 ff; Scherer and Ross (1990), 565 ff.

Covert change tends to give artificially restricted meanings to phrases, thereby exacerbating the characterisation problem.[92]

The process can be described in different ways, depending on the principles one uses for individuating rules,[93] and in particular on one's view of the role of interpretation in the individuation of rules. Where the change is from per se rule to rule of reason, it may be said that the original per se rule is abandoned and replaced by (a) a narrower per se rule covering a subclass of the original rule's scope and (b) one or more rules of reason covering some or all of the remainder of the original rule's scope. Alternatively it may be said that the original per se rule is retained but that (i) its substituend for 'kind K' is given a narrower interpretation and (ii) one or more rules of reason are introduced to cover some or all of those arrangements that instantiate the original but not the narrowed kind.

In this situation the court typically does not explicitly state an (R12)-type rule. Sometimes the reason may be that the court has not defined an appropriate kind of arrangement for inclusion in such a rule. In that case the court might be most accurately described as directly applying a criterial rule of reason to an individual arrangement which it would formerly have subjected to a per se rule, but in many situations the court also fails to make explicit a criterial rule. Nevertheless an (R12)-type rule and a criterial rule could be formulated to fit the court's judgment, and in this sense it can be said that the court is applying such rules implicitly.

It is an intricate question what the relation is between such a change of approach and a situation in which a court recognises an exception to a per se rule, applying a rule of reason to the exception.[94] On one view, this situation is an instance of the change of approach; on another, it is a distinct but related phenomenon. The former view is initially the more

[92] *Hyde* (note 28 above) exemplifies the artificiality of maintaining the form of a per se rule while adopting the substance of a rule of reason; see the remarks in that case of Justice O'Connor, who argued that the time had come to abandon the per se rule against tying, and of Justice Stevens, who held that the question whether the 'tying' label could be applied to the arrangement at issue was 'beside the point'. Wood Hutchinson (1994), 147, commenting on this and other cases in the same term, charges the Supreme Court with manipulating the law. See also Beschle (1987), 487, 514–15, Piraino (1991), 705 ff, and, for a broader discussion of the retention of rules after their doctrinal basis has been abandoned, Kelman (1987), 46 ff, and Kennedy (1973).

[93] See Black (1996).

[94] On the need to allow exceptions to per se rules, see *United States* v. *Jerrold Electronics Corp.*, 187 F Supp 545 (ED Pa 1960), 365 US 567 (1961).

attractive in the case of an exception comprising a kind of arrangement, the latter in the case of one comprising an individual arrangement. A decision between the two views would need to be based on a general account of exceptions. Such an account would include an assessment of the theory that, since there is no logical distinction between exceptions and the rules to which they are exceptions, there is likewise no logical distinction between creating an exception to a rule and changing the rule.[95] At issue here are the principles for individuating rules, so the choice between the two views is connected to the choice between the two ways, considered above, of describing the change of approach.

Question (6): contradiction

Question (6), in its restricted form, asks whether there is a contradiction between the use of (R12)-type rules and the use of per se rules. It was seen in the discussion of question (2) that a court cannot apply an (R12)-type rule and a per se rule to the same arrangement, but the allegation of contradiction has a broader theoretical basis. Certain writers in the school of critical legal studies have held that liberal legal thought contains and systematically represses a variety of contradictions.[96] The main alleged contradiction is between a commitment to mechanical rules and a commitment to situation-sensitive standards.[97] Some of these writers claim that the courts' use both of per se rules and of rules of reason is an instance of this contradictory pair of commitments.[98] Restricted to the terms of the present discussion, the claim is that the contradictory pair is instantiated by the courts' use of per se rules and (R12)-type rules.

I shall set aside the objections that the concept of liberal legal thought is very vague and that (R12)-type rules are not happily classified as standards, and shall focus on the concept of contradiction.[99] The traditional logic of propositions has it that propositions P and Q are contradictories if and only if both P is true if Q is false and P is false if Q is true. On this account it is unclear what it means to say that there is a contradiction between a commitment to rules and a commitment to standards (I shall omit the qualifiers 'mechanical' and 'situation-sensitive' from

[95] See Schauer (1991a). [96] See Kelman (1987), 3 ff.

[97] See Kelman, (1987), 3 ff, 15ff; Kennedy (1973), (1976).

[98] See Kelman (1987), 34; Kennedy (1976), 1703.

[99] Other words used in the literature are 'conflict' and 'antinomy': see Katz and Teitelbaum (1978); and Kelman (1987), 3.

now on), for commitments are neither true nor false.[100] The critical legal theorist must have in mind a different account of contradiction, applicable to commitments. Thus he might say that commitments C1 and C2 are contradictory if and only if both C1 is fulfilled if C2 is unfulfilled and C1 is unfulfilled if C2 is fulfilled.

'Commitment' is a murky word, but it seems that 'X has a commitment to rules' means something like 'X has a policy of applying rules' or 'X has a policy of exclusively applying rules'. A parallel pair of interpretations can be given to 'X has a commitment to standards'. Each interpreting phrase will in most contexts be implicitly indexed to a certain domain to which the policy is limited. To say that X's policy of doing Ax is fulfilled means that X does Ax. In that case the critical legal theorist is asserting one or other of the following theses:

(Con1) (a) X applies rules if X does not apply standards; and
(b) X does not apply rules if X applies standards.

(Con2) (a) X exclusively applies rules if X does not exclusively apply standards; and
(b) X does not exclusively apply rules if X exclusively applies standards.

(Con1)(b) and (Con2)(a) are false, so (Con1) and (Con2) are false. The reason, obviously, is that X may apply both rules and standards in a given domain. Indeed, if it is granted – as it must be if this discussion is to bear on per se rules and (R12)-type rules – that per se rules are rules and (R12)-type rules are standards, this is just what the US courts do in the domain of arrangements litigated under section 1.

The critical legal theorist might try to save his position by proposing some further account of contradiction. The difficulty, however, is that there appears to be no account that both, first, is close enough to the traditional one to qualify as explicating the concept of contradiction and, second, yields the conclusion that there is a contradiction between a commitment to rules and a commitment to standards.

The upshot is that there is no contradiction between these commitments and hence that the use both of per se rules and of (R12)-type rules

[100] Kennedy does not use the terminology of commitment, but uses such phrases as 'willingness to resort to standards', 'insistence on rigid rules', 'advocacy of rules' and 'preference for standards': Kennedy (1976), 1685, 1746, 1776. The point about truth-values applies equally to these. On commitments, see further note 9 of chapter 4 below.

is not an instance of such a contradiction. Absent any other reason to believe that the use of the two is contradictory, the answer to question (6) is no.

Question (7): discretion and right answers

Question (7), in its restricted form, asks whether the application of (R12)-type rules, but not of per se rules, involves discretion.[101] The answer yes is encouraged by the claim that per se rules, but not (R12)-type rules, are 'mechanical': see above. The answer yes in turn may encourage the view that, when an arrangement falls within a per se rule, there is a right answer to the question whether it is illegal under section 1, but that there is no right answer to that question in the case of an arrangement falling within an (R12)-type rule.

Ronald Dworkin describes discretion as a relative concept which only applies where someone is charged with the making of decisions subject to standards set by a particular authority.[102] He distinguishes three senses of 'discretion':

(D1) 'Sometimes we use "discretion" in a weak sense, simply to say that for some reason the standards an official must apply cannot be applied mechanically but demand the use of judgment.'[103]

Dworkin says that this sense is appropriate for example where orders are 'vague or hard to carry out'.[104] This is inaccurate, for vagueness as such does not import the use of judgment. It is, however, plausible to say that judgment is required when applying a vague expression to a borderline case. To justify this claim, which Dworkin would probably say is a tautology,[105] it would be necessary to give some account of the relevant concept of judgment.

(D2) 'Sometimes we use the term in a different weak sense, to say only that some official has final authority to make a decision and cannot be reviewed and reversed by any other official.'[106]

Dworkin contrasts these two weak senses with a strong sense:

[101] For the claim that the application of rules of reason involves discretion, see Handler (1941), 9 (Handler connects discretion to vagueness, as to which, see below); Joliet (1967), 4–5, 116; and Neale and Goyder (1980), 25 ff.

[102] R. Dworkin (1978), 31. [103] R. Dworkin (1978), 31. [104] R. Dworkin (1978), 32.

[105] See R. Dworkin (1978), 34. [106] R. Dworkin (1978), 32.

(D3) 'We use "discretion" sometimes . . . to say that on some issue [an official] is simply not bound by standards set by the authority in question.'[107]

Consider the relevance of these three senses of 'discretion' to the application of per se rules. The answer to question (1) pointed out that the expressions used in such rules to identify kinds of arrangement are vague. The application of a per se rule to a borderline case of the relevant kind of arrangement therefore involves discretion in sense (D1). Whether the application of a per se rule involves discretion in sense (D2) depends on the body applying the rule: an inferior court does not have such discretion, for its decision can be reviewed by a higher court, but the Supreme Court does have discretion in this sense.

Suppose a court is faced with an arrangement which the plaintiff alleges to infringe a certain per se rule. The court does not have discretion in sense (D3) when applying the rule, for the rule is dispositive in this sense: if the arrangement falls within it, the court is bound to find the arrangement illegal under section 1; if the arrangement does not fall within the rule, then, provided that the arrangement does not infringe some other rule, the court is bound to find it legal under section 1.[108] The arrangement may of course present the characterisation problem, for example because it is a borderline case of the kind specified by the rule, or because it also instantiates a kind specified by an (R12)-type rule (see the discussion of the third view of question (2)). If so, the court must use judgment in deciding whether the arrangement falls within the per se rule. But that is an exercise of discretion in sense (D1), not (D3).[109]

Much the same is true of (R12)-type rules: their application involves discretion in sense (D1) in borderline cases; it may or may not involve discretion in sense (D2), depending on the applying body; and it does not involve discretion in sense (D3). However, the application of these rules involves a greater amount of discretion in sense (D1) than does the application of per se rules. The reason is that the former involves the application of criterial rules of reason and that this can require judgment in two respects. First, as noted in the discussion of question (1), criterial rules are vague. Second, as noted before that, their application can involve

[107] R. Dworkin (1978), 32.

[108] This extends Dworkin's notion of a dispositive concept; see R. Dworkin (1986b), 119.

[109] Dworkin notes that philosophers commonly confuse these two senses of discretion: R. Dworkin (1978), 70.

the weighing of different factors against each other, and weighing, it is plausible to say, is a form of judgment.

The answer to question (7) is thus a qualified no. Whichever sense of 'discretion' is taken, there is no difference between (R12)-type rules and per se rules beyond the fact that application of the former involves a greater amount of discretion in sense (D1).

Finally a note on the existence of right answers. It was mentioned that the answer yes to (7) may encourage the view that, when an arrangement falls within a per se rule, there is a right answer to the question whether it is illegal under section 1, but that there is no right answer to that question in the case of an arrangement falling within an (R12)-type rule. The assumption is that, where the only legal rules relevant to a situation are such that their application to the situation involves discretion, there is no right answer to the question whether the situation is legal or illegal. The meaning and truth of this assumption have been extensively debated,[110] but it is plausible to hold that the assumption is true, if at all, only if discretion in sense (D3) is at issue.[111] Since neither the application of per se rules nor that of (R12)-type rules involves discretion in this sense, the assumption on its most plausible construal gives no reason to deny that, when an arrangement falls within a per se rule or an (R12)-type rule, there is a right answer to the question whether it is illegal under section 1.

[110] These issues are at the centre of the debate between Hart and Dworkin over legal positivism: see Hart (1961); R. Dworkin (1978), (1986a), (1986b). For commentary, see M. Cohen (1984).

[111] See R. Dworkin (1978), 34.

4

Agreements

Overview

Article 81(1) EC prohibits agreements with an anticompetitive object or effect, but does not define 'agreement': the meaning of the word has been left to emerge from the case-law. The advantage of this approach is that it allows a term's meaning to develop to fit the cases' contours: that development could be hampered by an explicit definition which every decision or judgment had to be made to fit. One disadvantage is that definition through cases is a haphazard process which is swayed by the specific facts that come before the authorities: the features of those facts tend to gain undue prominence in the jurisprudence. Another is that, as the diversity of the cases increases, the term's meaning can come to lack conceptual unity: the term is applied to a congeries of situations that have little significant in common. 'Agreement' in EC antitrust arguably displays both these faults, particularly the second: the textbooks standardly say that the word has a wide meaning and go on to list the diverse states of affairs that have been brought under it.[1] It is salutary, therefore, to step back

[1] Whish (2003), 92–3, gives the following examples of agreements: 'A legally enforceable contract of course qualifies as an agreement, including a compromise of litigation such as a trade mark delimitation agreement or the settlement of a patent action. "Gentleman's agreements" and simple understandings have been held to be agreements, though neither is legally binding; there is no requirement that an agreement should be supported by enforcement procedures. A "protocol" which reflects a genuine concurrence of will between the parties constitutes an agreement within the meaning of Article 81(1). Connected agreements may be treated as a single one. An agreement may be oral. The Commission will treat the contractual terms and conditions in a standard-form contract as an agreement within Article 81(1). An agreement which has expired by effluxion of time but the effects of which continue to be felt can be caught by Article 81(1). The constitution of a trade association qualifies as an agreement within Article 81. An agreement entered into by a trade association might be construed as an agreement on the part of its members. An agreement to create a European Economic Interest Grouping (EEIG), or the byelaws establishing it may be caught by Article 81(1). Guidelines issued by one person that are adhered to by another can amount to an agreement, and circulars and warnings sent by a manufacturer

from the cases' details and to reflect, at a more abstract level, on what an agreement is.

The first part of this chapter proposes two models of an agreement which develop the idea that an agreement exists where one party, X, gives a conditional undertaking and the other, Y, responds with an unconditional undertaking. In the first model (M4), X's undertaking is conditional on Y's undertaking to perform a certain action Ay. In the second model (M6), X's undertaking is conditional not on Y's undertaking to do Ay but on Y's *doing* Ay. (M4) and (M6) are defended against objections based on four alleged criteria for the adequacy of a model of an agreement: Symmetry, Obligation, Simultaneity and Interdependence. Symmetry is the requirement that both parties to an agreement do the same thing; Obligation, the requirement that an agreement directly generate performance obligations for the parties; Simultaneity, that the parties acquire their obligations at the same time; and Interdependence, that, if one party defaults on his performance obligation, the other ceases to have his original performance obligation. The models breach these criteria, but the criteria are unmotivated and misconceived and in any event certain of them are approximations to more plausible criteria which the models meet. Next I show that (M4) and (M6) accommodate plausible justifications for making and complying with agreements: the reasoning is set out that will lead X and Y, if they are rational, to make and comply with an agreement as modelled.

I then turn to the distinction drawn in Article 81 between the object and the effect of an agreement. I state what I call the Intuitive View, that the object limb of Article 81 catches agreements which the effect limb does not catch (and vice versa) but that, often at least, object is evidence for effect (but not vice versa). The first claim I call the Distinctness Thesis and the second the Evidence Thesis. The Intuitive View is plausible, so any view inconsistent with it is pro tanto implausible and needs defence. I then introduce three other views of an agreement's object: Odudu's View

to its dealers may be treated as part of the general agreement that exists between them. The fact that formal agreement has not been reached on all matters does not preclude a finding of an agreement, and there can be an agreement or concerted practice notwithstanding the fact that only one of the participants at a meeting reveals its intentions. Undertakings cannot justify infringement of the rules on competition by claiming that they were forced into an agreement by the conduct of other traders. Where an agreement is entered into unwillingly, this may be significant in influencing the Commission to mitigate a fine, not to impose a fine or not to institute proceedings at all. The Commission may abstain from fining parties which had no input in the drafting of the agreements into which they have entered.' Citations omitted. See also Faull and Nikpay (1999), paras. 2.27–2.40.

is that P is an object of agreement A if the parties to A, in making or implementing A, intend P; the Orthodox View is that 'P is an object of A' means the same as 'P is a necessary effect of A', where a necessary effect is one that can be reasonably foreseen as almost certain, or at least as highly likely (thus a necessary effect need not occur); and the Received View is that P is an object of A if P is a necessary effect of A.

Having dismissed the Orthodox View, I consider whether Odudu's View and the Received View are consistent with the Intuitive View. The discussion proceeds by way of four questions: (Q1) Is P an object of A if P is an effect of A? (Q2) Is P an effect of A if P is an object of A? (Q3) Is P's being an object of A evidence that P is an effect of A? (Q4) Is P's being an effect of A evidence that P is an object of A? The Distinctness Thesis, and hence the Intuitive View, is false if the answer to (Q1) or (Q2) is yes, and the Evidence Thesis, and hence the Intuitive View, is false if the answer to (Q3) is no or the answer to (Q4) is yes. On the Received View, the answer to (Q2), (Q3) and (Q4) is no; the Received View also supports the answer no to (Q1). Odudu's View supports the answer no to (Q1) if intention is not closed under the relation . . . causes . . . (the concept of closure is explained), but, if the very strong assumption is made that intention is closed under that relation, the answer to (Q1) on Odudu's View is yes. The answer to (Q2) and (Q3) on Odudu's View is no; the answer to (4) is no if intention is not closed under . . . causes . . . , and is probably the same if intention is closed under . . . causes . . . .

Thus, leaving aside qualifications, the Received View and Odudu's View are each consistent with the Distinctness Thesis and inconsistent with the Evidence Thesis. Each therefore is inconsistent with the Intuitive View and pro tanto implausible. The Received View fares worse because, in addition, it leaves it unclear why the object limb of Article 81 is needed: on this view, the effect limb is sufficient for Article 81 to do its job.

The final section of the chapter discusses the concept, introduced into UK antitrust by the 'cartel offence' specified in section 188 of the Enterprise Act 2002, of an agreement that is dishonest. The leading case on dishonesty is *Ghosh*, according to which a jury, in determining whether the prosecution has proved that the defendant was acting dishonestly, must first decide whether, according to the ordinary standards of reasonable and honest people, what was done was dishonest and, second, if so, whether the defendant must have realised that what he was doing was dishonest by those standards: the jury is to reach an affirmative conclusion if and only if both these conditions are met.

I argue that *Ghosh* falls to objections of circularity. As a preliminary, I distinguish four questions to which *Ghosh* might be taken to give an answer: a question of analysis (What is it to be dishonest?), a question of linguistic definition (What does 'dishonest' mean?), a question about conditions (Under what conditions is someone or something dishonest?) and an epistemic question (What is the, or a, test for dishonesty?). If *Ghosh* is read as answering the second question, it faces the circularity objection that the definition it gives contains non-redundant occurrences of the words 'honest' and 'dishonest'; a parallel objection applies to the reading of *Ghosh* as answering the first question. The third question is largely uninteresting to the extent that it differs from the first. We are left, therefore, with the fourth question, of the test for dishonesty. If *Ghosh* is read as answering this, it faces another circularity objection: the first limb of the test requires the jury to consider whether the defendant's action was dishonest by the ordinary standards of reasonable and *honest* people; but, if the jury is unsure how to tell that the defendant acted dishonestly, it will be at least as unsure how to tell that some other person is honest. The test is useless because it is as elusive as the thing to be tested.

Five replies to this objection are canvassed. The first is that the thing to be tested is a dishonest *action* whereas the test refers to honest *people*: it is easier to tell that a person is honest, or dishonest, than that an action is. The second is that the thing to be tested is a *dishonest* action whereas the test refers to *honest* people: it is easier to tell that someone or something is honest than that he or it is dishonest. The third invokes first-person privilege in ascriptions of honesty: although it may be no easier for X to tell that Y is honest than that Z's action is dishonest, it is easier for X to tell that he (X) is honest. The fourth reply is that, contrary to the literal wording of *Ghosh*, the jury is to decide whether by its own ordinary standards the defendant acted dishonestly: the concept of reasonable and honest people is not part of the content of, but is a gloss on, the first limb of the test, to the effect that it will be applied by people who are reasonable and honest. The final reply is that the test need only be applied to difficult cases, whereas the jury can use easy cases to identify honest people.

All these replies fail, so the objection of circularity stands. To avoid it, a different account of dishonesty is needed. A broad and a narrow concept of dishonesty can be distinguished: on the broad concept a dishonest action is simply one that is wrong; on the narrow concept it is wrong in a specific way that involves concealment. The narrow concept can be modelled by saying that a person's action is dishonest if (a) it is wrong and (b) he does it in a manner that he intends to conceal either (i) the fact that he is doing it or (ii) the fact that it is wrong. This gives an answer to all four of the questions identified above and avoids circularity in that 'wrong' is normally easier to understand and apply than is 'dishonest'. But the model is vulnerable to other objections, parallel to ones that other writers have raised to *Ghosh*, for example that it gives undesired results where jurors have lax views as to what is wrong.

In the face of this there are four options: to argue that, after all, such objections do not undermine *Ghosh* or the model; to try to frame a concept of dishonesty that avoids the objections; to live with the objections; or to expunge dishonesty from criminal law. So far as the Enterprise Act's cartel offence is concerned, the fourth option looks the best.

Models of agreement

If X undertakes to Y that X will do Ax if Y will do Ay, and Y undertakes the converse to X, they do not agree that X will do Ax and Y will do Ay, for both will comply with their undertakings if neither does anything. Nor is an agreement generated by complicating the conditionals, so that, for example, X undertakes that X will do Ax if, if X will do Ax, Y will do Ay, and Y undertakes the converse; for then, depending on the interpretation of 'if', either both parties can still comply by doing nothing or each party in effect merely undertakes to perform the action in question.[2] If X merely undertakes to Y that X will do Ax, and Y merely undertakes to X that Y will do Ay, there is just a pair of undertakings, not an agreement.

Can an agreement be modelled in terms of undertakings by the parties, in a way that avoids these problems and is otherwise satisfactory? Some philosophers[3] think not, but the orthodox opinion, so far as there is one, appears to be that such a model can be provided.[4] Talk of orthodoxy is perhaps out of place, for the philosophical literature on the nature of an

[2] The second horn of the dilemma applies if the 'if' is read truth-functionally, so that 'Q if P' means 'not both P and not Q'; for, on that reading, it is true that (P if (Q if P)) if and only if it is true that P. Compare Radford (1984), 580–1. A more elaborate complication of the conditionals is proposed by Prichard (1949a) in an analysis of exchange.

[3] Notably Gilbert: see Gilbert (1996a), (1996b).

[4] See Atiyah (1981), 204–5; Bach (1995); Baier (1985), 199; D. Lewis (1969), 34, 35, 84; Prichard (1949c); Radford (1984), 582; Raz (1984), 203; Robins (1984), 105; Velleman (2000a) (appendix), (2000b). For a similar view of the nature of contracts, see Beale (1999), para. 1-001.

agreement is relatively sparse; this is surprising, given the number and the importance of agreements. To state the obvious: agreements form one of the main types of social bond; they are central to the law – to antitrust and contract law,[5] of course, but also to criminal law (specifically, the rules on conspiracy) and to company law (the rules on concert parties); and the concept of agreement is prominent in various theoretical areas, such as the theory of cooperative games and social contract theories of political obligation.[6]

I shall defend the orthodox opinion by arguing for two models which develop the idea that there is an agreement where one party gives a conditional undertaking and the other responds with an unconditional undertaking. Once again the general remarks about models apply, specifically that a model is intended only to represent a central case of a central concept: I therefore leave open the possibility that certain agreements are better understood in other terms, for example as 'joint decisions' in Gilbert's sense.[7] Nor is the claim that every agreement within the meaning of Article 81 EC does or should conform exactly to one or other model. Rather, the models are intended as points of reference to help determine when something can properly be called an agreement and when the term is being extended implausibly far.

[5] A standard definition of a contract in common law is that it is an agreement giving rise to obligations that are enforced or recognised by law: Treitel (1995), 1. Contracts and agreements overlap but do not coincide; for example, unilateral contracts and deeds made by one person are not agreements in any normal sense. Also contract law has been extended since the late nineteenth century to protect detrimental reliance in the absence of an agreement, other than in an unusually broad sense: see Atiyah (1979) and Gilmore (1995), both passim, and Cooke and Oughton (1993), 47. For a review of objections to the identification of contracts with agreements, see Beale (1999), paras. 1-003–1-006. Contrast De Moor (1987), 115, where it is said that 'an agreement' adds little to the meaning of 'a contract'.

[6] In these areas the concept of an agreement or of a contract is more often presupposed than analysed. Game-theoretic accounts of bargaining throw some light on the nature of an agreement, but cooperative solutions such as Nash's assume an enforceable agreement between the parties: Nash (1950); Dixit and Skeath (1999), ch. 16. As to the social contract, Hobbes (1968), 192, gives a brief account of a contract as 'the mutual transferring of right'. Hume (1963), 454–5, distinguishes a strong and a weak sense of 'contract'. Rawls makes some remarks on the appropriateness of the term to describe his own theory: Rawls (1972), 16.

[7] Gilbert (1989), 380, (1996a), 292 ff, (1996b), 330 ff. There may be more than one concept of agreement, even if only everyday rather than legal agreements are in question. Gilbert (1996b), 314, talks of 'the everyday concept of an agreement', which implies that there is only one such concept. For one distinction between concepts of an agreement, see S. Freeman (1998), 663. I also shall not discuss here the relation between agreements and other forms of cooperation, as to which see Gauthier (1986), ch. 5. For the relation between agreements and joint action, see chapter 5 below.

The first model

Consider this first attempt:

(M1) X and Y agree that X will do Ax and Y will do Ay where:
(a) X undertakes to Y that X will do Ax if Y will undertake to X that Y will do Ay; and
(b) Y undertakes to X that Y will do Ay.

'Undertakes' will be left unanalysed. The obvious case of undertaking is promising: all promises are undertakings but it seems that some undertakings are weaker than promises – vows, for example, are weaker in that they need not be made to anyone[8] – and others, such as oaths, are stronger than mere promises. Since many agreements appear to involve nothing so solemn as a promise, the broader concept is preferable.[9]

(M1) and its successors are intended only to display the structure of the interaction between X and Y: it is not suggested that X and Y need *say* 'I undertake [etc.]'. The exchange is likely to be more informal, for example: X: 'Why don't you wash the dishes and I'll make the beds.' Y: 'Fine.' Indeed X and Y may say nothing, their undertakings being constituted by other actions.

Pretend however that X says 'I undertake that I will do Ax if you will undertake that you will do Ay'. Depending on the scope given to 'I undertake that' and 'if', the sentence can be interpreted to express an undertaking that is either externally conditional – 'If you will undertake that you will do Ay, I undertake that I will do Ax' – or internally conditional: 'I undertake that, if you will undertake that you will do Ay, I will do Ax.'[10] Each interpretation fits some agreements, but the internal one appears to fit more and will therefore be adopted here. So the model becomes:

(M2) X and Y agree that X will do Ax and Y will do Ay where:
(a) X undertakes to Y that, if Y will undertake to X that Y will do Ay, X will do Ax; and
(b) Y undertakes to X that Y will do Ay.

[8] See De Moor (1987), 109; and Fried (1981), 40–3.

[9] Binmore (1994), 60, characterises an agreement in terms of undertakings. Prichard (1949c), 172, says that 'undertake', 'promise' and 'agree' are all 'equivalent'. Another candidate for the model's right-hand side is the slightly different concept of commitment: see Bach (1995), 606–7; and Tuomela (1995), 113–14. The US Restatement (Second) of Contracts (1981) defines a promise in terms of a commitment (para. 2); Binmore does the opposite, in Binmore (1994), 161, (1998), 47. For distinctions between types of commitment, see Lieberman (1998), 5.

[10] This generalises to undertakings the distinction that Gilbert (1996b), 317 ff, draws between conditional promises.

(M2) has the defect mentioned earlier: a mere pair of undertakings does not amount to an agreement, even where the giver of each undertaking is the addressee of the other. The missing element is the idea (expressed in contract law by the principle that, for a contract to exist, there must be an offer that is accepted[11]) that Y gives his undertaking in *response* to X's. This can be developed by saying that Y's reason – or one of Y's reasons – for giving his undertaking is that X has given *his* undertaking. There are many kinds of reason; here the genus is practical reasons and the species comprises both justification and explanation: that X has given X's undertaking both justifies Y in giving and explains the fact that Y gives Y's undertaking. The nature of the justification will be discussed later, when I consider the forms of practical deliberation that would lead rational parties to give their undertakings.[12] As to explanation, the most promising thought is that it is causal. In more detail, let Ux and Uy be respectively X's and Y's acts of giving their undertakings: then the fact that Y does Uy is explained by the fact that there is an appropriate causal chain from Ux to Uy, where 'there is a causal chain from Ux to Uy' means 'Ux stands to Uy in the proper ancestral of the relation ... causes ...'[13] (roughly, this means that Ux causes Uy, or causes something that causes Uy, and so on). The requirement that the chain be appropriate is intended to exclude deviant cases in which the chain involves grossly irrational mental processes, or even no mental processes at all, on Y's part. A full account of appropriateness will not be attempted here,[14] but a necessary condition is that Y believe that X does Ux.[15] Normally Y will not only believe this,

[11] It appears to be a principle of English contract law that an act wholly motivated by factors other than the offer cannot amount to an acceptance: *Lark* v. *Outhwaite* [1991] 2 Lloyd's Rep 132, 140. Bach adopts an offer–acceptance model in his account of an agreement as an exchange of promises: the idea seems to be that X and Y exchange promises by X's making an offer and Y's accepting it, the offer and the acceptance themselves being promises: Bach (1995), 606–7.

[12] Broome holds that deliberation is not reason-giving, but rather is a matter of 'normative requirements': see Broome (2002) and the other papers cited in note 46 below. I here use 'reason' in a broad sense that glosses over the distinction. Clause (c), in the models of an agreement below, can be expanded to accommodate Broome's point explicitly.

[13] In Black (1987b), 104–10, and (1988), 429, this relation is used to explicate the notion of one belief's being based on another.

[14] See Peacocke (1979), ch. 2.

[15] This is a point at which contract law may diverge from the present concept of agreement. There is doubtful authority in English law for the principle that a party may accept an offer of which he is ignorant: *Gibbons* v. *Proctor* (1891) 64 LT 594, 55 JP 616; compare *Neville* v. *Kelly* (1862) 12 CB (NS) 740 and see Beale (1999), paras. 2-038–2-039. The authority is clear – e.g. in the posting rule – for the converse principle that a contract may arise where the offeror is ignorant of the acceptance: *Henthorn* v. *Fraser* [1892] 2 Ch. 27, 33; *Adams* v.

but his belief will be justified or amount to knowledge. Where the belief is justified, the justification will be epistemic rather than the practical kind of justification mentioned above; but it can be argued that, by virtue of the requirement of appropriateness, the explanatory element of the reason-relation here entails the element of practical justification. The model now becomes:

(M3) X and Y agree that X will do Ax and Y will do Ay where:
- (a) X undertakes to Y that, if Y will undertake to X that Y will do Ay, X will do Ax;
- (b) Y undertakes to X that Y will do Ay; and
- (c) Y's reason for giving the undertaking in (b) is that X gives the undertaking in (a).

(c) says 'X gives' whereas the previous discussion used 'X has given'; but, given that 'Y's reason' signifies a causal chain from Ux to Uy, and that effects normally succeed their causes,[16] (c) can be taken to imply that Ux precedes Uy (see the remark in chapter 1 on the use of the timeless present in the models). 'Y's reason' is intended to include the case where Y also has other reasons. Note that the relation specified in (c) between the two undertakings is external in a sense stronger than the one, discussed earlier, in which X's undertaking is not externally conditional: the latter sense concerns the respective scopes of 'I undertake that' and 'if' – matters that are internal to the content of X's undertaking – whereas the relation in (c) is external to the contents of Ux and Uy in that it connects the acts themselves. Note also that because this relation is strongly external, and because it is not one of simple conditionality, (M3) does not have the defect of the reciprocally conditional undertakings mentioned earlier, that both parties will comply if neither does anything.

It may be suggested that the model should mention not only Y's reason but also X's – not for doing Ux but for doing Ax. The thought is this: suppose that, first, X knows that, if Y does Uy, Z will force X to do Ax, where Ax is something that X hopes not to do and believes it would be bad for him to do; second, X, in order to inform Y of this, tells Y that, if Y does Uy, X will do Ax; and third, for the reason that X tells this to Y, Y vindictively takes advantage of X's predicament by doing Uy. Then

Lindsell (1818) 1 B & Ald 681; *Potter* v. *Sanders* (1846) 6 Hare 1; *Harris's Case* (1872) LR 7 Ch. App 587. See Beale (1999), paras. 2-043–2-057 and, for other situations in which the offeror's ignorance does not preclude the creation of a contract, para. 2-042A.

[16] It may be argued that sustaining, rather than efficient, causes can occur at the same time as their effects: e.g. a weight's lying on a cushion causes the cushion to be indented. See Black (1987b), 117, 183–4.

it seems that (M3) is satisfied, but X and Y surely do not agree that they will respectively do Ax and Ay. One proposal for dealing with this case is to exclude it by rewriting the end of (M3)(a) to say that X, solely for the reason that Y will have done Uy, will do Ax. But the proposal is unnecessary because the case is not a counterexample to (M3). Without analysing the concept of an undertaking, it is clear enough that X's utterance does not amount to an undertaking that, if Y does Uy, X will do Ax: rather, it is a conditional prediction and perhaps a warning.

As noted earlier, (M3)(c) implies that Y believes that X does Ux, and Y's belief will normally be justified or amount to knowledge. It may be suggested that a corresponding condition should be imposed on X – that X believe, or believe with justification, or know, that Y does Uy; for otherwise, it may be said, the model fails to capture the fact that an agreement involves a meeting of minds. This step can lead to an infinite regress: if X must believe that Y does Uy, perhaps Y must believe that X believes this, and perhaps X must believe that Y believes that X does Ux, and so on. Such thinking motivates the addition of a clause attributing to X and Y the common belief, or justified belief, or knowledge, that they respectively do Ux and Uy, and perhaps also that Y's reason for doing Uy is that X does Ux: roughly, X and Y have the common belief that P if and only if X believes that P, Y believes that P, Y believes that X believes that P, X believes that Y believes that P, etc., and likewise for common justified belief or knowledge.[17] How far one should go along this path depends first on whether an agreement involves a meeting of minds[18] and second on how strong a sense 'meeting of minds' has: the answers are partly a matter of stipulation, for the phrase is more venerable[19] than clear, and it can be given a meaning weak enough to

[17] Gilbert's account of an agreement attributes common knowledge to the parties: Gilbert (1996a), 296; see also Gilbert (1996e), 109. On common knowledge generally, see chapter 1, note 23, above.

[18] The principles in note 15 above support the view that a meeting of minds is not needed for a contract to exist; see further Beale (1999), para. 1-004, which cites *Byrne* v. *Van Tienhoven* (1880) 5 CPD 344 in support of the principle that a contract can arise where the parties are not 'ad idem'. Also it appears to be a principle of English contract law that where the offeree believes the offeror to have the relevant intention – that the offer is to become binding on acceptance – it is not necessary that the offeror be aware of the offeree's belief (*The Hannah Blumenthal* [1983] 1 AC 854, 924; Beale (1999), para. 2-003): this pulls against a requirement of common belief. A variant is the concept of a meeting of wills, which is more prominent in French than in English contract law: see note 1 above and De Moor (1986) and (1987), 115–16. For an example from EC antitrust, see Case T-41/96, *Bayer* v. *Commission* [2001] CMLR 176, where the court held that an agreement involves a 'concurrence of wills'.

[19] See Gordley (1991), 135–6, which cites Plowden and Comyns.

apply to (M3). To add a clause attributing common belief (etc.) to X and Y would capture an unusually strong concept of agreement and would also raise the general difficulties with common propositional attitudes, notably that it seems psychologically unrealistic to hold that people ever have them.[20] A more attractive proposal is to add just the clause that X has the justified belief that Y does Uy: intuitively, this captures the idea that not only Y but both parties are aware of what is going on.[21] The model becomes:

(M4) X and Y agree that X will do Ax and Y will do Ay where:
- (a) X undertakes to Y that, if Y will undertake to X that Y will do Ay, X will do Ax;
- (b) Y undertakes to X that Y will do Ay;[22]
- (c) Y's reason for giving the undertaking in (b) is that X gives the undertaking in (a); and
- (d) X has the justified belief that (b).

(M4) is the first of the two models I propose.

Alleged criteria of adequacy

Four criteria may be proposed for the adequacy of a model of agreement: Symmetry, Obligation, Simultaneity and Interdependence. (M4) breaches all of them, so either (M4) is inadequate or the criteria are misconceived. The latter is the case, but certain of the criteria are approximations to more plausible ones which (M4) meets.

[20] See Schiffer (1987), 246, and chapter 5 below. Proposals for psychologically plausible forms of common knowledge or belief are found in Bennett (1976), 127; Kemmerling (1986); Loar (1981), 250; and Tuomela (1995), 41–51. On the broader issue of a person's having an infinity of beliefs, see Black (1987b), ch. 8, (2003e).

[21] A strong version of this idea is embodied in Gilbert's '"knowledge of agreements" assumption', that, if a person enters into an agreement, he knows that he does: Gilbert (1996a), 284.

[22] Where the undertakings are promises, Raz appears to hold that (a) and (b) are sufficient for an agreement: Raz (1984), 203. He appears to take the same view of (a) and (b) in (M6) below. But Raz explicitly disregards the distinction between the internally and the externally conditional (which, in the case of duties, he conflates with a distinction between present and future duties): Raz (1984), 196, n. 1. Bach likewise appears to think that an agreement may involve promises which respectively have the structures of the undertakings in (a) and (b) in (M4): Bach (1995), 606–7. In Gilbert (1996b), 327, case 8, read as involving an internally conditional promise, instantiates (a) and (b) in (M4). Surprisingly, Gilbert does not examine a case instantiating the corresponding clauses of (M6).

The idea of Symmetry is that both parties do the same thing.[23] It is hard to make this precise, but there is no need to, as it is clear that the criterion is breached by (M4): specifically, the content of Ux is conditional and that of Uy is not, and, whereas Y does Uy for the reason that X does Ux, the converse need not be true. So much the worse for Symmetry. (M4) does, and the criterion does not, reflect the fact that normally in the making of an agreement one party – X in the model – goes first.[24] Contract law recognises this in the doctrine of offer and acceptance.

The remaining three criteria have been proposed by Gilbert, as part of an argument against that version of the orthodox opinion which holds that an agreement is an exchange of promises. Gilbert expresses Obligation by saying that 'the agreement directly generates the relevant performance obligation for each of the parties', a performance obligation being 'an obligation to perform the specified act'.[25] The specified acts in the model are Ax and Ay. Now the following principles are plausible:

(O1) If a person undertakes that he will φ, he has an obligation to φ.[26]
(O2) If a person undertakes that if P he will φ, then:
(a) he has an obligation, namely to φ if P; and
(b) if P, he has an obligation to φ.[27,28]

[23] Radford talks of the 'parallel nature' of the things said by the parties (Radford (1984), 581), but he in effect rejects Symmetry.

[24] Compare Bach (1995), 606–7. Bach describes a counterexample in which a third party suggests a plan and effects its joint acceptance.

[25] Gilbert (1996b), 315.

[26] Raz (1984), 202, states a similar principle for promises. Tuomela says that it is constitutive of the notion of agreement that an agreement creates an obligation for the parties.

[27] Different views may be taken as to the ground of the obligations. On one view, they arise from the fact that an undertaking causes, or is intended or can be foreseen to cause, reliance: see Atiyah (1979), especially chs. 1, 6, 22, (1981), especially chs. 3 and 7, (1986); Demarco and Fox (1992), 48; Fogelin (1983); Knapp (1984); MacCormick (1972); McMahon (1989); and Scanlon (1990), (1998), ch. 7, (2001). For criticism, see Altham (1985); Ardal (1976); Cartwright (1984); Downie (1985); Fox and Demarco (1993), 82; Fried (1981), chs. 1–2; Morris (1991); Patterson (1992); Raz (1972), (1977); Warnock (1971), ch. 7; and Woozley (1981). On the relations between reliance and obligation generally, see the appendix to chapter 5 below.

[28] Consider the following objection to (O2)(b). Suppose that I am a dentist and I undertake to you, my patient, that, when you raise your hand, I shall stop drilling. I do not discharge this obligation if, when you raise your hand, I stop for some different reason and while ignoring the fact that you have raised your hand. But I would discharge it if the obligation were merely to stop when you raise your hand. So my obligation is a stronger one, to stop for the reason that you raise your hand. There are two replies to this. First, my having the stronger obligation does not preclude my having the weaker one – on the contrary, my having the weaker follows from my having the stronger – so the example does not impugn

In (b) the obligation is externally conditional and in (a), considered by itself, the obligation is internally conditional; but the obligation in (a) is externally conditional with respect to the antecedent (i.e. the 'if'-clause) of (O2). The distinction between externally and internally conditional obligations corresponds to that between externally and internally conditional undertakings.[29] (O1) and (O2) concern pro-tanto rather than on-balance obligations; the question can here be left open whether the obligations are moral.[30] Assume that the type of obligation in the principles is the same as in Gilbert's criterion.[31]

Gilbert does not explain what she means by 'directly generates', but it appears that (M4) meets the criterion so far as Y is concerned: by (M4)(b), Y undertakes that he will do Ay; so, by (O1), Y has an obligation to do Ay. X, however, only gives the conditional undertaking in (M4)(a); hence by (O2)(a) he has the internally conditional obligation, to do Ax if Y will undertake to him that Y will do Ay. But this is not X's performance obligation, which is simply to do Ax. So (M4) appears to fail Obligation.

But Gilbert gives no reason for imposing such a stringent test. (It is a weakness of her discussion that she says little about the supposed sources

(O2)(b). Second, it is doubtful that I do have the stronger obligation. An alternative and plausible view is that the weaker obligation is the only one that, in Gilbert's phrase, is directly generated by my undertaking: if I stop only for some different reason, I thereby and luckily fulfil it. It can be conceded that I am morally at fault in failing to pay adequate attention to that obligation. The fault might perhaps be described in terms of a meta-obligation (which might, in order to avoid a regress, be taken to apply to itself) to pay attention to my obligations.

29 The question whether an obligation is conditional or unconditional is distinct from the question whether or not the obligation motivates. The distinction is blurred in Gilbert (1996b), 319, 328–9.

30 See further chapter 5, especially the appendix. The distinction between pro-tanto and on-balance obligations corresponds to the distinction between pro-tanto and on-balance goods: see chapter 2, note 6. A pro-tanto obligation is one that may be overridden by other factors, and especially by other obligations; an on-balance obligation is one that applies once all relevant factors are taken into account. If X promises to meet Y at the cinema, X is obliged pro tanto to meet Y there; but if on the way X finds Z dying in the street, X is likely to be obliged on balance to help Z, thereby failing to keep his promise. For criticism of the related concept of prima-facie obligation, see Searle (1968). For a distinction between the prima-facie and the pro-tanto, see Hurley (1989), 130 ff.

31 In Gilbert (1996a), 299–300, Gilbert allows that the obligations of agreement are pro-tanto and doubts that they are moral; see also Gilbert (1996b), 631–2, n. 13, (1996d), 79, (1996e), 108–9, (1996g), 181. Raz (1977), 225, denies that promissory obligations as such are moral.

of her proposed criteria; she might, for example, have argued that they somehow flow from the purposes served by the concept of an agreement[32] or by agreements themselves.) Granted that an agreement imposes obligations on each party, a more plausible criterion, in the case of the party giving the conditional undertaking, is that he has the corresponding conditional obligation and that, when the other party gives the unconditional undertaking, he has the performance obligation. (O2)(a) ensures that (M4) meets the first limb, as just noted, and (O2)(b) that it meets the second. Gilbert's criterion is an approximation to this more plausible one, and indeed may be interpreted to amount to the same thing if 'the agreement directly generates the relevant performance obligation' is construed broadly enough to cover the second limb. Gilbert probably means something narrower.

The next criterion is Simultaneity: the parties to an agreement acquire their obligations under the agreement at the same time.[33] (O1) and (O2) say nothing about the times at which the obligations they mention arise, but temporal references can plausibly be introduced,[34] thus:

(O3) If at time T1 a person undertakes that he will φ, at T1 he gets an obligation to φ.

(O4) If at T2 a person undertakes that if at T3 event E occurs he will φ, then:
(a) at T2 he gets an obligation, namely to φ if at T3 E occurs; and
(b) if at T3 E occurs, at T3 he gets an obligation to φ.

These principles can be refined (in particular, to specify the time at which the person is to φ) but they are accurate enough for present purposes. The temporal references in (M4) can likewise be made more precise. Using names for times that match those in the principles (so that T1 = T3):

[32] Compare the approach taken to knowledge in E. Craig (1990), ch. 1, and to truth in B. Williams (2002).

[33] Gilbert (1996a), 290, (1996b), 315–16. Gilbert may – her wording is not clear – have in mind a stronger criterion, that the parties both acquire and lose their obligations at the same time; if so, the following discussion is unaffected. The distinction between lasting for the same period and lasting for adjoining or overlapping periods seems to resolve the conflicts between requirements of simultaneity and succession that Benson (2001b) finds in contract law. It thus avoids the need for the baffling solution Benson proposes, that '"Simultaneity" must . . . mean something other than "at the same time"' (148) and that 'Value is the unity of temporal succession and simultaneity' (195).

[34] On the time of an obligation, see Prichard (1949d).

(M5) At T1 X and Y agree that X will do Ax and Y will do Ay where:
- (a) At T2 X undertakes to Y that, if at T1 Y will undertake to X that Y will do Ay, X will do Ax;
- (b) At T1 Y undertakes to X that Y will do Ay;
- (c) Y's reason for giving the undertaking in (b) is that X gives the undertaking in (a); and
- (d) X has the justified belief that (b).

Ux precedes Uy, as already noted, so T2 precedes T1. By (M5)(a) and (O4)(a) X gets an obligation at T2, and by (M5)(b) and (O3) Y gets an obligation at T1. So (M5) fails Simultaneity.

But again the test is too stringent. A more plausible criterion, to which Simultaneity approximates, is that the parties get their *performance* obligations at the same time. (M5) meets this criterion: both X and Y get their performance obligations at T1 – Y by (M5)(b) and (O3), X by (M5)(a), (M5)(b) and (O4)(b). In support of Simultaneity, Gilbert says 'In many cases, a given party will have no desire to take on some particular obligation before the other party has taken on a corresponding obligation.'[35] But, if X wants to make an agreement with Y, X must be willing to take the steps needed to achieve this – specifically, to do Ux and thereby to acquire a conditional obligation. Since the obligation is only conditional, it is not burdensome, for it does not require X to do anything unless Y does Uy. It might be argued that the conditional obligation entails certain unconditional obligations on X – in particular the obligation not to put himself in such a position that, if Y does Uy, X will be unable to do Ax – and that in some circumstances such obligations will be a burden on X; but, even if this is true, it is not a good enough reason to prefer Simultaneity to the weaker criterion.

Gilbert's third criterion is Interdependence: 'if one party defaults on his performance obligation, the other ceases to have his original performance obligation.'[36] Reverting for simplicity to (M4), it appears that the model fails the criterion so far as a default by Y is concerned. By (M4)(a), (M4)(b) and (O2)(b), if X does Ux and Y does Uy, X gets the performance obligation to do Ax: nothing in the model or in the normative principles so far proposed implies that this obligation falls away if Y fails to do Ay. It

[35] Gilbert (1996b) 315–16.

[36] Gilbert (1996b), 317; see also Gilbert (1996a), 291, and compare Fried (1981), 117. In Gilbert (1996a), 291, and (1996b), 316, a stronger version of Interdependence is proposed: if either party defaults, he nullifies the obligations of *both* parties.

might be replied that, if Y fails to do Ay, Y thereby ceases to undertake to do Ay,[37] in which case (O2)(b) ceases to generate the performance obligation on X. There is no need to consider whether this reply can be sustained – specifically, by reintroducing temporal references and/or by elaborating the concept of an undertaking (for example, so as to distinguish between the act and the resultant state) – for it is clear that the model breaches Interdependence so far as default by X is concerned: by (O1), if Y does Uy he gets the performance obligation to do Ay whether or not X does Ax. ((O1) says that, if a person undertakes that he will φ, he has an obligation to φ.) It makes no difference that, as (M4)(c) provides, Y does Uy for the reason that X does Ux.

Gilbert's case for Interdependence is based on our 'common understanding'[38] of an agreement, but it is doubtful whether we do commonly understand that agreements meet the criterion: a plausible view is that, at least in some cases, if one party defaults on his performance obligation the performance obligation of the other party persists. This view is supported by English contract law, which provides that a breach justifying rescission[39] does not automatically determine a contract[40] and moreover that, where a contract is rescinded, the injured party remains liable to perform obligations that accrued before rescission.[41] Possible counterexamples are agreements of coordination – as where the parties agree to meet at a certain place and time – for there a breach by one party makes the other's compliance pointless; but these are not enough to sustain Interdependence as a general criterion for the adequacy of a model of agreement. The performance obligations of the parties in (M4) are

[37] See the discussion of the caducity of promises, in Black (2003d).

[38] Gilbert (1996b), 316.

[39] The use of 'rescind' in this context has been criticised (see Beale (1999), para. 25-046, and Treitel (1995), 674–6), but is a common and convenient shorthand for those remedies that, broadly, absolve the injured party from performance of obligations under the contract that have not accrued. See the cases cited in Black (2003d), n. 22.

[40] Cases are cited in Treitel (1995), 757, n. 9. Where the contract comprises promises that depend on each other, rescission is sometimes but not always available, the main deciding factor being the seriousness of the failure to perform: Beale (1999), paras. 25-036–25-045; and Treitel (1995), 681–739. In the unusual case where the promises are independent of each other, neither party is entitled to rescind for failure by the other party to perform: the defaulting party can still enforce the injured party's promise. The distinction between dependent and independent promises is analysed in Black (2003d), which cites cases in nn. 2 and 4; it is argued there, however, that a contract comprising independent promises does not amount to an agreement.

[41] Beale (1999), paras. 25-001, 25-050; Treitel (1995), 762–3.

interdependent in a looser sense (to which, however, Interdependence cannot be viewed as an approximation): Y's performance obligation arises from an undertaking which he gives for the reason that X gives an undertaking which, together with Y's undertaking, gives rise to X's performance obligation.

The view that where X fails to do Ax Y remains obliged to do Ay strains our intuitions. The strain is partly eased by recognising that X's default does not free X from all obligations relating to the agreement: in most cases he is obliged to make some form of reparation to Y (in the context of the law on rescission, this is a secondary obligation to pay damages). But it may now be objected that X may breach this obligation in turn, but by (O1) Y remains obliged to do Ay, and that this is just as hard to accept. A better response to the intuitive resistance is to attribute it, at least in part, to a confusion between those obligations Y has and those it is fair for him to have: it can be granted that here it is unfair for him to be obliged to do Ay, but it does not follow that he is absolved from the obligation. Obligations are often unfair: obvious examples can be found among cases (unlike the present one) in which an obligation arises otherwise than through the will of the obligor, such as certain obligations to look after one's parents. If an intuition still supports Interdependence, I think the intuition should be abandoned.

The second model

In (M4) X's undertaking is conditional on Y's undertaking to do Ay. The second proposed model, which fits some cases better, is a simpler variant in which X's undertaking is conditional on Y's *doing* Ay,[42] thus:

(M6) X and Y agree that X will do Ax and Y will do Ay where:
- (a) X undertakes to Y that, if Y will do Ay, X will do Ax;
- (b) Y undertakes to X that Y will do Ay;
- (c) Y's reason for giving the undertaking in (b) is that X gives the undertaking in (a);[43] and
- (d) X has the justified belief that (b).

[42] X's undertaking in the first sentence of the section 'Models of agreement', above, is of this kind.

[43] The conversation in Radford (1984), 582, has the structure of (a) and (b). There is some similarity between the causal-explanatory component of (c) and Radford's requirement that the party making the unconditional statement have an appropriate motivation. Compare note 11 above.

(M6), like (M4), fails to meet the four alleged criteria, and again the right response is to reject the criteria. There are some differences of detail: as to Obligation, the revised criterion which (M6) meets, in the case of X, is that he has the corresponding conditional obligation and that, if Y fulfils Y's performance obligation, X gets X's performance obligation. As to Simultaneity, X and Y need not get their performance obligations at the same time, so (M6) does not even meet the weaker version of that criterion proposed earlier; by (O3), Y gets his performance obligation at T1, and by (O4)(b) X gets his at T3, but unlike the case of (M5) there is no implication that T1 = T3. ((O3) says that, if at T1 a person undertakes that he will φ, at T1 he gets an obligation to φ; (O4)(b) – with the headpiece of (O4) – says that, if at T2 a person undertakes that if at T3 event E occurs he will φ, then, if at T3 E occurs, at T3 he gets an obligation to φ.) As to Interdependence, if Y defaults on his performance obligation, nothing in the model or the normative principles implies that X ever gets a performance obligation; thus (M6) substantially meets the criterion so far as default by Y is concerned – 'substantially' because, if X never gets the obligation, it is inaccurate to say that he ceases to have it. The parties' performance obligations are now interdependent in the looser sense that Y's arises from an undertaking which he gives for the reason that X gives an undertaking which, if Y fulfils Y's obligation, gives rise to X's obligation.

Justifications for making and complying with agreements

(M4) and (M6) accommodate intuitively plausible justifications for making and complying with agreements. The justifications to be discussed are arguments that would lead a rational agent to make or comply with an agreement; they are not justifications, on grounds of morality or public policy, for the promotion or enforcement of agreements. The basic idea is that X wants, and believes that doing Ux is the best means of getting, Y to do Ay, and correspondingly for Y. I shall develop the idea for (M4) only and begin with the parties' arguments to their respective undertakings. Since (M4)(a) embeds Y's undertaking in X's ((M4)(a) says that X undertakes to Y that, if Y will undertake to X that Y will do Ay, X will do Ax), the approach will be to show how Y reasons to his undertaking and then to show how X, in reasoning to X's undertaking, takes Y's reasoning into account. Ux precedes Uy, as noted above, and the undertakings are in the future tense, but for simplicity I shall cast the arguments in the timeless present: this will not affect their substance.

Y may rationally argue to his undertaking as follows:

(1) I want X to do Ax. (Premiss.)
(2) X does Ux. (Premiss.)
(3) If I do Uy, X does Ax. (From (2).)
(4) My doing Uy is a means for me to secure that X does Ax. (From (3).)
(5) No other means for me to secure this is at least as good as my doing Uy. (Premiss.)
(6) The best means for me to secure that X does Ax is for me to do Uy. (From (4) and (5).)
(7) Other things are equal. (Premiss.)
(8) I will do Uy. (From (1), (6) and (7).)

(3) follows from (2) on the assumption that X's undertaking is reliable, where to say that a person's undertaking that if P he will φ is reliable means that if he gives it and it is the case that P then he will φ. That assumption is in turn underpinned by X's argument (24)–(28), discussed below, to the conclusion that he will do Ax: it is underpinned by the argument in the sense that the assumption follows from the propositions (i) that if X and Y respectively do Ux and Uy then X carries out the argument and (ii) that the intention expressed by the argument's conclusion is reliable in the sense that if X forms it then he will carry it out.

As to the move from (3) to (4), 'If I φ then P' does not by itself entail 'My φ-ing is a means for me to secure that P': possible counterexamples to a supposed entailment are the case where 'I φ' is substituted for 'P' and the case where there is some sufficient cause of both my φ-ing and its being the case that P, but no other causal relation and no constitutive relation between my φ-ing and its being the case that P. Nevertheless it seems clear that 'If I φ then P' can be supplemented to yield an entailment (which is not to say – what is false – that 'My φ-ing is a means for me to secure that P' entails 'If I φ then P'). What the supplementary assumptions are will depend on the analysis of the means–end relation, which will not be pursued here; the obvious approach is to analyse it in terms of the relation . . . causes . . . and perhaps also the relation . . . constitutes . . . . In any event, let the appropriate substitution-instances of the supplementary assumptions – whatever exactly they are – be granted to Y.

(6) follows from (4) and (5) on the assumption that the other means mentioned in (5) are commensurable, in respect of their goodness, with Y's doing Uy; there is no need here to amplify the relevant concepts of

commensurability and goodness.[44] (7) is required by the principle of means–end reasoning used to derive (8):

(PR) (a) I want that P.
(b) The best means for me to secure that P is for me to φ.
(c) Other things are equal.

So
(d) I will φ,

where (a) expresses a desire, (b) and (c) beliefs, and (d) an intention. (c) is needed to exclude such cases as the one where I want that P less than I want not to φ. Without an informative description of the types of 'thing' that need to be equal, (c) – and thus (PR) – is fairly trivial, but that does not matter for the present purpose. I shall simply assume that (PR) is valid, without attempting to explain why or in what sense. Clearly it is not valid in deductive logic: following Broome, one might say that (PR)'s validity is a matter of the 'formal', rather than logical, relations that hold among (a)–(d);[45] but so far that is only a label. It is plausible to say – adopting another idea of Broome's – that reasoning in accordance with (PR) is correct in that the mental states expressed by (a)–(c) 'normatively require' the intention expressed by (d), in the sense that I ought to see to it that I have that intention if I have that desire and those beliefs.[46]

X may rationally argue to his undertaking thus:

(9) I want Y to do Ay. (Premiss.)
(10) If I do Ux, Y reasons as at (1)–(8). (Premiss.)
(11) If Y reasons as at (1)–(8), he intends to do Uy. (From (10).)
(12) If Y intends to do Uy, he does Uy. (Premiss.)
(13) If Y does Uy, he does Ay. (Premiss.)
(14) If I do Ux, Y does Ay. (From (10)–(13).)
(15) My doing Ux is a means for me to secure that Y does Ay. (From (14).)
(16) No other means for me to secure this is at least as good as my doing Ux. (Premiss.)

[44] On commensurability, see Chang (1997). [45] Broome (2001a), 182.

[46] Broome (2000), (2001a). (PR) is similar to the schema of best-means reasoning in Broome (2002): the main differences are that Broome's first premiss expresses an intention whereas mine expresses a desire and, consequently, that (PR) contains the premiss that other things are equal. (PR) is similar in other respects to the basic schema for practical reasoning in Audi (1989), 99, the main difference being that the conclusion in Audi's schema is normative: 'I should φ.' For strictures on the detachment of normative conclusions in means–end reasoning, see Broome (2000), (2001a), (2001b), (2002), (2004).

(17) The best means for me to secure that Y does Ay is for me to do Ux. (From (15) and (16).)
(18) Other things are equal. (Premiss.)
(19) I will do Ux. (From (9), (17) and (18).)

(10) assumes that Y is rational enough to carry out the argument at (1)–(8). (11) makes explicit the fact, already noted, that (8) – the conclusion of Y's reasoning to Uy – expresses an intention. The import of (12) is that Y's intention is reliable in the sense specified above, and of (13) that Y's undertaking is reliable in a similar sense: that assumption is underpinned by Y's argument (20)–(23), discussed next, to the conclusion that he will do Ay; the point here is parallel to the one made above about the assumption that X's undertaking is reliable. (14) follows from (10)–(13) given transitivity of the conditional: this assumption may need to be qualified, depending on the interpretation given to 'if'.[47] The rest of the argument is parallel to (4)–(8).

Once X and Y have given their undertakings, they may rationally argue their way to fulfilling them. Y may argue:

(20) I do Uy. (Premiss.)
(21) I have an obligation to do Ay. (From (20).)
(22) Other things are equal. (Premiss.)
(23) I will do Ay. (From (21) and (22).)

(21) follows from (20) by (O1) (if a person undertakes that he will φ, he has an obligation to φ). (22) is required by the principle of normative reasoning used to derive (23):

(NR) (a) I have an obligation to φ.
(b) Other things are equal.

So
(c) I will φ.

The remarks on (PR) apply mutatis mutandis to (NR).[48]

X may argue:

[47] Transitivity is defined in chapter 1, note 59. Unqualified transitivity does not hold for counterfactual conditionals: Stalnaker (1991), 38; and D. Lewis (1973), 32–5.

[48] The schema of normative practical reasoning in Broome (2001a) is similar to (NR), but uses 'ought' instead of 'obligation' and does not have the provision that other things are equal. Compare principle 2 in M. Smith (1994), 12. On the relation between 'ought' and 'obligation', see the appendix to chapter 5 below.

(24) I do Ux. (Premiss.)
(25) Y does Uy. (Premiss.)
(26) I have an obligation to do Ax. (From (24) and (25).)
(27) Other things are equal (Premiss.)
(28) I will do Ax. (From (26) and (27).)

(26) follows by (O2)(b), and (28) by (NR). ((O2)(b) – with the headpiece of (O2) – says that, if a person undertakes that if P he will φ, then, if P, he has an obligation to φ.)

These arguments show that it is rational to make agreements and, having made them, to keep them.

Object and effect of an agreement

Object of an agreement: four views

That completes the general account of the nature of agreements and the justifications for making and complying with them. I begin the discussion of the distinction, drawn in Article 81 EC between the object and the effect of an agreement, by identifying four views of an agreement's object.

The Intuitive View and Odudu's View

Article 81(1) prohibits agreements that have an anticompetitive object or effect. It seems clear that the object limb of Article 81 catches agreements which the effect limb does not catch, and vice versa,[49] but also that, often at least, object is evidence for effect (but not vice versa). Call the first claim the Distinctness Thesis, the second the Evidence Thesis and their conjunction the Intuitive View.

The Intuitive View is plausible: any view inconsistent with it is pro tanto implausible and thus in need of defence. The Distinctness Thesis is plausible because, if it were false, Article 81 would contain redundant wording, and it is reasonable to assume that legislation generally does not contain redundancies. This assumption has two components: that legislators intend not to create redundancies and that their intention is successful.

The Evidence Thesis makes two claims: first, that P's being an object of agreement A is evidence that P is an effect of A and, second, that P's

[49] This is distinct from the point that the limbs are disjunctive rather than cumulative, as to which see Case 56/65, *Société Technique Minière (LTM)* v. *Maschinenbau Ulm GmbH (MBU)* [1966] ECR 235, 249; Roth (2001), para. 2-097.

being an effect of A is not evidence that P is an object of A.[50] 'Evidence' here has a weak sense. The first claim is only that P's being an object of A is some reason to believe that P is an effect of A: there may be an overriding reason to believe that P is not an effect of A, for example that the implementation of A causes a third party to intervene to prevent P. Thus construed, the claim is plausible. It might perhaps be grounded in an assumption that agreements are efficient in the sense that usually, if P is an object of A, P is an effect of A (the 'usually' is needed to avoid contradicting the Distinctness Thesis). Suppose we know that P is an object of A: then, given the assumption of efficiency, we have reason to believe that P is an effect of A. The second claim of the Evidence Thesis is plausible *despite* the weakness of the sense of 'evidence'. Agreement A may have any number of remote and unforeseeable effects: P's being an effect of this kind is no evidence that P is an object of A.

The Distinctness Thesis in particular seems to chime with Odudu's View that 'subjective intention is sufficient to satisfy the object requirement' in Article 81[51] – or, to put it in a form more amenable to analysis and assessment: P is an object of A if the parties to A, in making or implementing A, intend P.[52] (The distinction between making and implementing is not material to the discussion, which can therefore be limited to the parties' intentions in implementing A.) On this basis Odudu offers

[50] I shall assume that the objects of agreements, and the terms of the relations . . . causes . . . and . . . is evidence for . . . are propositions; 'P', 'Q' etc. are accordingly used interchangeably as schematic sentences and schematic names for propositions. The assumption about the terms of the relations, and arguably the assumption about objects, is artificial, but these assumptions make for simplicity and do not invalidate the discussion, which can be recast to avoid them. Probably a more accurate view is that causes and effects are events (see Davidson (1980a)) and that the terms of the evidential relation are states of affairs.

[51] Odudu (2001a), 70, citing Cases 96–102, 104, 105 and 110/82, *NV IAZ International Belgium and others* v. *Commission* [1983] ECR 3369, Case 35/83, *BAT Cigaretten* v. *Commission* [1985] ECR 363, Case T-1/1989, *Rhône-Poulenc* v. *Commission* [1991] ECR II 867, and Case T-8/89, *DSM NV* v. *Commission* [1991] ECR II, 1833. The Commission's Guidelines on the application of Article 81(3) of the Treaty 2004/C 101/08, OJ C101 27.4.2004, 97, state, at para. 22, that evidence of the parties' subjective intention is relevant to, but not a necessary condition of, the agreement's object; they are silent on the question whether subjective intention is a sufficient condition.

[52] For simplicity I likewise assume, again harmlessly but perhaps artificially in some cases, that the content of an intention is a proposition. I also assume that the parties have the same intention. Odudu claims that the object limb of Article 81 is met only where the latter assumption holds: Odudu (2001b), 384, citing Joined Cases 29 and 30/83, *Compagnie Royale Asturienne des Mines SA and Rheinzink GmbH* v. *Commission* [1984] ECR 1679, 1703.

two justifications for prohibiting an agreement with an anticompetitive object but no anticompetitive effect:

> The first is that Article 81(1) is not only concerned with seeking out those who have caused restrictive effects, but with preventing restrictive effects from occurring . . . A second, non-consequentialist justification is that failure to restrict competition, after attempting to do so is a function of chance rather than choice and the choice is sufficient in itself.[53]

The first justification runs together two arguments, one causal, the other epistemic. The causal argument is that, since anticompetitive effects are bad, and since normally an anticompetitive intention is causally antecedent to an anticompetitive effect, prohibiting such an intention is good as a way of preventing such an effect. This argument is irrelevant to the situation in question, where the agreement would not have an anticompetitive effect. The epistemic argument is the same except that its second premiss is that an anticompetitive intention is reliable evidence of an anticompetitive effect: given such an intention, it may reasonably be inferred that the agreement is anticompetitive in effect. In that case the primary concern of this argument, as of the causal argument, is not the object but the effect of the agreement: the arguments might therefore be said, as Odudu himself says of the Orthodox View considered below, to 'fail to take seriously' the object/effect distinction.[54] In any event, both arguments miss their mark because they connect an agreement's effect not with its object but with the parties' intention, which according to Odudu is only a sufficient condition for an object.

The second justification begs the question. Let the debatable claim be granted that, if it is bad for the parties to have an anticompetitive intention, they should not escape merely because by chance they fail to realise their intention. That gives no reason to think that it *is* bad for them to have such an intention. Moreover it seems false that failure to realise an intention is always a matter of chance: there may be a predictable causal chain leading to the failure. Further discussion would require an account of the concept of chance.

These objections attack the justifications which Odudu raises on his view that subjective intention is sufficient for an object, but they do not attack the view itself. The view has implications as to the breadth of an agreement's object that vary depending on the closure attributed to intention under various relations. To say that the property F is closed

[53] Odudu (2001a), 71. [54] Odudu (2001b), 382.

under the relation G is to say that, if one thing both has F and bears G to another thing, then the other thing has F. For example the property of being a dog is closed under the relation . . . is a sibling of . . . , for anything of which a dog is a sibling is a dog; conversely the property of being male is not closed under that relation, for some males are siblings of females. Now suppose that two people in implementing an agreement intend to share information of a certain kind and that it is reasonable to believe that their sharing such information causes a restriction on competition. (What it is reasonable to believe will depend on who the potential believer is and what he already believes.) If the property of intending P in φ-ing is closed under the relation expressed by 'it is reasonable to believe that . . . causes . . .', it follows that the parties intend the restriction on competition, but this does not follow if the property is not closed under that relation. Likewise, on Odudu's View, it follows in the first case but not the second that the agreement's object is to restrict competition.

On an intuitive concept, intention (more strictly, the property just specified) is not closed under that relation. In turning the key I intend to open the door, it is reasonable to believe that my opening the door causes wear to the hinges, but I do not intend the wear to the hinges: it is an unintended side-effect of my action.[55] This example can be adapted to show that, similarly, intention is not closed under . . . causes . . . . The fact that Odudu talks of 'subjective' intention suggests that he would agree that intention is not closed under these relations, which might be called objective (in one sense of that word). But, if intention is not closed under the relation expressed by 'it is reasonable to believe that . . . causes . . .', Odudu's View is uninterestingly weak: for instance, as has been seen, it does not imply that the information-sharing agreement has an anticompetitive object. Odudu thus has reason to extend the intuitive concept so that it is closed at least under that relation.[56] Where the intuitive

[55] The doctrine of double effect, in one of its versions, distinguishes foreseen side-effects from effects intended as a means to an intended end: Bratman (1999c), 140. That is a narrower distinction, as it leaves open the possibility that a side-effect is intended otherwise than as such a means. Other versions of the doctrine characterise the side-effects as unintended: Harman (1986), 99–100.

[56] English criminal law allows a court to find the defendant's intention to be closed under a more complex relation involving causation. J. Smith (2002), 71, summarises the current law thus: '(1) A result is intended when it is the actor's purpose to cause it. (2) A court or jury *may also find* that a result is intended, though it is not the actor's purpose to cause it, when (a) the result is a virtually certain consequence of that act, and (b) the actor knows that it is a virtually certain consequence.' (Emphasis in original.) Black (1995a), 357, discusses intention's closure under other relations.

concept does not apply but the extended one does, the subject could be said to have an 'imputed' intention.

The Orthodox View and the Received View

Odudu contrasts his view with what he calls the Orthodox View,[57] that 'object means necessary effect',[58] i.e. that 'P is an object of A' means the same as 'P is a necessary effect of A'. By 'necessary effect' he appears to understand an effect that agreements of the kind in question invariably produce (in the next paragraph he talks of practices that are 'invariably injurious'). A better synthesis of the authorities is to say that a necessary effect of an agreement is one that can be reasonably foreseen – on the basis of economic theory, experience of similar agreements and the facts of the particular case – as almost certain, or at least as highly likely.[59] On this interpretation, mildly paradoxically, a necessary effect need not occur. Odudu's View and the Orthodox View, thus interpreted, are mutually inconsistent because (a) that P is an object of A only if P is a necessary effect of A is entailed by the Orthodox View and (b) it is not the case that only if P is a necessary effect of A do the parties to A, in implementing A, intend P: given these premisses a contradiction can be deduced from the two views.

The Orthodox View is highly implausible and, contrary to Odudu's claim, it is doubtful that anyone has ever held it. If 'object' means 'necessary effect', then an agreement without a necessary effect cannot have an object. The consequent (i.e. the 'then'-clause) of this conditional seems false; certainly an agreement may have an object while lacking the sorts of necessary effect that concern antitrust law – the hard-core restrictions such as price-fixing and market-sharing.[60] In that case Odudu is attacking a straw man. A more plausible view, supported by authority,[61] is that a necessary effect is sufficient for an object, i.e. that P is an object

[57] I have added the initial capitals. [58] Odudu (2001a), 62.

[59] See the Commission's Guidelines on the application of Article 81(3) of the Treaty (note 51 above), para. 21; Goyder (1998), 121; Roth (2001), para. 2-064 ff; and Whish (2003), 112.

[60] *Franz Völk* v. *SPRL Ets J. Vervaecke* [1969] ECR 295 is a case in point.

[61] Most clearly Case 123/83, *Bureau National Interprofessionnel du Cognac* v. *Clair* [1985] 2 CMLR 430, 445 (Slynn AG). See also *Technique Minière* (note 49 above); Case 19/77, *Miller International Schallplatten GmbH* v. *Commission* [1978] ECR 131; Joined Cases T-374/94, T-375/94, T-384/94, T-388/94, *European Night Services Ltd (ENS), Eurostar (UK) Ltd, formerly European Passenger Services Ltd (EPS), Union Internationale des Chemins de Fer (UIC), NV Nederlandse Spoorwegen (NS) and Société Nationale des Chemins de Fer Français (SNCF)* v. *Commission* [1998] ECR II-3141. Para. 21 of the Commission Guidelines (note 51 above) seems to support the Received View, but might also be read as supporting the Orthodox View.

of A if P can be reasonably foreseen as an almost certain effect of A (call this the Received View). Since Odudu's View and the Received View each only give a sufficient condition for an object, they are mutually consistent.

By the same token, neither provides a complete account of what an agreement's object is. The cases are unclear[62] but appear to indicate that, in addition to necessary effects and the parties' intentions, the following factors are relevant in identifying an object:[63] the agreement's content, i.e. what it says;[64] the parties' desires;[65] the circumstances, particularly the legal and economic ones, in which the agreement is implemented;[66] the agreement's foreseeable and actual effects;[67] its origin;[68] actions taken, and statements made, by the parties in connection with the agreement.[69] The authorities are not precise enough to separate these into those factors that enter into the analysis of the concept of an object, those that define the word 'object', those that give a test for an object and those that are mere conditions, of some kind or other, for the existence of an object.[70] Likewise it may be wrong to regard them, or any subset of them, as necessary and/or sufficient for an object: a more accurate interpretation may be that each is a factor that the court may take into account and that will have different weights in different cases. On that reading, each of the four views is over-tidy (an excess of virtue that will be tolerated in the following discussion).

[62] Two examples of unclarity: (a) the use of the word 'effect' to explicate the concept of an object, in *Technique Minière* (note 49 above), 249–50; (b) the talk of 'concrete effects' – as opposed to what other effects? – in Cases 56 and 58/64, *Consten and Grundig* v. *Commission* [1966] ECR 299, 342, [1966] CMLR 418, 473.

[63] For commentary on the cases, see Faull and Nikpay (1999), para. 2.60 ff; Roth (2001), para. 2-056 ff; and Whish (2003), 108 ff.

[64] See *Technique Minière* (note 49 above), 249; *IAZ* (note 51 above), para. 23; Commission Guidelines (note 51 above), para. 22.

[65] See *IAZ* (note 51 above), para. 24.

[66] See *Technique Minière* (note 49 above), 249; *IAZ* (note 51 above), para. 23; *CRAM* (note 52 above), 1703–4; Commission Guidelines (note 51 above), para. 22. Cf Joined Cases 100–103/80, *SA Musique Diffusion Française and others* v. *Commission of the European Communities* [1983] ECR 1825, para. 112.

[67] See *Technique Minière* (note 49 above), 249; Commission Decision IV/29.883, *AROW/BNIC*, para. 65.

[68] See *IAZ* (note 51 above), para. 23.

[69] See *IAZ* (note 51 above), paras. 24–5; *AROW/BNIC* (note 67 above), para. 61; Commission Guidelines (note 51 above), para. 22.

[70] The distinctions between analyses, definitions, conditions and tests are exploited further in the discussion of the cartel offence at the end of this chapter. Similar distinctions are drawn in Parfit (1997), 108.

Relations between object and effect

The relations between object and effect, and between the four views, can be illuminated by considering four questions, two about conditionality and two about evidence. The questions of conditionality are whether an agreement's object is a necessary condition of its effect – or, equivalently, whether its effect is a sufficient condition of its object – and vice versa;[71] the questions of evidence are whether an agreement's object is evidence of its effect, and vice versa. More precisely:

(Q1) Is P an object of A if P is an effect of A?
(Q2) Is P an effect of A if P is an object of A?
(Q3) Is P's being an object of A evidence that P is an effect of A?
(Q4) Is P's being an effect of A evidence that P is an object of A?

It does not follow from an affirmative answer to (Q1) that in order to prove an effect one has to prove an object, or from an affirmative answer to (Q2) that in order to prove an object one has to prove an effect, for a thing can be proved without proving its necessary conditions: it is a necessary condition of my existence that my great-grandfather had children, but it can be proved that I exist without proving anything about my great-grandfather. The interest of all four questions lies, rather, in their bearing on the Intuitive View: the Distinctness Thesis is false if the answer to (Q1) or (Q2) is yes, and the Evidence Thesis is false if the answer to (Q3) is no or the answer to (Q4) is yes. Hence, if any of the other three views gives these answers to the questions, the view in question is inconsistent with the Intuitive View and thus implausible.

The Received View

The answers to the questions vary depending on whether the Received View or Odudu's View of an object is taken (the Orthodox View has been dismissed) and, in the latter case, on the kinds of closure attributed to intention. Starting with the Received View, if its antecedent is substituted into (Q1) the question is whether P can be reasonably foreseen as an almost certain effect of A if P is an effect of A. The answer is clearly no. It does not follow that the answer to (Q1) is no, for the Received View gives only a sufficient condition for P to be an object of A: it might still be that

[71] Other questions of conditionality, which will not be pursued here but which could further illuminate the relation between object and effect, concern more complex conditions, e.g. inus conditions, in the sense given in Mackie (1974), or independent necessary parts of sufficient conditions, in the sense given in the appendix to chapter 5 below.

P is an object of A if P is an effect of A. Nevertheless the Received View *supports* the answer no to (Q1).

The answer to (Q2) is a definite no on the Received View. With the same substitution as before, the question now is whether P is an effect of A if P can be reasonably foreseen as an almost certain effect of A. The answer is no: as noted earlier, a necessary effect need not occur. It is easily proved that (Q2) has the same answer, as follows. By the Received View, P is an object of A if P can be reasonably foreseen as an almost certain effect of A. As just stated, it is not the case that, if P can be reasonably foreseen as an almost certain effect of A, P is an effect of A. Suppose that the answer to (Q2) is yes, i.e. that P is an effect of A if P is an object of A. By the Received View, the supposition just made and transitivity of the conditional,[72] P is an effect of A if P can be reasonably foreseen as an almost certain effect of A. So it both is and is not the case that, if P can be reasonably foreseen as an almost certain effect of A, P is an effect of A. By reductio ad absurdum, the answer to (Q2) is no.

If the same substitution is made into (Q3), the question is whether P's being reasonably foreseeable as an almost certain effect of A is evidence that P is an effect of A. The answer is clearly yes. Again it does not follow that the answer to (Q3) is yes, but now the obstacle is not merely that the Received View gives only a sufficient condition for P to be an object of A: even if the biconditional is supposed, that P is an object of A if and only if P can be reasonably foreseen as an almost certain effect of A, it does not follow that P's being an object of A is evidence that P is an effect of A. The inference would have this form: Q is evidence for R; Q if and only if S; so S is evidence for R. That schema is invalid, as the following counterexample shows: that all swans I have seen are white is evidence that all swans are white; all swans I have seen are white if and only if all non-white things are not swans I have seen; but that all non-white things are not swans I have seen is not evidence that all swans are white.[73] Two possible responses are to argue, contrary to intuition, that the former *is* evidence for the latter, or to add to the schema a restriction which ensures that the schema both is valid and continues to license the inference to the conclusion linking object and effect. Neither course looks promising.

A different argument might be proposed, as follows, that the Received View yields a definite yes to (Q3). For any propositions Q and R, if it is the case that if Q then R, then R is evidence for Q (call this principle (CE1)).

[72] As to which, see note 47 above. [73] Compare Hempel (1983).

So, by the Received View, P's being an object of A is evidence that P can be reasonably foreseen as an almost certain effect of A. As has been seen, P's being reasonably foreseeable as an almost certain effect of A is evidence that P is an effect of A. So, by transitivity of the evidential relation, P's being an object of A is evidence that P is an effect of A.

This argument has two weak links, the first being the claim that the evidential relation is transitive. Here is a counterexample: George's being an antitrust lawyer who does not know the *IAZ* case is evidence that George is an antitrust lawyer; his being an antitrust lawyer is evidence that he knows *IAZ*; but his being an antitrust lawyer who does not know *IAZ* is not evidence that he knows *IAZ*.[74] The second is the principle (CE1). Suppose that R concerns a matter in a remote and unknown galaxy: surely R is not evidence for anything. A plausible view, which (CE1) fails to acknowledge, is that evidence is a three-place relation: R is evidence for Q to so-and-so. On this view, whether one proposition is evidence for another depends – as does what it is reasonable to believe (see above) – on the relevant person's epistemic position. But even if (CE1) is expanded to accommodate this relativity, for example by providing that both Q and R are in some suitable sense accessible to the relevant person, it seems that the principle, if true at all, is true only of a very weak form of evidence (weaker than the form ascribed by the Evidence Thesis): if R has a large number of mutually incompatible sufficient conditions, R is at best very weak evidence for any one of them. To pursue these issues it would be necessary to move beyond an intuitive understanding of the concept of evidence,[75] but provisionally the proposed argument can be rejected.

The Received View thus provides no grounds to hold that P's being an object of A is evidence that P is an effect of A. Assuming that the answer no should be given to (Q3) unless grounds for the answer yes are provided, the answer to (Q3) on the Received View is no. Nevertheless, given that P's being reasonably foreseeable as an almost certain effect of A is evidence that P is an effect of A, the Received View entails that the obtaining of a specified sufficient condition of P's being an object of A is evidence that P is an effect of A.

By similar reasoning, the answer to (Q4) on the Received View is also no. But the Received View does not entail that P's being an effect of A is

[74] Similar examples are used in relation to confirmation in Black (1988), 431, and to justification in Klein (1976), 806–7.

[75] Achinstein (1983) is an introduction to the philosophical literature.

evidence that a specified sufficient condition of P's being an object of A obtains (the converse of the evidential proposition just mentioned). In particular it does not entail that P's being an effect of A is evidence that P can be reasonably foreseen as an almost certain effect of A.

Odudu's View

To answer the four questions on Odudu's View, it is useful to distinguish between intentions that the parties have in implementing A: their *formal* intention is simply that they implement A;[76] the content of each of their *content-specific* intentions is some part of the content of A, for example 'The price for widgets shall be £1'; and their *ulterior* intentions concern things they hope to achieve in or by implementing A, for example an increase in profits. Normally the parties will have intentions of all three kinds.

If the antecedent of Odudu's View is substituted into (Q1), the question is whether, if P is an effect of A, the parties in implementing A intend P. On the intuitive concept of intention identified earlier, the answer is no. Odudu's View thus supports but does not entail the answer no to (Q1): the reasoning is as for the answer to (Q1) on the Received View. The result is the same if intention is taken to be closed under the relation expressed by 'it is reasonable to believe that . . . causes . . .'.

But the answer is yes if intention is taken to be closed under . . . causes . . . . Assume that P is an effect of A. Grant that P is an effect of A if and only if the parties' implementing A causes P. So their implementing A causes P. In implementing A they have the formal intention that they implement A. By closure, in implementing A they intend P. By Odudu's View, P is an object of A. So P is an object of A if P is an effect of A. The assumption that intention is closed under . . . causes . . . is, however, true only on an artificial and very strong concept of intention: this concept allows that a person may intend an effect of his action even if he does not foresee the effect and could not reasonably do so. Unlike the other assumption of closure, this one does not seem necessary in order to make Odudu's View strong enough to be interesting (see above).

The answers to (Q2) and (Q3) are not sensitive to the forms of closure attributed to intention. If the antecedent of Odudu's View is substituted into (Q2), the question is whether P is an effect of A if the parties

[76] I controversially assume that one person's intention can concern another person's action. Justification for this assumption is given in Bratman (1999b), (1999e); and Tuomela (1995), ch. 2. See also the discussion of 'plural subjects' in Gilbert (1989), ch. 4, and (1996c).

in implementing A intend P. The answer is no, as intentions can fail to be fulfilled. Reasoning as for the Received View, the answer to (Q2) is no.

Again by reasoning as for the Received View, Odudu's View provides no grounds to hold that P's being an object of A is evidence that P is an effect of A; so the answer to (Q3) is no. But it might be argued that, as with the Received View, Odudu's entails (on certain assumptions) that the obtaining of a specified sufficient condition of P's being an object of A is evidence that P is an effect of A. The argument is this. Suppose that the parties, in implementing A, intend that P is an effect of A. By Odudu's View, this is sufficient for it to be an object of A that P is an effect of A. Assume that the parties are efficient in the sense that if they intend something their intention is fulfilled (this is a different sense of 'efficient' from the one used earlier to ground the first claim of the Evidence Thesis). Then P is an effect of A if they intend, in implementing A, that P is an effect of A. Assume that, for any propositions Q and R, if it is the case that if Q then R, then Q is evidence that R (call this principle (CE2)). Then the parties' intending, in implementing A, that P is an effect of A is evidence that P is an effect of A. So the specified sufficient condition of P's being an object of A is evidence that P is an effect of A.

(CE2) is more plausible than its converse, (CE1) (which says that, if it is the case that if Q then R, then R is evidence for Q), but it shares (CE1)'s flaw of failing to acknowledge that whether one proposition is evidence for another depends on the epistemic position of the relevant person. For the argument to work, therefore, it must be recast in terms of some acceptable modification of (CE2). It is doubtful that this can be accomplished.

If intention is taken not to be closed under . . . causes . . . , the answer to (Q4) is no: the reasoning is the same as for the Received View. Again as for the Received View, it is not plausible to hold that Odudu's View entails that P's being an effect of A is evidence that a specified sufficient condition of P's being an object of A obtains. Where the condition in question is that the parties in implementing A intend that P is an effect of A, the entailment can be secured via the assumptions that the parties are efficient and that (CE1) is true. But, to repeat, (CE1) is unacceptable.

It might be argued as follows that, if intention is taken to be closed under . . . causes . . . , the answer to (Q4) is yes. Given closure, P is an object of A if P is an effect of A: see the answer to (1). Given (CE2), P's being an effect of A is evidence that P is an object of A. But again, leaving aside the implausibility of the closure assumption, this argument fails because of the flaw in (CE2), and again it is unclear that (CE2) can be acceptably revised in a way that allows the argument to go through.

Conclusions

The result is this. The Received View is that P is an object of A if P can be reasonably foreseen as an almost certain effect of A; Odudu's View is that P is an object of A if the parties to A, in making or implementing A, intend P. On the Received View, the answer to (Q2), (Q3) and (Q4) is no. The Received View also supports the answer no to (Q1). A qualification to the answer to (Q3) is that the Received View entails, on an acceptable assumption, that the obtaining of a specified sufficient condition of P's being an object of A is evidence that P is an effect of A. Odudu's View supports the answer no to (Q1) if intention is not closed under . . . causes . . . . If the very strong assumption is made that intention is closed under that relation, the answer to (Q1) on Odudu's View is yes. The answer to (Q2) and (Q3) on Odudu's View is no, and it is doubtful that the answer to (Q3) is subject to the qualification that applies on the Received View. The answer to (Q4) on Odudu's View is no if intention is not closed under . . . causes . . . , and is probably the same if intention is closed under that relation.

Refinements aside, therefore, the Received View and Odudu's View are each consistent with the Distinctness Thesis and inconsistent with the Evidence Thesis. (The Distinctness Thesis says that the object limb of Article 81 catches agreements which the effect limb does not catch, and vice versa; the Evidence Thesis says that, often at least, object is evidence for effect but not vice versa.) Each, then, is inconsistent with the Intuitive View (the conjunction of the Distinctness Thesis and the Evidence Thesis) and pro tanto implausible. The Received View fares worse because, in addition, it leaves it unclear why the object limb of Article 81 is needed. In the first place, the condition which the Received View states to be sufficient for P's being an object of A is expressed in terms of A's effects; in the second, as already seen, the obtaining of the condition is evidence of A's effects. As to the second point, the fact that a restriction of competition is reasonably foreseeable as an almost certain effect of A can be good enough evidence that the restriction *is* an effect of A for it to be reasonable to condemn A under the effect limb of Article 81 (provided that the restriction and the potential effect on trade between member states are appreciable). The issue here is not the Distinctness Thesis, for the evidence may in fact be misleading: a necessary effect need not occur. In that case, although the object limb applies according to the Received View, the effect limb does not, even though it is reasonable to judge that it does. But there is still nothing in the Received View to motivate the inclusion of the object limb.

Dishonest agreements: the cartel offence in the Enterprise Act

Ghosh and its problems

The introduction of the cartel offence in the Enterprise Act 2002 has awakened an interest among antitrust lawyers, and renewed the interest of criminal lawyers, in the concept of dishonesty in English law. *Ghosh* remains the leading case: the crucial passage is:

> In determining whether the prosecution has proved that the defendant was acting dishonestly, a jury must first of all decide whether according to the ordinary standards of reasonable and honest people what was done was dishonest. If it was not dishonest by those standards, that is the end of the matter and the prosecution fails. If it was dishonest by those standards, then the jury must consider whether the defendant himself must have realised that what he was doing was by those standards dishonest . . . It is dishonest for a defendant to act in a way which he knows ordinary people consider to be dishonest.[77]

This passage has attracted many overlapping objections in the context of the UK Theft Acts, notably that it makes for more, longer and more difficult trials; it creates an unacceptable risk that decisions will be mutually inconsistent; it assumes that there exist community norms of dishonesty; the fact that 'dishonestly' is an ordinary word does not preclude disagreement on its application in particular contexts; the passage gives inadequate guidance to juries in specialised cases; jurors may have low standards of honesty, so that, if they apply their own standards, the scope of dishonesty offences is reduced in an unintended way and, if they apply higher standards, they are hypocritical; it creates uncertainty – in particular it requires, but does not give guidelines for, moral estimations and thus allows anarchic verdicts that are not technically perverse; it allows an unacceptably open-ended range of defences – in particular it does not exclude the 'Robin Hood' defence and it allows something like

[77] *R.* v. *Ghosh* [1982] 2 All ER 689, 696.

a mistake of law to be a defence; it is a threat to standards of honesty, in giving weight to the defendant's possibly idiosyncratic beliefs about them; it does not adequately protect unpopular victims; it makes it unduly hard to secure convictions; it wrongly conceives the classification of an act as dishonest to be a factual rather than a legal matter; it creates inconsistency within the Theft Acts; it departs radically from previous law; it is inept as an attempt to remove confusion in previous law; and it obscures the relation between dishonesty in theft and in other crimes in the Theft Acts.[78] Various alternative accounts of dishonesty have been proposed in order to avoid these objections.[79]

All these objections except the last four apply equally or a fortiori to section 188 of the Enterprise Act, under which an individual is guilty of an offence if he dishonestly agrees with one or more other persons to make or implement, or cause to be made or implemented, arrangements constituting a hard-core cartel as characterised in sections 188 and 189.[80] The problem of community norms is especially acute here: most people have not reflected on the norms to apply to cartels and, in so far as they have, opinions are likely to differ as to the dishonesty of, say, dividing markets: few people, perhaps, will see anything dishonest in the practice where the purpose is to preserve jobs, and a vigorous entrepreneur may see nothing dishonest in it in any circumstances.[81] Also, to the extent that community norms of dishonesty exist, they change at both the individual and the governmental level: a couple of generations ago, practices falling within sections 188 and 189 were officially encouraged in the interest of planning and the elimination of wasteful duplication.[82] It appears that one aim of the government in creating the cartel offence was precisely to shift public opinion as to the heinousness of hard-core cartels.[83]

[78] Most of these objections are reviewed in Griew (1985). See also Elliott (1982); J. Smith (2002), 551 ff; G. Williams (1983), 728 f.

[79] See the works in note 78 above.

[80] Further objections have been raised that apply only to the use of dishonesty in the cartel offence, e.g. that dishonesty is usually associated with acquisitive offences: Dean (2003), 910; Joshua (2003), 626.

[81] See Joshua (2003), 626; Peretz and Lewis (2003), 99; and Taylor and Mansell (2003), 24. MacCulloch (2003), 622, notes, however, the authority for the view that the reasonable and honest person, for the purposes of *Ghosh*, is the person in the street, not the business person.

[82] See Peretz and Lewis (2003), 99; and Whish (2003), 11.

[83] See Hammond and Penrose (2001), para. 2.5; Joshua (2003), 625, 640; Taylor and Mansell (2003), 24.

Various tests of dishonesty have been proposed for the application of section 188, in particular that the defendant tried to conceal his activity,[84] or knew it to be illegal[85] – most likely under Article 81 EC or section 2 of the UK Competition Act 1998 – or acted for personal gain.[86] Each of these causes difficulty. As to the first two, if the defendant knew that the activity infringed Article 81, he is likely to have tried to conceal it in order to avoid the legal consequences, but it does not follow that, as *Ghosh* requires, either reasonable and honest people would regard it as dishonest or he must have known that they would: he may have believed that any reasonable and honest person would hold Article 81 to be an unjust, and justly evaded, constraint on freedom of contract. This is a variant of the Robin Hood defence. (The account of dishonesty proposed later uses the concept of concealment but abandons the *Ghosh* approach, thereby avoiding this difficulty.) The third test appears to draw the offence too narrowly, for it would not catch the case where an over-zealous employee forms a hard-core cartel not for his own sake but for that of his employer and its shareholders.

Circularity objections

I shall advance objections of a more conceptual nature, which may loosely be called objections of circularity. They apply to the passage in *Ghosh* generally, not just to its application in the context of the cartel offence. As a preliminary, four questions to which the passage might be taken to give an answer need to be distinguished. The first is one of analysis: what is it to be dishonest? Different views may be taken as to the subject of this question and to the character of an adequate answer. The subject may be viewed, for example, as the concept of dishonesty or as the fact that someone or something is dishonest: an answer can be given without settling this ontological issue. An adequate answer will specify a set of conditions for dishonesty: on a stringent view they will be severally necessary and jointly sufficient; on a more lenient one they will merely model a central case of dishonesty (see the Introduction). To constitute an analysis the

[84] Beard (2003), 156–7; Peretz and Lewis (2003), 99; Taylor and Mansell (2003), 24, where it is said that dishonest intent might be inferred from 'use of code'. The inference from use of code alone is very weak: it is common and innocent to use code-names in an unannounced major transaction.

[85] Taylor and Mansell (2003), 24. Joshua doubts that knowledge of illegality is sufficient for dishonesty: Joshua (2003), 4.

[86] Dean (2003), 910.

conditions cannot be, say, causal conditions but must be of a particular kind: standard views are that they are truth-conditions or assertability-conditions for sentences of the form 'X is dishonest'.

The second question is one of linguistic definition: what does 'dishonest' mean? This differs from the analytical question as it concerns a particular word in a particular language, but the answers to the two questions will be substantively the same. The third is a question about conditions: under what conditions is someone or something dishonest? Depending on the type of conditions at issue, some versions of this question will coincide with some versions of the first. The fourth question is epistemic: what is the, or a, test of dishonesty?

There is no clear sign in *Ghosh* that the judges separated the four questions in their minds. Lawyers generally tend to be insensitive to the differences between questions of the four kinds, but the differences are substantial: for example it may be a test of there having been a mouse in the larder that the cheese has been gnawed, but 'A mouse has been in the larder' does not mean the same as 'The cheese has been gnawed'. The judgment's description of section 2 of the Theft Act 1968 as giving a 'partial definition' of dishonesty gives a slender reason to think that the quoted passage is intended to answer the second question.[87] If so, the answer is inadequate. Strictly, if the passage is read in this way, the definiendum is 'dishonestly'. The objection is that the definiens contains non-redundant occurrences of the words 'honest' and 'dishonest', which are too close to 'dishonestly' to illuminate its meaning: 'dishonest' is just the adjective from which the adverb is formed, and 'honest' is a contrary (but not the contradictory:[88] see below) of 'dishonest'.

The point can be amplified in terms of a regress. 'Dishonestly' means 'in a dishonest way'. If for simplicity we consider only the first limb in the passage and regiment its words, the result is that 'X acted in a dishonest way' means the same as 'By the ordinary standards of reasonable and honest people X acted in a dishonest way' (call this sentence (S1)). That is

[87] Note 77 above, 696c. Elliott (1982), 396, similarly describes section 2(1) as giving a 'partial negative definition'. Compare Williams, who objects that *Feely* (note 90 below) 'mistakes the meaning of honesty': G. Williams (1983), 726–7. In the Australian case *R.* v. *Salvo* [1980] VR 401, the court explicitly discussed the meaning of 'dishonestly'.

[88] To say that two propositions are contraries is to say that they cannot both be true; to say that they are contradictories is to say that one is true if the other is false, and false if the other is true (see the discussion of question (4) in chapter 3). A parallel distinction can be drawn as to the applicability of adjectives.

unilluminating unless 'honest' and/or 'dishonest' in (S1) is defined. The only way to try to do this, given the materials in the passage, is to apply (S1) to the occurrence in (S1) of 'X acted in a dishonest way', yielding (S2) 'By the ordinary standards of reasonable and honest people, by the ordinary standards of reasonable and honest people X acted in a dishonest way'. This mere iteration of the first clause creates two problems. First, it is obscure what its first occurrence in (S2) means: are the standards mentioned supposed to be meta-standards, not for judging dishonesty but for judging standards for judging dishonesty? Second, (S2) still contains an undefined 'dishonest'. Clearly an attempt to solve the second problem by applying (S1) to the occurrence of 'X acted in a dishonest way' in (S2) prolongs a regress at each stage of which the two problems recur.

Griew takes passing account of this problem when he notes that 'there is an unhelpful tautological element in the question as it was worded in *Ghosh*: was what was done dishonest "according to the . . . standards of . . . honest people"?'[89] He dismisses it as a 'preliminary matter' on the ground that the words in *Ghosh* were intended by the court to be equivalent to an earlier formulation which did not contain a cognate of 'dishonestly': in *Feely* the court spoke of 'the current standards of ordinary decent people'.[90] But this fails to solve the problem because, first, 'ordinary decent people' means much the same as and is no clearer than 'reasonable and honest people' and, second, it leaves a cognate of 'dishonestly' in the definiens: a jury must decide whether according to the current standards of ordinary decent people what was done was *dishonest*.

The objection that the passage from *Ghosh* fails to give an adequate answer to the question of linguistic definition is easily adapted to show that it fails adequately to answer the question of analysis. The third question, about conditions, is for legal purposes largely uninteresting to the extent that it differs from the analytical question. That leaves the epistemic question, of the test for dishonesty. It is plausible to read the passage as an answer to this question, for a court is concerned with the practical matter of finding out whether the defendant acted dishonestly. The reading is also supported by the passage's words (italicised here) '*In determining whether* the prosecution has proved that the defendant was acting dishonestly, the jury must first of all *decide whether . . .*'.

But now there is another objection of circularity. A test only needs to be specified if the jury is unsure how to tell that the defendant acted

[89] Griew (1985), 342. [90] *R.* v. *Feely* [1973] QB 530, 536–7. See further note 91 below.

dishonestly.[91] Applying the test's first limb, the jury considers whether the action was dishonest by the ordinary standards of reasonable and honest people. The jury must therefore identify such people. One problem is that the concepts of reasonableness and honesty are epistemologically problematic: it may be held that there is no fact of the matter as to whether someone is reasonable and honest (irrealism), or that there is such a fact but either no one knows it (scepticism) or it is somehow local to some reference group (relativism): these claims may in turn arise from a concern that, at any rate in pluralistic Western societies, there is a lack of consensus about reasonableness and honesty (compare the objection about the lack of community norms).[92] This problem can be set aside, for it is distinct from the objection of circularity, which is this: if the jury is unsure how to tell that the defendant acted dishonestly, it will be at least as unsure how to tell that some other person is honest. The test is therefore useless because it is at least as elusive as the thing to be tested.

Replies to the second circularity objection

One reply points out that the thing to be tested is a dishonest *action* whereas the test refers to honest *people*: it may be suggested that it is easier to tell that a person is honest, or that he is dishonest, than that an action is. But the reverse is true. Roughly, an honest person is one who is disposed to act honestly and a dishonest person one who is disposed to act dishonestly: to decide that someone is honest or that he is dishonest, one must decide that his actions (actual or hypothetical) are.[93] Since the first requires the second, it cannot be easier than the second. To this it might be replied in turn that a person's honesty or dishonesty can be ascertained not only through his actions but through his thoughts, attitudes, emotions and feelings. But that fails to answer the objection, because these are themselves identified largely through his actions and in any event their

91 In *Feely* the court appeared to think that the jury would not be unsure about this: 'Jurors, when deciding whether an appropriation was dishonest can be reasonably expected to, and should, apply the current standards of ordinary decent people. In their own lives they have to decide what is and what is not dishonest. We can see no reason why, when in a jury box, they should require the help of a judge to tell them what amounts to dishonesty': note 90 above, 537. This passage is intended, however, to explicate the statement 'We do not agree that judges should define what "dishonestly" means' (536) – an instance of the failure to distinguish the epistemic question from the question of linguistic definition.

92 Compare also the discussion in chapter 2, of irrealist, sceptical and subjectivist views of welfare and their connection with a concern about lack of consensus.

93 Some virtue theorists would deny this: see Crisp (1998); and Crisp and Slote (1997).

honesty or dishonesty is no more readily detectable than the honesty or dishonesty of actions.

A second reply to the objection of circularity points out that the thing to be tested is a *dishonest* action whereas the test refers to *honest* people: the suggestion is that it is easier to tell that someone or something is honest than that he or it is dishonest. One objection to this is that the test also refers to actions that, by the standards of such people, are *dis*honest; but let that pass. To assess the reply, the relation between honest and dishonest must be clarified. Being dishonest is more than not being honest: a desk is neither honest nor dishonest. Roughly, X is dishonest in a certain respect if and only if X is not but could be honest in that respect. This biconditional seems to support the reply in that it makes dishonesty appear more complex than honesty; but the appearance is deceptive, for the biconditional can be reversed to give the opposite appearance: X is honest in a certain respect if and only if X is not but could be dishonest in that respect. (It appears that in the relevant sense of 'could', which can be left unanalysed here, X could be honest if and only if X could be dishonest.)

A different way of trying to support the reply is to maintain that people are generally honest, so that we are entitled to presume that someone is honest in the absence of reason to think otherwise. That may be true but it is irrelevant, for it does not support the reply: a presumption of honesty may cloud our assessment of the evidence in a particular case that a person is honest just as it may cloud our assessment of the evidence that he is dishonest.

Yet another way of trying to support the reply is by analogy. Suppose that disease D is hard to diagnose because its symptoms are similar to those of another disease: in that case it is hard to tell that someone has D. But, if the symptoms of either disease are obvious, it is easy to tell that he does not have D. Examples such as this establish that, for some properties, it is easier to tell that something does not have them than that it does.[94] It may be argued that this principle is true of dishonesty. The claim is initially plausible in the case of those things that could not be dishonest: it is easy to tell that a desk is not dishonest, but impossible to tell that it is dishonest. One objection that might be raised to this is that it is off point: the thesis at issue is that it is easier to tell that someone or something is honest, not that he/it is not dishonest, than that he/it is dishonest: as examples such as the desk show, some things are neither

[94] Compare B. Williams (1978), 309 ff.

honest nor dishonest. But it will be seen shortly that this objection falls away. Another objection is that it can be argued that it is possible to tell, of something that could not be dishonest, that it is dishonest. Granted, it is impossible that I am able to know that the desk is dishonest. But 'I can tell that the desk is dishonest' is plausibly read as a conditional, roughly along the lines of 'If the desk is dishonest, I am able to know that it is'. Simplifying, assume that 'Q if P' is equivalent to 'Not possibly (P and not Q)'. Then the conditional becomes 'It is impossible that (the desk is dishonest and I am able to know that it is)'. Since it is impossible that the desk is dishonest, this statement is true, in which case I *can* tell that the desk is dishonest. A way of blocking this conclusion is to reject the proposed equivalent of 'Q if P' on the ground that it gives counterintuitive results precisely in cases, such as this, where the antecedent is necessarily false.[95] The dialectic need not be pursued, for it depends on an exotic case: such cases aside, there is no reason to think it easier to tell that someone or something is not than that he/it is dishonest. But, if those cases are excluded, dishonesty and non-honesty coincide (which is why the objection of irrelevance falls away). Likewise, therefore, there is no reason to think it easier to tell that someone/something is honest than that he/it is dishonest.

A third reply to the objection of circularity invokes first-person privilege in ascriptions of honesty. The suggestion is that, although it may be no easier for X to tell that Y is honest than that Z's action is dishonest, it is generally easier for X to tell that he (X) is honest. ('He' here is a 'quasi-indicator':[96] it cannot be replaced by 'X', for if X does not know that he is X it may be very hard for him to tell that X is honest.) So a juror, in applying the first limb of the *Ghosh* test, ascertains that he himself is reasonable and honest and decides whether, by his standards, the defendant acted dishonestly. The test avoids the objection because it is easier for the juror to tell that he is honest than that the defendant's action was dishonest.

One problem with this reply is that the juror may be dishonest (see further below). Leaving that aside, it is clear that, in respect of some properties, first-person privilege exists in the weak sense that it is generally easier for a person to tell that he has such a property than that someone else does.[97] Typically the properties are mental, for example

[95] The classic treatment of this issue is Lewis and Langford (1959), 174 ff, 248 ff, 503 ff.

[96] See chapter 1, note 19.

[97] Philosophers have contemplated other forms of first-person privilege, such as incorrigibility, indubitability, directness, self-warrant and certainty. See Alston (1989); and Black (1988), 424.

that of having a headache; so it seems that honesty is in the right category, as it is a mental property (the point is debatable). But a property's being mental is not sufficient for it to be subject to first-person privilege: self-deception is mental, but it is not generally easier for one person to tell that he is deceiving himself than that another is. Self-deception is, or is close to, a form of dishonesty,[98] so it might be argued that dishonesty generally is not subject to first-person privilege, and from there that honesty likewise is not subject to it. Regardless of whether those inferences can be sustained, there are two reasons to think that first-person privilege does not apply to honesty: first, honesty shades into its absence in subtle ways – specifically, our motives are usually a mixture of the reputable and the disreputable – and, second, honesty, unlike the property of having a headache, is not essentially manifest to consciousness. It is characteristic of a certain kind of honesty that it is uncomplicated by reflection: someone who exhibits it need not be aware that he is being honest.

In any event the objection of circularity does not deny that first-person privilege applies to honesty. The objection is not that it is no easier for a juror to tell that someone, and in particular that he himself, is honest than that the defendant is, but that it is no easier for the juror to tell that someone, and he himself in particular, is honest than that a particular action of the defendant was dishonest. The crucial distinction here is not between honest and dishonest – the subject of the second reply – but between a person and an action. As the objection to the first reply showed, it cannot be easier to tell that someone is (dis)honest than to tell that his actions are. It is plausible to think that in many cases a juror's hypothetically greater ability to tell that he is (dis)honest than that the defendant is will be outweighed by the juror's greater ability to tell that an action is (dis)honest than that a person is. In such cases the objection stands.

A fourth reply pursues the first-person approach adopted in the previous one but does not make a claim of privilege. The suggestion now is that the first limb of the *Ghosh* test does not mean what it says: rather, the jury is to decide whether by its own ordinary standards the defendant acted dishonestly. The concept of reasonable and honest people is not part of the content of, but is a gloss on, that limb of the test, to the effect that it will be applied by people who are reasonable and honest (a jury consists

[98] This claim might be challenged on the basis of the House of Lords' view in *Scott*: see below.

of twelve good men and true). This perhaps was the thought in *Feely*, where the court said that jurors 'can be reasonably expected to . . . apply the current standards of ordinary decent people'.[99] On this account the objection of circularity does not arise, as a jury is not required to identify honest people.

The reply is exposed to various other objections. First, as already noted, the jury may not be reasonable and honest, in which case the gloss is false. Second, the reply flies against the express words in *Ghosh*. Next, it causes a problem in the construal of the test's second limb: if that is construed correspondingly, the question for the jury is whether the defendant must have realised that he was acting dishonestly by the ordinary standards of the jury. But that is absurd, for the defendant cannot be expected at the time of his action to have had any view about the jury's standards: most likely he will not even have known that its members existed. If on the other hand the second limb is taken at face value, to refer to the ordinary standards of reasonable and honest people, there is a rupture between the second limb and the first. It might be replied that a rupture is prevented by the proposed gloss on the first limb, for the gloss expresses a presumption that the jury is reasonable and honest. But that reply fails, for the jury may be reasonable and honest while yet its ordinary standards of reasonableness and honesty are not those of reasonable and honest people: it may be that the jurors, although meeting high standards in their own conduct, are unusually indulgent in their assessments of people's reasonableness and honesty (this is an instance of one of the objections mentioned at the start, that jurors may have low standards of honesty). In such a case – this is a fourth objection – the test under the proposed interpretation can produce counterintuitive verdicts; for, whichever way the second limb is construed, the defendant will be acquitted if he only just manages to meet the jury's lax standards. It might be suggested that this case is excluded by the fact that the test refers to standards that are ordinary. But that defence misses the mark; for if, as is being proposed, the content of the first limb concerns the jury's own standards rather than those of reasonable and honest people, 'ordinary' there must signify what is ordinary for the jury, not for such people.

A fifth reply to the objection of circularity, and the last to be considered, starts from the claim that the test need only be applied to difficult cases: the Court of Appeal has often stated that it is not necessary to give a *Ghosh* direction to the jury in every situation.[100] Consider, then, a difficult

[99] Note 90 above. [100] See J. Smith (2002), 553.

case in which the jury is unsure how to tell whether the defendant acted dishonestly. To apply the test's first limb, the jury must identify honest people. Normally the honesty of a person is revealed by actions of his that are plainly honest. So, to determine that he is honest, the jury need not consider difficult cases. Hence the jury will be surer that the person in question is honest than that the defendant's action was dishonest. The argument can be reinforced by a rough analogy. Suppose I cannot tell whether a dimly illuminated object is red. A test would be to improve the light and then to decide whether the object looks red. Clearly it would be a feeble objection of circularity to say that, if I am unsure whether the object is red in bad light, I shall be at least as unsure whether it is red in good light.

This is a strong reply to the objection of circularity as the objection has been stated, but it does not vindicate the test; for, as already noted, the test also essentially contains another cognate of 'dishonestly': the defendant's action must have been *dishonest* by the ordinary standards of reasonable and honest people. Even if it is easier to tell that some person is honest than that the defendant's action was dishonest, it is surely no easier to tell that the defendant's action was dishonest by the ordinary standards of that person.

A non-circular account of dishonesty

The result is that the passage in *Ghosh*, whether it is taken to give a definition or a test of dishonesty, faces an objection of circularity to which there is no ready answer. If it is thought necessary to supply a definition or a test to juries, the one given must not contain non-redundant occurrences either of cognates of 'dishonest' or (as in *Feely*) of words that are no easier to understand or apply.

As a start to providing an account that avoids circularity, it is useful to distinguish roughly between a broad and a narrow concept of dishonesty. On the broad concept a dishonest action is simply one that is wrong. On the narrow concept it is wrong in a specific way that involves concealment: a dishonest action involves deception, lying, fraud or something similar. The distinction appears among the meanings given in *Chambers* – not honest, lacking integrity, disposed to cheat, insincere, unchaste: cheating and insincerity do, unchastity does not, and lack of integrity may not, import the concept of concealment. The cases and commentaries in criminal law do not consistently use one or other concept: the Criminal Law Revision Committee appeared to hold that, although 'dishonestly' is clearer than 'fraudulently', they have the same meaning,[101] and Viscount Dilhorne, in *Scott*, explicitly stated that they do.[102] This suggests that the narrow concept is intended, but the position is clouded by the courts' broad use of 'fraud' to cover, for example, the forcible taking of property without deception.[103] Elliott claims that the old larceny cases never gave to 'fraudulently' a definite meaning distinct from 'without a claim of right':[104] if so, and if 'dishonest' means the same as 'fraudulent', the concept of dishonesty at issue is not the narrow one but also seems narrower than the broad one. A broad reading of the word is weakly supported by the House of Lords' view in *Scott* that dishonesty is sufficient, but deceit is not necessary, for conspiracy to defraud;[105] for this suggests that dishonesty is broader than deception. Williams defines 'honesty' to mean three things: respect for property rights; refraining from deception, at least where this would cause loss to another; and keeping a promise, at least where the promisee has supplied consideration or will suffer loss if the promise is not kept.[106] Taking the corresponding definition of 'dishonest', the first element does not fall within the narrow concept but is narrower than the broad one; the second falls within the narrow concept; and the third can be argued to do so from the controversial premiss that breaking a promise is, or is akin to, a form of lying.[107]

A central case of the narrow concept can be modelled in a way that gives an answer to all four questions distinguished at the start of the discussion. Roughly, a person's action is dishonest if (a) it is wrong and (b) he does it in a manner that he intends to conceal either (i) the fact that he is doing it or (ii) the fact that it is wrong. This model is weakly analogous to *Ghosh* in that it contains one limb that may be called objective and another that may be called subjective: (a) is objective in the sense that it concerns the wrongness of the action, not the agent's belief as to its wrongness; (b) is subjective in the thin sense that it refers to the agent's intention. The model can be refined in various ways: for example 'wrong' might be amplified to cover other moral categories, such as certain actions that are bad in some respect without being wrong; clause (b) might be expanded to provide for a specified category of people from whom the relevant fact is concealed; and more might be said about the distinction between an action and the manner in which it is performed. This last appears partly

[101] Criminal Law Revision Committee (1966), para. 39.
[102] *Scott* v. *Commissioner of Police for the Metropolis* [1974] 3 All ER 1032, 1038.
[103] See G. Williams (1983), 705–6. [104] Elliott (1982), 403. [105] Note 102 above, 1037.
[106] G. Williams (1983), 726–7. [107] See Warnock (1971), ch. 7.

a matter of stipulation: if I run quickly, my action can be described as a quick running or the action – running – can be distinguished from the manner – quick. There is no need to tie these loose ends. Applying the model to the cartel offence, suppose competitors make a price-fixing agreement with each other, taking care to conceal the agreement from anyone else: then, if price-fixing is wrong, (a) their action is wrong and (b)(i) they conceal the fact that they are doing it. Now suppose they agree to limit production, disguising the relevant clauses as provisions to ensure quality and safety:[108] then, if limiting production is wrong, (a) their action is wrong and (b)(ii) they conceal the fact that it is.

Remaining problems

The model captures an important and intuitive concept of dishonesty and avoids circularity in that 'wrong' is normally easier to understand and apply than is 'dishonest': we may be uncertain whether to classify some action as dishonest while being confident that it was wrong to do it. The achievement is modest, of course, for our grasp of the concept of wrong is still insecure at both the theoretical and the practical level. The position is worse when the model is considered as a test to be used by juries, for it is little better able than *Ghosh* to withstand objections of kinds listed at the start: for example the problem of community norms remains and jurors may have lax views as to what is wrong.

There are four options: to argue that, contrary to appearances, the objections do not undermine *Ghosh* or the model just proposed; to try to frame a concept of dishonesty that avoids the objections; to live with the objections; or to expunge dishonesty from criminal law. So far as the cartel offence is concerned, the fourth seems the most attractive. The UK Government considered an alternative to the offence in its current form, which was to make it unlawful for a person to participate in an agreement whose purpose is a hard-core cartel activity, where the agreement also involves a breach of either Article 81 EC or section 2 of the Competition Act. This was rejected, principally on the ground that it could require a jury with no antitrust expertise to consider potentially complex economic arguments[109] (a concern which tacitly acknowledges the objection that

[108] See e.g. the *IAZ* case (note 51 above). See also para. 165 of the European Commission's Guidelines on horizontal cooperation agreements 2001/C3/02, OJ 6.1.2001.

[109] Department of Trade and Industry (2001), para. 7.19 ff. See also Hammond and Penrose (2001), para. 2.6. MacCulloch (2003), 621, suggests, however, that the

Ghosh gives inadequate guidance to juries in specialised cases[110]). But, as commentators have observed, the current offence does not exclude that possibility: specifically, it may be relevant to a defendant's dishonesty whether it was reasonable to believe that his action was not caught by or was exemptable under Article 81 or section 2.[111] Since the current offence has the main fault of the alternative, but not conversely, there is a case for adopting the alternative. How likely this is to happen will depend in part on the Office of Fair Trading's degree of success in securing convictions under the present law.[112]

form-based approach of the cartel offence reduces the level of economic evidence that the jury will need to examine. The Government was also concerned that, before the abolition of notification, the defendant's employer could frustrate court proceedings by notifying an agreement to the European Commission: *ibid.*, para. 7.32. Joshua (2003), 622, advances the further objections that political sensitivities would be aroused by imprisoning people for frustrating a 'Euro-agenda' and that Article 81 and section 2 are too broadly drawn to form the basis of a criminal offence.

[110] See MacCulloch (2003), 622. Contrast Scanlan (2002), 119, where it is argued that *Ghosh* works well in complex cases of fraud.

[111] See Beard (2003), 157; Joshua (2003), 629; MacCulloch (2003), 621; MacDonald and Thompson (2003), 96; and Peretz and Lewis (2003), 100. On the bearing in this context of Article 3(2) of Council Regulation 1/2003/EC, see Peretz and Lewis (2003), 100; and MacCulloch (2003), 620.

[112] See Joshua (2003), 620, on the scant record of enforcement in other jurisdictions that have criminal legislation against cartels.

5

Concerted practices

Overview

Antitrust, to be effective, must capture not only legally enforceable contracts but also informal understandings. Article 81 EC accordingly applies to both agreements and 'concerted practices' (CPs): a CP is normally prohibited if it both is anti-competitive and may affect trade between member states. Similarly section 43 of the UK Restrictive Trade Practices Act 1976, now repealed, defined 'agreement' to include 'any agreement or arrangement, whether or not it is or is intended to be enforceable . . . by legal proceedings'. EC legislation does not define 'concerted practice': as with 'agreement', the meaning of the phrase has been left to emerge from the case-law. The advantage and the disadvantages of this approach were noted in chapter 4: on the one hand, it allows a term's meaning to develop to fit the cases; on the other, definition through cases is a haphazard process swayed by specific facts and, as the diversity of the cases increases, the term's meaning can come to lack conceptual unity. Certainly the meaning of 'concerted practice' does not emerge clearly from the judgments and decisions. The standard definition is from the judgment in *Dyestuffs*:

> a form of coordination between undertakings which, without having reached the stage where an agreement properly so-called has been concluded, knowingly substitutes practical cooperation between them for the risks of competition.[1]

This is unhelpful, for the relevant concept of cooperation is no easier to grasp than that of concertation:[2] there is a cluster of words beginning with 'co' – concert, cooperate, coordinate, concord, correlate, collude, conspire, consensus – which are often used in antitrust, economics and game theory, but without any clear indication of their meanings and

[1] Cases 48/69 etc., *ICI* v. *Commission* [1972] ECR 619, [1972] CMLR 557, para. 64.
[2] Compare the circularity objections in chapter 4 to the *Ghosh* account of dishonesty.

relations to each other (this point is pursued in chapter 6). Moreover the force of 'knowingly' in the quoted passage is obscure: it appears that the cooperation as well as the substitution is being described as knowing; in which case, unless second-order knowledge is in question, the wording seems pleonastic, for it is plausible to suppose that cooperation, in the sense in question, is by definition a knowing activity.

The commentaries shed little light. Faull and Nikpay say:

> First, some form of direct or indirect contact between undertakings is required. Secondly, there must be some meeting of minds or consensus between the parties to cooperate rather than compete.[3]

'Meeting of minds' is a hallowed but cloudy phrase, as noted in chapter 4, and the gloss 'consensus' is unhelpful; nor is the difficulty removed by truistically saying, as Whish does, that the consensus is 'mental'.[4] Phlips says that a CP exists where:

> a concordance of wills leads to collusive outcomes without there being any explicit cooperation between the colluders.[5]

'Concordance of wills' is just as bad, and Phlips compounds the problem by failing to explain the relations between concordance, cooperation and collusion.

Given that antitrust in the United States is generally more advanced than in Europe, it might be hoped that the cases on conspiracy under section 1 of the Sherman Act could be used to illuminate the concept of a CP. The hope is forlorn, as the US courts resort to phrases that are similarly obscure: for example:

> Where the circumstances are such as to warrant a jury in finding that the conspirators had a unity of purpose or a common design and understanding, or a meeting of minds in an unlawful arrangement, the conclusion that a conspiracy is established is justified.[6]

> The unlawful agreement may be shown if the proof establishes a concert of action, with all the parties working together understandingly with a single design for the accomplishment of a common purpose.[7]

This chapter does for CPs what chapter 4 did for agreements: it models them, thereby providing a reference point to help decide when behaviour can properly be said to constitute a CP and when the term is being stretched

[3] Faull and Nikpay (1999), para. 2.49. [4] Whish (2003), 100.
[5] Phlips (1995), 2. [6] *American Tobacco Co. et al.* v. *US*, 328 US 781, 809–10 (1946).
[7] *US* v. *Charles Pfizer & Co. et al.*, SD New York, from 6200–1 of the trial record.

too far. Two models are offered. The first is an analogue of a theory in the philosophy of language, Grice's analysis of speaker-meaning. According to Grice a speaker means something by an utterance when he makes it with certain complex intentions: first, that the hearer should form a certain belief; second, that the hearer should recognise the first intention; and, third, that the hearer's recognition should be part of what induces him to form the belief. The analysis is exposed to counterexamples which can be excluded by refining it. The first model of a CP attributes to the parties intentions similar to those described by Grice.

This model is intuitively appealing, but the second model is more powerful because it reinforces the appeal to intuition with a theory, to the effect that CPs are instances of the broader phenomenon of joint action. The core of joint action is mutual reliance. I give a model of reliance, then I develop it into a model of joint action, defending this model against certain objections, and then I argue that CPs are instances of joint action so conceived. The argument shows that the model both fits the cases on CPs and, more generally, suits the purposes of antitrust: specifically, it distinguishes CPs both from agreements and from individual conduct; it illuminates the 'oligopoly problem' (a matter taken up in chapter 6); it reflects the importance of exchanges of information; it encompasses the view that CPs involve reciprocity and often also mutual deterrents; and it applies to provisions similar to Article 81 in other jurisdictions.

The next section shows that the model does not apply to agreements, a conclusion that has consequences for both contract law and antitrust. As to the former, the conclusion casts doubt on the widely held view that reliance is at the heart of contract. As to the latter, it reinforces the point that CPs and agreements are distinct phenomena. This point impugns the claim, often heard, that the boundary between an agreement and a CP can be hard to draw and that, since both are covered by Article 81, this is unimportant in practice. The claim can be accepted, but only if it is not construed to mean that CPs and agreements fall on a single spectrum, CPs being a pale kind of agreement. Indeed, an argument that the model of joint action does not apply to agreements supports the converse view that an agreement is a pale CP, people only making agreements when they do not have enough in common for them to act jointly.

The Gricean model and the reliance-based model are distinct from each other, but, as the following section shows, they coincide in two significant respects: both models incorporate the view, supported by legal authority, that CPs involve communication between the parties and neither model implies that CPs involve obligations. In the latter respect the models conflict with authority, but I maintain that the authority is confused and misleading. Central to the argument that CPs do not involve obligations is the proposition that there is no interesting relation of conditionality connecting reliance and moral obligation. This proposition – which is important to the many areas of law (extending well beyond antitrust) in which the concept of reliance is prominent – is defended in the appendix to the chapter.

The defence runs as follows. Assume that a state of affairs may or may not be actual, let SR be the state of affairs that X in doing Ax relies on Y to do Ay, and let SO be the state of affairs that Y is morally obliged to do Ay. It is easily shown that SR is neither necessary nor sufficient for SO. SR is, however, a necessary part of a sufficient condition of SO, that is, there is some further state of affairs S3 such that, first, if SR and S3 obtain then SO does and, second, it is not the case that if S3 obtains then SO does; but this is a trivial result, for it can also easily be shown that every state of affairs is a necessary part of a sufficient condition of every other. A more interesting question is whether SR is an *independent* necessary part of a sufficient condition of SO, where this means that SR is a necessary part of some sufficient condition of SO that is not represented by a sentence conjoining 'X in doing Ax relies on Y to do Ay' and a logically compound sentence of which that sentence is a component. Here the argument is more difficult, but the conclusion is that the answer is no. Assume that there are no other interesting relations of conditionality that yield a different answer. Then there is no interesting relation of conditionality that connects reliance and moral obligation.

Why, then, is reliance so prominent in morality and law? Its prominence in law is partly explained by considerations of public policy that may extend beyond morality, but there are two reasons for its prominence that apply equally to morality and law. First, the concept of obligation falls in a hierarchy of moral concepts of roughly increasing strength – 'reason for', 'should', 'ought', 'obliged', 'duty' – and the result extends only to some of these. For example it is not true of mere reasons: SR is sufficient for there to be a reason for Y to do Ay. Second, it is commonly the case that, where SR obtains, additional elements are present which, with or without SR, are sufficient for SO to obtain: reliance is thus a fairly reliable *indicator* of obligation.

A Gricean approach

The first model will be developed by starting with conditions that seem uncontroversially necessary for a CP and adding in stages further intuitively appealing conditions until it appears that an adequate model has been reached. (The methodological limitations of this approach will be discussed at the end of this section.) As explained in the Introduction, a model can be adequate without its conditions' being severally necessary and jointly sufficient. For simplicity I consider only a CP between two individuals, but the analysis can be generalised to cover cases involving a greater number of parties, some or all of which are firms or groups (this applies equally to the models of reliance and joint action proposed later in the chapter). Again for simplicity, the discussion will be in terms of particular actions. There is some artificiality in this, for it is plausible to hold that human behaviour often occurs as a *durée* that cannot be parcelled into separate actions (a point noted in chapter 1). Moreover CPs may consist in courses of conduct over extended periods. These can cause special problems for antitrust authorities. One is that behavioural uniformities may develop into conventions. Certain conventions, for example among oligopolists, may be anti-competitive, but a convention can persist in the absence of anything that might, save by ad hoc fiat of definition, be called a CP between its parties.[8] Similarly a convention can start without a CP and, even where a CP brings a convention into being, its causal role in sustaining the convention can diminish over time to zero.[9] In such a case a competition authority seeking to prohibit the convention by reference to the CP faces a dilemma. It can hold that, since the initiating CP was anti-competitive, the convention issuing from it is too; but that is unsatisfactory, as the convention is now no different from one that started without a CP. Or it can hold that the convention was illegal only for as long as the sustaining influence of the CP exceeded a certain threshold. But that creates an insuperable problem of evidence and is anyway unsatisfactory if, as is being assumed, the authority wants to prohibit the convention altogether. This example is one ground for the conclusion that anti-competitive aspects of oligopoly are better treated by structural than by behavioural remedies. It is a weakness of EC antitrust that it has no structural weapon comparable to the market investigation provisions of the UK Enterprise Act 2002.

Consider the following two conditions:

(1) X does Ax;
(2) Y does Ay.

[8] This is shown by D. Lewis (1969), ch. 1. Lewis demonstrates how a convention may arise in an oligopoly (46).

[9] Compare D. Lewis (1969), 83–8.

These seem necessary but obviously are not sufficient: if they were, any pair of actions would constitute a CP. What is missing is a reference to the fact that in a CP the parties act on the basis of beliefs about each other's conduct. This motivates the addition of:

(3) X believes that Y does Ay;
(4) X's belief is part of X's reason for doing Ax,

and corresponding clauses reversing 'X' and 'Y' (this rider will be omitted from now on). Thus X does Ax because he believes that Y does Ay, and Y does Ay because he believes that X does Ax. In some cases, either or both of the beliefs will be expectations: as noted in chapter 1, the use of the timeless present in the models admits various temporal relations. Where X expects Y to do Ay, 'expects' in this context has a purely positive, not a normative, sense: there is no implication that X believes that Y ought or is obliged to do Ay. (The relation between CPs and obligations is discussed later.)

It may be said that the clauses still do not give an adequate model of a CP, for they merely characterise a case of mutual beliefs and say nothing as to how the beliefs arise. This remains true even if (3) is modified to introduce a belief that Y's action is conditionally connected to X's, for example:

(3′) X believes that, if he does Ax, Y does Ay,

or:

(3″) X believes that Y does Ay only if he (X) does Ax,

or both. What is needed, it may be suggested, are further conditions, to the effect that X's belief results from Y's behaviour:

(5) Y does Ay′;
(6) X's belief (described in (3)) is produced by Ay′,

where 'produced' signifies an appropriate causal chain (as to which, see chapter 4). It may be that Ay′ and Ay are the same action.

But this, it may be said, is inadequate, for (1)–(6) might be satisfied merely as a result of X's and Y's observation of each other, as happens in the case of non-collusive coordination in oligopolies (considered later in this chapter and in chapter 6). Y might do Ay′ without any intention to produce in X the belief that he does Ay. So it seems that the further condition is needed:

(7) Y does Ay′ with the intention to produce X's belief.

But it may be said that this is still inadequate, as there would not be a CP if nevertheless X failed to recognise Y's intention. This prompts the addition of:

(8) X recognises Y's intention in (7).

But now it may be said that there would be no CP if, although X recognised Y's intention, Y did not intend X to do so. In that case a further condition is needed:

(9) Y does Ay′ with the intention that X should recognise his (Y's) intention in (7).

But it may be said that there would still be no CP unless Y also intended that X's recognition should be effective in producing X's belief. So:

(10) Y does Ay′ with the intention that X's recognition of his (Y's) intention in (7) should be effective in producing X's belief.

There is a structural similarity between this model of a CP and Grice's analysis of speaker-meaning. Grice held that Y does Ay, meaning thereby that P, if and only if in doing Ay he intends:

(i) that some audience X should come to believe that P;
(ii) that X should recognise intention (i); and
(iii) that X's recognition in (ii) should be part of what induces X to believe that P.[10]

Grice's analysis is vulnerable to the following counterexample, due to Strawson.[11] Y intends by a certain action to induce in X the belief that P; so he satisfies (i). He arranges convincing-looking 'evidence' that P, in a place where X is bound to see it. Y does this knowing that X is watching him at work, but knowing also that X does not know that Y knows that X is watching him at work. Y realises that X will not take the arranged 'evidence' as genuine or natural evidence that P, but Y realises and intends that X will take Y's arranging of it as grounds for thinking that Y intends to induce in X the belief that P. Thus Y intends X to recognise his intention in (i). So Y satisfies (ii). Y knows that X has general grounds for thinking that Y would not want to make X believe that P unless it were known by Y to be the case that P, and hence that X's recognition of Y's intention

[10] Grice (1957). [11] Strawson (1971), 28–9.

in (i) will seem to X a sufficient reason to believe that P. And Y intends X's recognition of Y's intention in (i) to function in just this way. So Y satisfies (iii).

Y meets Grice's three conditions but is not trying to communicate with X in that sense of 'communicate' which, Strawson suggests, Grice is seeking to explain. The reason roughly is that, in cases of communication in this sense, there is transparency between the parties,[12] while in Strawson's example Y contrives that he and X are at cross-purposes. The objection applies to the model of CPs, and for the same reason: in a CP the parties must communicate with each other (see below).

Strawson proposes the addition of a further condition to Grice's analysis, that Y intends:

(iv) that X should recognise intention (ii).[13]

Adapting the proposal to the model of CPs:

(11) Y does Ay′ with the intention that X should recognise his (Y's) intention in (9).

But this still seems inadequate, for, whatever is stipulated about Y's intentions, there may still be some element that Y intends X to get wrong; i.e. a more elaborate Strawsonian counterexample can always be constructed in which Y contrives that he and X are at cross-purposes.[14]

Various ways of further refining Grice's analysis have been advanced, which apply equally to the model of CPs. One is to point out that in the regress of counterexamples a stage is soon reached at which reference is made to mental states too complex for anyone to have. The suggestion then is that it is only necessary to add to the analysis enough further conditions to guard against states that are psychologically possible. There are, however, two objections to this approach. The first is that it is theoretically inelegant to rely on psychological contingency. The second is that people have different mental capacities: the proposed solution would therefore either require a series of analyses, one for each level of intelligence, or entail that only the most intelligent can communicate. Another proposal is to add a condition that Y intends X and Y to have common knowledge of Y's intentions[15] (on common epistemic states, see chapter 4 above). This

[12] See below for the varieties of communication, including some that seem not to involve this kind of transparency.

[13] Strawson (1971), 29. [14] See Schiffer (1972), 17–23.

[15] See Schiffer (1972), 30–42. Compare D. Lewis (1969), 52–60.

too is vulnerable to two objections: first, that it is doubtful whether people ever have common knowledge and, second, that it admits the possibility of a counterexample in which Y intends that X should mistakenly believe that Y did not intend it to be common knowledge that Y had the relevant intentions.[16] The most promising solution is to add a condition that Y does not have any intention belonging to a certain recursively specifiable sequence.[17] To this it may be objected that no one could ever know that the condition was met and hence that no one could know that a person meant something or that two people were parties to a CP.[18] That objection is little more cogent than the old, and false, saw that one cannot prove a negative: so far as the proposed condition is concerned, a claim to knowledge is secured by the absence of evidence for an intention belonging to the sequence. (This is not to deny that the problem of finding evidence for a CP can be severe: see below.)

Assume that the model can be supplemented, in this or some other way, to exclude Strawsonian counterexamples. Three methodological objections may still be raised, all concerning the use of intuitive judgments in the model's development. It was explained in the Introduction that a model should take such judgments into account, but the main point of the objections is that the intuitions invoked here are inadequate to support the model. The first objection is that the expression 'concerted practice' has become a technical term of EC antitrust and its descendants; hence our intuitive understanding of it is either irrelevant – because it pertains to the expression's ordinary meaning – or too feeble to furnish a criterion for an analysis. The second objection is that the model pays insufficient attention to the courts' dicta on the meaning of 'concerted practice': courts have semantic authority in that they can rule that the legal meaning of an expression diverges from its ordinary sense: in a legal context, if there is a conflict between dictum and intuition, the dictum wins. Third, it may be objected that some of the conditions in the model are so complicated that they baffle intuition.

There are weaknesses in these objections. The reply to the last is that intuitive judgments can be complex. As to the first, it has already been noted that 'concerted practice' is not defined in the legislation; hence the expression must be taken to have its ordinary meaning. As to the second, it is true that the courts can make the legal meaning of a term diverge

[16] Schiffer tries to avoid this objection (Schiffer (1972), 39–42), but his solution is called into doubt in Harman (1974), 224–9.

[17] See Bennett (1976), 126–7. [18] See Schiffer (1987), 246.

from its ordinary one; but the objection tells only half the story, for it says nothing about the criteria the courts apply to rule on meanings. In this respect the objection is like that crude form of legal realism which defines the law as whatever the courts decide. Where, as here, there is no statutory definition, a court's interpretation must be based at least in part on an intuitive understanding.

The main point of the objections nevertheless has some force: the intuitions used to justify the model's various clauses are debatable and have not themselves been supported. A more powerful account would present a model based not only on intuitive judgments, as to when a CP does or does not exist, but also on a theory – for example, to the effect that CPs are instances of a broader phenomenon that is well understood – and would show how the model both reflects the legal authorities and, more generally, suits the purposes of antitrust. To provide such an account is the project of the rest of the chapter. The model that will be proposed is quite different from the one just given (an advantage in the eyes of those hostile to Gricean semantics) but, as will be shown in the final section, they converge in two important respects: both incorporate the thesis that CPs involve communication and neither implies that CPs involve obligations.

A reliance-based approach

The central idea of the second account is that of joint action. Reliance, I shall argue, is the core, and CPs are instances, of this phenomenon. I shall accordingly approach the account of CPs in stages: first I give a model of reliance, then I expand it into a model of joint action, and then I argue that CPs are instances of joint action as modelled.

Reliance

The model of reliance is this:[19]

X, in doing Ax, relies on Y to do Ay where:
(I) X does Ax;
(II) X has the goal Gx;
(III) If X does Ax, Gx is achieved if and only if Y does Ay;
(IV) X believes (III);

[19] For other accounts of reliance, see Hertzberg (1988); Holton (1994); Lagenspetz (1992); MacCormick (1982), 195; McMahon (1989); Regan (1985); Rotenstreich (1972); Stoljar (1988); and Strasser (1985).

(V) X believes that Y does Ay;
(VI) (I) is true because (II), (IV) and (V) are true.

As before, the general remarks about models apply. In particular, not all of (I)–(VI) are instantiated in every case of reliance. For example it may sometimes be misleading to say that X has a goal: a broader locution may be more accurate, that S wants a certain state of affairs to be actual: this would require a revision of (II), (III) and – below – (VIII). In some situations X relies on Y even though X does not have the belief described in (IV), provided it is true – as (III) states – that, if X does Ax, Gx is achieved if and only if Y does Ay. Conversely, in other situations X relies on Y even though (III) is false, provided (IV) is true; here X's belief described in (IV) is mistaken. Again, X sometimes relies on Y where (V) is false but X has some mental state that falls short of belief; for example X *hopes* that Y does Ay.[20] Such points do not, however, impugn the claim that (I)–(VI) model a central case of reliance.

The model is exemplified by a case imagined by MacCormick:

> Suppose that Jones has been swimming from a beach at the foot of a cliff on a stormy day. He has failed to notice the speed with which the tide is rising, and is now in such a position that a desperate dash along the beach will perhaps enable him to reach the path up to safety before he is cut off by the tide. Macdonald happens just then to be strolling along the cliff-top carrying a few hundred feet of stout climbing-rope. He spots Jones's predicament and lowers the rope down the cliff-face to him. Jones sees what he is doing and waits for the rope to reach himself, thus losing time so that he can no longer conceivably reach the path before the tide comes in. He then starts to climb the rope.[21]

MacCormick clearly intends this to be a case of reliance: we are to take it that Jones, in waiting for the rope (and later in climbing it), relies on Macdonald to keep hold of the rope until Jones has climbed to safety. The example does not explicitly contain elements corresponding to all of the model's clauses, but is naturally conceived as containing them implicitly.[22] Substituting in the model:

(I*) Jones waits for the rope.
(II*) Jones has the goal of avoiding drowning.

[20] For the view that reliance need not involve belief, see Holton (1994). Holton would also maintain that (V) underdescribes the *content* of X's mental state.

[21] MacCormick (1982), 198.

[22] In Unger's phrase, substitution-instances of the clauses are 'boring' implications of MacCormick's description: Unger (1996), 25–6.

(III*) If Jones waits for the rope, he avoids drowning if and only if Macdonald holds the rope.
(IV*) Jones believes (III*).
(V*) Jones believes that Macdonald will hold the rope.
(VI*) Jones waits for the rope because he has the goal described in (II*) and the beliefs described in (IV*) and (V*).

An aspect of the example that the model fails to capture is the fact that Jones has an alternative means of achieving his goal, namely running to the path. It may be claimed that there is reliance only where such an alternative exists. The claim is doubtful, but can be accommodated by adding further clauses to produce a model of 'strong' reliance:

(VII) X can do Ax′. (Jones can run to the path. This simplifies the example by omitting the uncertainty whether Jones can get to the path before he is cut off by the tide.)
(VIII) If X does Ax′, Gx is achieved even if Y does not do Ay. (If Jones runs to the path, he avoids drowning even if Macdonald does not hold the rope.)
(IX) If X does Ax, X does not do Ax′. (If Jones waits for the rope, he does not run to the path.)
(X) X believes (VII), (VIII) and (IX).

For present purposes the simpler model, containing only clauses (I)–(VI), is sufficient.

Joint action

The model

The concept of joint action is commonplace in everyday life and important in law, social theory and certain parts of philosophy. A fundamental question concerns the relation between joint and individual action, and in particular the possibility of reducing the former to the latter. This has been much discussed,[23] and I shall not add to the discussion here: the answer will depend on the meanings given, out of the many conflicting ones that have been advanced, to the question's terms.[24] Crudely

[23] Gateways to the large literature are Gilbert (1989), especially chs. 1 and 7, and Tuomela (1995).

[24] The question needs to be distinguished from that of the relation between joint (or collective) and individual agents. For example, in a football game, the members of a team are individual agents who act jointly, whereas there is a sense in which the team is a joint agent which may act individually or jointly with the other team.

speaking, the model to be proposed here is individualist, in the sense that it represents joint action in terms of the actions, goals and beliefs of the individual parties:[25] this is appropriate, given the aim of describing CPs, which typically involve firms pursuing their own interests. Granted the general caveats about models, the possibility can be left open of there being other cases of joint action which cannot adequately be captured by an individualist model.[26]

Consider a very simple example of joint action. X and Y are loading a van. Among the things to be loaded is a box too heavy for either to lift by himself. X: 'We're going to have to lift this together: why don't you take that end and I'll take this end.'[27] Y: 'All right.' They get into position. X: 'After three: one, two, three – heave!' They lift the box in.

Four features of the example are significant. First, each person, in lifting his end of the box, relies on the other to lift *his* end: thus there is reciprocal reliance. Second, the goal that each has in relying on the other is the same, that the box be in the van.[28] (On the potential difficulties of determining whether goals are the same, see chapter 1.) Third, each person knows the previous two propositions to be true. Fourth, X has this knowledge partly because Y communicates to X those elements of the first two propositions that relate to Y, and conversely.[29]

Of course, the scene could be developed or varied in such a way that it lacked certain of these features. As to reciprocal reliance, Y might not believe that the box is too heavy for him to lift by himself, in which case he will not believe the relevant instance of (III) – that if he lifts his end the box gets into the van if and only if X lifts the other end – and hence will not be relying on X to lift that end. As to the shared goal, Y's purpose might be to thwart the loading of the van while appearing to be helpful. As to knowledge, X might wrongly believe that this is Y's

25 The individualist approach is standard in game theory: see e.g. Binmore (1994), 142; Binmore (1998), 96; Gilbert (1996f); and Scherer and Ross (1990), 210.

26 For distinctions between kinds of joint action, see S. Miller (1992); and Tuomela (1995), 88–93.

27 In the terminology of McMahon (1989), X makes a 'coordination proposal'.

28 This claim is weaker than the claim that they have a 'group goal' or even a 'cogoal' in the senses specified in Tuomela (1995), ch. 6. In game-theoretic terms this is a situation of pure coordination. On the spectrum from such games to games of pure conflict, see D. Lewis (1969), 13–14; and Schelling (1980), 83–118, 291–303.

29 Communication is necessary but not sufficient for a game to be cooperative; another condition, not assumed in the example, is that the players can make binding agreements: Luce and Raiffa (1985), 89, 114. As with pure coordination and pure conflict, it is plausible to hold that there is a spectrum from full cooperation to non-cooperation: *ibid.*, 105. On the reducibility of cooperative to non-cooperative games, see Binmore (1998), 42–3.

purpose and hence not know that Y shares the goal that the box be in the van; or X's epistemic state might fall short of knowledge, instead being justified belief, or merely belief. (Conversely, it may be suggested that X and Y have not only knowledge, but common knowledge.[30]) Finally, it is arguable that X and Y might do nothing that amounts to communication: they could both simply walk up to the box, take an end each and lift it into the van.

Communication comes, however, in various forms and degrees. The palmary case is where the speaker says something to the hearer in words which they both understand in the words' normal sense; this can be assumed to be true of the words uttered in the example, but the communication identified as the example's fourth feature is not of that sort. Communication need not, however, be linguistic or – a different point – be in words: it covers a range from the case just mentioned to somewhere short of the case where one person simply causes another to believe something (or to have some other mental state).[31] It may be indirect – X tells Y, who tells Z – or non-specific – someone makes a general announcement – or inexplicit, so that the hearer needs to make large inferences in order to reach the speaker's meaning. ('Tacit' might be used as a synonym for 'inexplicit' here, but it is better avoided as it also has an attributive sense, in which 'tacit communication' means behaviour that appears to be, but is not, communication. This sense of 'tacit' is frequent in discussions of tacit coordination by oligopolists,[32] a point discussed in chapter 6.) Communication may also suffer from various forms of linguistic failing – vagueness, ambiguity, defect of grammar or vocabulary – or be misleading, by either mistake or design. Once this range is recognised, as it must be in an account of joint action and of CPs in particular, it is plausible to suppose, for example, that Y – possibly by nods and eye-contact, possibly by just lifting his end of the box at the appropriate moment – communicates to X that he is relying on X.

The model of joint action is produced by generalising and making more precise the description of the example's four features:

[30] Gilbert (1989), ch. 4, argues that joint action involves common knowledge.

[31] It may be argued that Strawson's counterexample to Grice's analysis falls towards the latter end of, rather than off, the range. Lewis's 'signalling' falls nearer the former end without amounting to full linguistic communication: D. Lewis (1969), ch. 4. Bennett (1976), 127–8, argues that there is a sense in which X communicates to Y that P provided merely that X gets Y to believe that P.

[32] See e.g. Faull and Nikpay (1999), para. 1.76.

X and Y act jointly where:

(a) X, in doing Ax, relies on Y to do Ay;
(b) Y, in doing Ay, relies on X to do Ax;
(c) X, in relying on Y to do Ay, has the goal Gx;
(d) Y, in relying on X to do Ax, has Gy;
(e) Gx = Gy;
(f) X knows (a)–(e);
(g) Y knows (a)–(e);
(h) (f) is true partly because Y communicates (b) and (d) to X;
(i) (g) is true partly because X communicates (a) and (c) to Y.

The model is untidy at certain points. In particular, if it is assumed that X's knowledge in (f) is articulate, so that he knows not merely (a) but each clause of the model of reliance, then X knows (III). Granted that knowledge implies belief,[33] clause (IV) follows – that X believes (III). In that case (f) makes (IV) redundant. A parallel point is true of Y. These loose ends may be left untied.

Objections and replies

Objections to the model are to the effect either that certain of its clauses do not represent necessary conditions, or that its clauses do not together represent a sufficient condition, of joint action. The objection as to sufficiency raises the question already mentioned, of the relation between joint and individual actions, and specifically the possibility of reducing the former to the latter. Someone who rejects the individualist approach is likely to claim that the model fails to give a sufficient condition because it fails to express the 'jointness' of joint action;[34] but such claims are obscure and are rebutted by showing, as this chapter is meant to do, that the model adequately describes cases which we intuitively judge to be central ones of joint action.

As to necessary conditions, it has already been allowed that the example could be developed or varied so that it lacked certain features included in the model: the question is whether, in that case, there would still be an example of joint action. Intuition is liable to falter here, so it is helpful to consider other cases which might be advanced as counterexamples.

At a party X starts to sing a song and Y joins in. This seems to be a case of joint action. But X, who enjoys attention, wishes that Y would stop, so X is

[33] This has sometimes been denied; see e.g. Radford (1966).

[34] See Gilbert (1989), especially ch. 4; (1996f).

not relying on Y to carry on singing. Therefore, the objection runs, clause (a) (X in doing Ax relies on Y to do Ay) is not instantiated and does not represent a necessary condition of joint action (a parallel objection could be raised to (b)). One response would be to concede the example and to dismiss it as peripheral; another would be to argue that this is a case not of joint action but of a weaker concept, say coordinated action. The relation between the two would need to be explained; as already noted, various terms are used in this area without any clear indication of their meanings and relations to each other. The best reply to the objection is that, if the singing of X and Y is a case of joint action, X does instantiate (a): he may not be relying on Y to carry on singing, but it is plausible to assume that he is, for example, relying on Y, for as long as Y persists in singing, to sing in tune and at a volume that does not drown X's contribution, to continue singing the same song rather than starting a different one, and so on.

Imagine now that X and Y are politicians who vote together on some issue for their own divergent ends: here it may be said that they act jointly but without a shared goal, in which case (e) (Gx = Gy) is not instantiated and hence does not represent a necessary condition of joint action. As before, it may be replied that this is a peripheral case; or – as is plausible if the voting did not result from some agreement or arrangement between them – that it is an example not of joint action but of something weaker; or that (e) is instantiated, since X and Y share the goal of getting the vote passed, even if their other goals are different.[35] To this last reply it might be objected that X could vote unwillingly: he does not want the vote passed, and only votes by way of log-rolling. In that case there are three further responses. One is to distinguish the goal of a person from the goal of his action: X's act of voting has the goal of getting the vote passed even if X himself does not. This response, however, requires (c) and (d) to be revised, for they are currently expressed in terms of a person's goals; and it might also be objected that strictly speaking only people, not their actions, have goals.[36] Another approach is to distinguish having something as a goal from wanting that thing: X has the goal of getting the vote passed, but pursues it reluctantly (compare the discussion of unwilling competition, in chapter 1). Alternatively a distinction may be drawn between not having Gx as a goal and having not-Gx as a goal: X, being unwilling to vote, has the goal of not getting the vote passed – or, if that sounds artificial, he desires that it should not be passed – but, since he

[35] Compare the remarks on the 'joint action "bottom"' in Tuomela (1995), 149.

[36] See Frankfurt (1999d), 83.

does vote, he also has the goal of getting it passed. He thus has conflicting goals, a familiar predicament.

We can return to the van and the box to discuss whether clauses (f) and (g) represent necessary conditions of joint action. (These clauses say respectively that X and that Y knows (a)–(e).) Two variants of the scene were considered which fail to instantiate (f): in one X has a mistaken belief about Y, and in the other X's epistemic state falls short of knowledge, instead being justified belief or mere belief. If either constitutes joint action, (f) fails to represent a necessary condition (a parallel objection can be made to (g)). As regards the antecedent of this conditional, there is a significant intuitive difference between the variants. If X has a justified belief, or even a mere belief, that (b), (d) and (e) are true, it is plausible to say – assuming all the other clauses are instantiated – that X and Y act jointly: accordingly this should be accepted as an example of 'weak' joint action which is modelled by adjusting clauses (f) and (g). If, however, X has a mistaken belief about (b), (d) or (e), there is a sense in which he and Y are at cross-purposes (compare Strawson's counterexample to Grice's analysis): intuition indicates that this is not an example of joint action, in which case it is not a counterexample to the original model. Finally, as regards clauses (h) and (i), the earlier brief discussion of the forms and degrees of communication was intended to forestall counterexamples; a more detailed treatment of the concept of communication will not be attempted here.

Concerted practices

The theory

The obscure dicta cited at the start of the chapter are clarified if the model of joint action is applied to CPs. Suppose that X and Y are duopolists who, without making an agreement, act in concert to share geographic markets: X supplies only into France and, in doing so, relies on Y to supply only into Germany, and conversely; they each have the goal of sharing the markets between them; and they each know all this, partly because each has in some way communicated to the other that he is thus relying on him for that purpose.

The theory is that CPs are instances of joint action. This is more modest than the claim that 'concerted practice' is synonymous or even coextensive with 'joint action': as noted earlier, 'concerted practice' has become a technical term of EC antitrust and its descendants; hence, whereas 'joint action' has general application, it is arguable that the application of 'concerted practice' is now limited to the sorts of situation to which such laws and policies apply. The theory has several attractions: first, the model distinguishes CPs both from agreements and from individual conduct, thus protecting Article 81 against the objection that there is no need for an intermediate category. Second, as explained in the next chapter, it illuminates the 'oligopoly problem' – the fact that in certain circumstances oligopolists will display parallel behaviour which is anti-competitive but results from decisions that are plausibly described as made on an individual basis.[37] Third, the requirement of communication reflects the attention given, in cases under Article 81, to exchanges of information.[38] Fourth, the symmetry between the clauses about X and those about Y encompasses the view that a CP involves reciprocity between the parties.[39] Fifth, the model accommodates the plausible view that CPs often involve mutual deterrents:[40] each party knows or believes that, if any of them deviates from the conduct in question, the others will retaliate. In such circumstances there is reason for each to believe that the others will perform their part of the CP. A reason is thus supplied for the belief specified in clause (V) of the model of reliance: the fact that Y believes that X will retaliate if Y fails to do Ay is a reason for X to believe that Y does Ay. Sixth, the model can be applied to provisions similar to Article 81 – not only the many copies in subsequent national legislation, but also section 1 of the Sherman Act (and the provisions on 'arrangements' under the Restrictive Trade Practices Act: see below).

Objections and replies

Some objections to this theory of CPs have the same form as those to the model of joint action generally: they are to the effect either that certain clauses of the model do not represent necessary conditions, or that the

[37] Discussions of this problem are often marred by the terminological unclarity described at the start of the chapter (see further chapter 6) and/or by a failure to separate the constitutive and evidential questions distinguished below.

[38] See Freeman and Whish (2002), div. II, ch. 3.

[39] See paras. 170–1 of the Opinion by Darmon AG in *Wood Pulp*: Cases 89/85 etc., *Ahlström* v. *Commission* [1993] ECR I-1307, [1993] 4 CMLR 407.

[40] I do not know any direct authority for this view. The judgment in Case T-342/99, *Airtours plc* v. *Commission* [2002] ECR II-2585, [2002] 5 CMLR 317, identified deterrence as an element of collective dominance, which it associated with 'tacit coordination' (para. 62), but it distinguished such coordination from a CP (para. 61). A similar distinction was drawn in Case T-102/96, *Gencor Ltd* v. *Commission* [1999] ECR II-753, [1999] 4 CMLR 971, para. 277. In any case, tacit coordination in the specified sense does not fit the model of joint action. See further chapter 6 below.

clauses do not together represent a sufficient condition, of a CP. Another form of objection claims that, if the model accurately represents CPs, the concept of a CP is useless as a tool of antitrust.

As regards necessary conditions, there is authority for the principle that an undertaking may be party to a CP even though it participates unwillingly:[41] in that case, the objection runs, it will not share the goal of the other parties, contrary to clause (e) of the model. If for example Y forces X into a CP for fixing prices, X will not have price-fixing as a goal. The available responses here are parallel to those considered earlier to the objection, based on the example of the two politicians, to the model of joint action. One is to distinguish the goal of a person from the goal of his action. Another is to distinguish having something as a goal from wanting that thing: X has the goal of fixing prices, but pursues it reluctantly. A third is to distinguish not having Gx as a goal from having not-Gx as a goal: X, being unwilling to participate, has the goal of not fixing prices, but, since X does participate, he also has the goal of fixing prices.

A second objection as to necessary conditions is that, contrary to clauses (a) and (b), the parties to a CP need not act in reliance on each other: it is enough for them to communicate their intentions to act. Thus it was held in the *Sugar Cartel* case that a CP exists where there is:

> any direct or indirect contact between such operators, the object or effect whereof is either to influence the conduct on the market of an actual or potential competitor or to disclose to such a competitor the course of conduct which they themselves have decided to adopt or contemplate adopting on the market.[42]

In the same vein Whish invokes the *Hüls* judgment to support the principle that a CP need not be 'put into effect'.[43]

Various replies are again available. One is to say that, in cases where the parties merely communicate their intentions, the acts of communication correspond to clauses (a) and (b) of the model; but this is unsatisfactory, first, because it seems that the parties in communicating need not, as (a)

[41] Case 16/61, *Modena* v. *High Authority* [1962] ECR 289, [1962] CMLR 221; Joined Cases 100-103/80, *Musique Diffusion Française* v. *Commission* [1983] ECR 1825, [1983] 3 CMLR 221, paras. 90 and 100.

[42] Cases 40/73 etc., *Suiker Unie* v. *Commission* [1975] ECR 1663, 1942, [1976] 1 CMLR 295, 425.

[43] Cases C-199/92 P etc., *Hüls AG* v. *Commission* [1999] ECR I-4287, [1999] 5 CMLR 1016; and Whish (2003), 102.

and (b) require, be relying on each other and, second, because clauses (h) and (i) refer to communication about the acts in (a) and (b), thus implausibly implying the existence of second-order communication in such cases. A more promising response is to impugn the idea that a CP need not be put into effect, which Whish acknowledges to create 'semantic, or indeed philosophical, problems': there are no such problems as regards agreements – there is a simple distinction between agreeing to do something and doing it – but the distinction becomes murky in the case of CPs. Regardless of this difficulty, it is doubtful that *Hüls* is authority for the principle that a CP need not be put into effect: as Whish observes, the court acknowledged that the concept of a CP implies that there will be conduct on the market.[44] A distinction must be drawn between the question whether a CP involves conduct on the market – and specifically actions corresponding to clauses (a) and (b) – and the question whether such conduct has anti-competitive effects:[45] the answer to the first question may be yes even if the answer to the second is no. Thus the points noted by Whish – that the court recognised that a CP may merely have an anti-competitive object,[46] and that in *British Sugar* the European Commission concluded that a CP can exist in the absence of an anti-competitive effect[47] – do not support the objection.

Despite these replies, the passage from the *Sugar Cartel* judgment clearly implies that a CP may exist where the parties do not act in mutual reliance but only communicate to each other their intentions to act. It is also clear however that the authorities are interested in these cases only because the communication of the intention is normally a step towards the action intended:[48] if, for some extraordinary reason, it were known that the parties never acted on their own or each other's expressed intentions, these cases would not have been brought within the concept of a CP. They may therefore be accepted as peripheral examples which can be represented by a weakened version of the model.

[44] See *Hüls* (note 43 above), para. 161. According to Whish the court added that there must be a presumption that, where the parties make contact with each other, such conduct will follow. In fact the court, in para. 162, made the converse point that, where the parties are active on the market, it can be presumed that they take account of information exchanged with each other. Another authority for the proposition that a CP requires conduct on the market is Case C-49/92 P, *Commission* v. *Anic Partecipazioni SpA* [1999] ECR I-4125, para. 118.

[45] The distinction was drawn in *Hüls* (note 43 above), para. 165.

[46] *Hüls* (note 43 above), para. 164.

[47] *British Sugar plc, Tate & Lyle plc, Napier Brown & Co. Ltd, James Budgett Sugars Ltd* OJ (1999) L76/1, (1999) 4 CMLR 1316, paras. 95–7.

[48] See para. 97 of *British Sugar* (note 47 above).

A third objection to the effect that not all the clauses of the model represent necessary conditions of a CP is that, contrary to clauses (h) and (i), a CP may exist where the parties do not communicate. This objection complements the previous one, for there communication of a certain kind was argued to be sufficient whereas here communication is argued not to be necessary. In *Soda-Ash/Solvay* the European Commission said:

> An infringement of Article [81] may well exist where the parties have not even spelled out an agreement in terms but each infers commitment from the other on the basis of conduct.[49]

A weaker form of the objection states that, even if there is communication in one direction, it need not be reciprocal. Faull and Nikpay give the following imagined examples of a CP:

> [I]f X unilaterally tells its competitor, Y, that it will be raising its price in a month's time, with the aim of getting Y to do so as well, a concerted practice can be found to have taken place if Y responds by increasing the price of its goods. If X, instead of telling its competitor direct, makes a public announcement of its intention to behave in a particular manner, a concerted practice may be held to have taken place if X did so in the knowledge that its competitors would follow and they do so.[50]

One response is to repeat that communication comes in many forms and degrees which may fall short of explicit statement; but this does not dispose of the objection, for even when the point is acknowledged it is implausible to hold that Y communicates anything to X if X merely knows something about Y's conduct or Y merely responds to a statement by X. It is better either to reject these as cases of CPs or at most to allow that they are again peripheral examples which can be represented by a weakened version of the model. They should only be accepted with reluctance, for, once it is allowed that a CP may exist without reciprocal communication, the oligopoly problem is harder to manage: see the next chapter.

The next form of objection claims that the model's clauses do not jointly represent a sufficient condition of a CP: in some cases further elements, not included in the model, are critical to there being a CP – notably features of the market's structure;[51] or 'facilitating practices' such

[49] *Soda-Ash/Solvay*, OJ (1991) L152/1, para. 59.

[50] Faull and Nikpay (1999), para. 2.49. For uniformity 'X' and 'Y' have been substituted for 'A' and 'B'.

[51] Emphasis is given to the concentration of the market in the European Commission's Guidelines on horizontal cooperation agreements, 2001/C 3/02, OJ 6.1.2001, paras. 27–31. On the importance of market structure in the assessment of exchanges of information, see Whish (2003), 487.

as information exchanges, most-favoured-customer clauses or uniform delivered prices;[52] or conduct or profits that are abnormal.[53] Arguably the claim is more sympathetically construed to be that references to these elements can replace, rather than that they must supplement, clauses in the model, in which case objections of this form concern necessity and not sufficiency. The following discussion covers either version.

The suggestion that market structure is a constituent of a CP confuses structural and behavioural issues: the structure of the market may be important in an assessment of the anti-competitive effects of a CP, but cannot determine whether a CP exists; at most it might sometimes be part of the evidence for a CP's existence.[54] The distinction between the constitutive question – What constitutes a CP? – and the evidential one – What goes to prove that a CP exists?[55] – also provides a response in the cases of facilitating practices and abnormal conduct or profits: these elements may properly be mentioned in an answer to the latter but not to the former. In so far as they are relevant, they bear on matters already represented in the model; for example, facilitating practices typically involve or permit communication between undertakings.[56]

Finally an objection to the model may be raised on the basis not of counterexamples but of pragmatism. The claim is that, if the model accurately represents CPs, the concept of a CP is useless as a tool of antitrust: the model contains too many clauses (and the model of reliance expands each of clauses (a) and (b) into another six), and they concern matters too hard to verify (the parties' beliefs, goals, knowledge and motivating reasons), to be applicable in practice.

It might be replied that the position is no worse here than in some other areas of law: for example in criminal law it can be hard to prove certain types of mens rea. But the model of joint action is more complex than the accounts of all or most types of mens rea; and, if it is now replied that this is only because those accounts have not been pushed to

[52] See Rees (1993), 27, 35–7; and Whish (2003), 516–17. US law appears to take a more lenient approach than EC law towards facilitating practices: see Scherer and Ross (1990), 345–6, but compare Faull and Nikpay (1999), para. 1.104.

[53] The authority for the view that abnormal conduct or profits indicate a CP is uncertain, but see paras. 65 and 66 of the *Dyestuffs* judgment (note 1 above). The position is also uncertain in US law: see Scherer and Ross (1990), 346.

[54] As is implied by para. 66 of *Dyestuffs* (note 1 above).

[55] The questions were clearly distinguished in paras. 65 and 66 of *Dyestuffs* (note 1 above).

[56] 'What all these devices have in common is the exchange of information as the central element': Faull and Nikpay (1999), para. 1.98.

such an explicit degree of analysis, the reply can be turned on its head: it implies that those types of mens rea are exposed to the same objection. A different response is to say that the standard of proof in competition cases is low enough for the problem to be managed; but that is unsatisfactory, first, because it amounts to washing one's hands of the difficulty – we cannot tell whether a CP exists, so we take a view[57] – and, second, because proof beyond reasonable doubt is likely to be required where participation in a CP gives rise to a criminal offence.[58] A more radical response is to revise the concepts of antitrust. One version of this approach is to simplify the model of a CP; but that would risk creating an artificial concept divorced from our intuitive understanding of joint action, which the model articulates. Another, more stringent, version is to abandon the concept of a CP and to make do with that of an agreement, together possibly with an increased range of structural remedies. To this it might be replied that a CP is in effect a diluted agreement, so that there is reason to expect that the concept of an agreement is subject to the same objection; but it will be shown below that this reply is misconceived. The simplest response to the objection is that it is overstated: if CPs are instances of joint action, as represented by the model, it is indeed hard to prove that a CP exists, but that does not make the concept of a CP useless: it has a use in antitrust, just as the concept of joint action does in other contexts.

The result is that the theory withstands the objections. The model fits the authorities well, and it can be accepted that certain peripheral cases do not instantiate every clause: as already acknowledged, there may be more than one concept of a CP and in any case a model of this kind need not purport to specify necessary and sufficient conditions for every application of a given concept. There is, of course, further work to be done; in particular, the forms of communication, mentioned in clauses (h) and (i), the relation signified by the 'because' in those clauses, and the presumably different relation signified by the 'because' in clause (VI) of the model of reliance, could be explored in more detail. Also, it should go without saying, a general model of joint action cannot capture the

[57] On the risk of over-zealous inference from parallel conduct to collusion in oligopolistic markets, see Whish (2003), 513.

[58] As noted in chapter 4, section 188 of the UK Enterprise Act 2002 makes an individual guilty of an offence if he dishonestly agrees with one or more other persons to make or implement, or to cause to be made or implemented, arrangements constituting a hard-core cartel as characterised in sections 188 and 189. It is unclear whether a CP is sufficient for an agreement or an arrangement in the relevant senses.

varieties of fact and shades of interpretation that go into a finding of a CP in an individual case: the textbooks are meant to do this.

Joint action and agreement

The question whether an agreement is, like a CP, an instance of joint action is ambiguous: it may concern the making of the agreement or the actions that the parties agree to perform. The latter reading appears more favourable to the answer yes, and will therefore be adopted here, as it will be argued that even on this reading the answer is no. More accurately, the conclusion will be that a central case of action pursuant to an agreement – a case compatible with the models of agreement that were given in chapter 4 – fails to instantiate the model of joint action; a variety of things have been called agreements, and it may be that the model fits some of them.[59]

Suppose that X and Y agree that X will pay £10 to Y and that Y in return will supply 10 widgets to X. If the model of joint action applies, then by clause (a) X, in paying £10 to Y, relies on Y to supply 10 widgets to X. Substituting in the model of reliance:

(I**) X pays £10 to Y.

Clause (II) of that model says that X has the goal Gx. The account in chapter 4, of the practical reasoning that would lead a rational X to make an agreement, suggests that X's goal is that Y supplies 10 widgets to X; but X is also likely to have a more specific goal than this, that Y supplies 10 widgets to X in return for X's paying £10 to Y. Glossing 'in return for' as a biconditional, the goal is that Y supplies 10 widgets to X and (Y supplies 10 widgets to X if and only if X pays £10 to Y), which simplifies to: Y supplies 10 widgets to X and X pays £10 to Y. So (II) becomes:

(II**) X has the goal that Y supplies 10 widgets to X and X pays £10 to Y.

Clause (III) says that, if X does Ax, Gx is achieved if and only if Y does Ay. Given that the relevant substitution-instance of 'Y does Ay' is 'Y supplies 10 widgets to X', (III) becomes:

(III**) If X pays £10 to Y, (Y supplies 10 widgets to X and X pays £10 to Y) if and only if Y supplies 10 widgets to X,

[59] Tuomela's 'proper' joint action involves agreement, in a wide sense, but does not instantiate the model: Tuomela (1995), 73–81.

which is a tautology. Unless an uninterestingly weak concept of belief is used, whereby a person believes any tautology, it may well be false that X believes (III**), in which case it is false that:

(IV**) X believes (III**).

But (IV**) is the relevant substitution-instance of (IV) and hence, if the agreement is an instance of joint action as modelled, should be true. Thus the model of reliance, and by the same token the model of joint action, fails to fit a paradigm agreement. The models break down at other points too; for example the relevant substitution-instance of clause (V) in the model of reliance is:

(V**) X believes that Y will supply 10 widgets to X.

But X may not believe this; he may know that Y will default and be hoping that the law will provide a remedy. Likewise, if it is false that X is relying on Y, it is false that Y knows that X is relying on him, in which case clause (g) of the model of joint action fails to apply.

The result is that, on plausible assumptions about the parties' beliefs, a central case of action pursuant to an agreement fails to instantiate the model of joint action. Thus action pursuant to an agreement is insufficient for joint action as modelled. Conversely, the latter is insufficient for at least some cases of the former. (From this it does not follow that such cases do not instantiate the model, unless that is taken narrowly to mean 'satisfy the model's clauses and nothing more'.) On the models of agreement that were given in chapter 4, part of what it is to make an agreement is for the parties to give undertakings to each other, but it is clear that joint action as modelled here can occur without any undertaking's being given by either party, specifically without X's committing himself to doing Ax or Y's committing himself to doing Ay: indeed the parties may explicitly state that they are not thus committing themselves and hence that they rely on each other at their peril. It follows that, on those models of agreement, joint action is not action pursuant to an agreement.[60]

These results have consequences for both contract law and antitrust. As to the former, a lemma of the argument about the widgets was that reliance is unnecessary for action pursuant to an agreement. This casts

[60] Compare the observation in *Dyestuffs* (note 1 above), para. 65: 'By its very nature, then, a concerted practice does not have all the elements of a contract.'

doubt on the common view that reliance is at the heart of contract.[61] It might be replied that the lemma concerns actions pursuant to an agreement, whereas the view in question concerns the ground of contractual obligation; but that defence is unpromising, given the argument summarised in the next section of this chapter, that there is no interesting general relation of conditionality between reliance and obligation.

As to antitrust, it is often said that the boundary between an agreement and a CP can be hard to draw and that, since both are covered by Article 81, this is unimportant in practice.[62] The point can be accepted, but only if it is not interpreted to mean that CPs and agreements fall on a single spectrum, CPs being a pale or diluted kind of agreement.[63] Although the argument about undertakings might be invoked to support this interpretation, the argument about the widgets, that action pursuant to an agreement is insufficient for joint action as modelled, supports the converse view that an agreement is a pale CP, people only making agreements when they do not have enough in common for them to perform a joint action. In any event, the combined effect of the two arguments, which is to distance agreement from joint action, indicates that CPs and agreements are distinct phenomena.

Communication and obligation in concerted practices

The proposition that CPs involve communication is built into the model of joint action, at clauses (h) and (i), and similarly motivated the inclusion in the Gricean model of provisions to forestall Strawsonian counterexamples. All this is as it should be, given the importance ascribed to communication in the authorities: the *Sugar Cartel* case emphasises the

[61] The locus classicus is Fuller and Perdue (1936). For an account of the history and values behind this view, see Atiyah (1979). As mentioned in note 5 of chapter 4 above, Atiyah shows how contract law has been extended since the late nineteenth century to protect detrimental reliance in the absence of an agreement, other than in an unusually broad sense. This qualifies but does not dispel the doubt I have raised. For a contrasting view of contract, see Fried (1981).

[62] See the opinion of Reischl AG in Cases 209/78 etc., *Van Landewyck* v. *Commission* [1980] ECR 3125, 3310, [1981] 3 CMLR 134, 185; Faull and Nikpay (1999), paras. 2.54–2.55; and Whish (2003), 94 ff.

[63] 'Agreements and concerted practices are intended to catch forms of collusion having the same nature and are only distinguishable from each other by their intensity and the forms in which they manifest themselves': *Commission* v. *Anic* (note 44 above), para. 131. This statement is hard to reconcile with the one quoted from *Dyestuffs* in note 60 above.

element of communication in CPs, as noted earlier, and there is the same emphasis in cases on the concept of an 'arrangement' under the repealed UK Restrictive Trade Practices Act 1976 (RTPA) (for present purposes there is no significant difference between an arrangement and a CP). In *Basic Slag* Cross J said:

> Whether it is an agreement or an arrangement, it must, I think, result from some communication between the parties – some meeting of the minds . . . As I see it, all that is required to constitute an arrangement not enforceable in law is that the parties to it shall have communicated with one another in some way, and that as a result of the communication each has intentionally aroused in the other an expectation that he will act in a certain way.[64]

The condition which Cross J here states as sufficient for an arrangement is, of course, much weaker than the conjunction of those given in either model.

There is also authority for the view – which, as will now be argued, is nevertheless false – that CPs involve obligations.[65] The clearest statements are in cases on the concept of an arrangement under the RTPA. In *Austin* Upjohn J held that:

> an arrangement must at least connote an arrangement whereby the parties to it accept mutual rights and obligations.[66]

As with the passage quoted earlier from *Dyestuffs*, this is unhelpful if taken as a definition, first because it is circular – the definiendum 'arrangement' reappears in the definiens – and second because the concepts of right, obligation and mutuality are no clearer than that of an arrangement. Upjohn J denied that he was giving a definition, but the two criticisms still apply if he was only attempting a non-definitional explanation of what an arrangement is.

His dictum was upheld in *Basic Slag*, where Cross J appeared to accept that mutual rights and obligations were necessary for an arrangement.[67]

[64] *Re British Basic Slag Ltd's Application* [1962] 1 WLR 986, 995. See also *Re Agreement of the Mileage Conference Group of the Tyre Manufacturers' Conference Ltd* [1962] 2 All ER 849, 859, where it was stated that communication in an arrangement need not be verbal – a point acknowledged in the discussion above of the forms and degrees of communication.

[65] Various writers have held that obligation is an element of joint action generally. An example is Gilbert, whose view is based on a non-individualist account of joint action: Gilbert (1989), 162, 380, 411–15.

[66] *Re Austin Motor-Car Co. Ltd's Agreements* [1958] 1 Ch. 61, 74.

[67] Note 64 above, 996.

That claim sits uneasily with Cross J's remark, quoted above, that intentional arousal of expectation by communication is 'all that is required to constitute an arrangement'; for, if that is sufficient, it is unclear why mutuality of rights and obligations should be necessary. Unless Cross J believed that mutual rights and obligations somehow flow from the fact that by communication the parties have intentionally aroused expectations in each other, the claim of sufficiency must be taken to presuppose the claim of necessity; i.e. his thought must have been that intentional arousal of expectation by communication is sufficient for an arrangement, provided that there exist mutual rights and obligations.

Upjohn J's dictum was also endorsed by Whish, who wrote in an earlier edition of his book:

> In saying that an arrangement must involve the acceptance of mutual rights and obligations Upjohn J was simply reiterating the terms of the [RTPA] that at least two parties must accept restrictions if an agreement is to be registrable. Anyone who accepts a restriction is put under an obligation, at least of a moral kind, and if two people do so there must be a sense of mutuality.[68]

This is unsatisfactory in various respects. First, Upjohn J's statement does not simply reiterate the terms of the RTPA. Second, while it is plausible to hold that anyone under an obligation is thereby restricted, it seems false that an obligation must arise from acceptance of a restriction. Whish's thesis is made hard to assess by the notorious obscurity of the RTPA's sense of 'restriction'.[69] Certainly it is false in the case of some restrictions, for accepting a restriction may simply prevent someone from doing a certain action, rather than obliging him not to do it. If I allow myself to be chained to a fence, I am under no obligation not to walk away: I *cannot* do so. Third, the reference to moral obligation is unhelpful. To say that anyone who accepts a restriction is put under an obligation 'at least of a moral kind' is by implication to use the category of moral obligation as a catch-all, as if any obligation that was not legal were moral, and as if moral obligations were weaker than legal ones. Neither of these claims is true. Moreover Whish appears to think that the concept of morality is clear enough to explain the existence in arrangements of obligations that are not legal. That proposition is doubtful. Fourth, the phrase 'a sense of mutuality' is obscure, but, whatever exactly it means, it is untrue that such a sense exists whenever two people accept a restriction. Suppose X, Y and

[68] Whish (1993), 129. [69] See Black (1993), (1994b), (1995a), (1995b); and Lever (1969).

Z enter an agreement under which X supplies goods to Y and Z, and both Y and Z accept restrictions (this was the case with the original agreements in *Austin*). Then two people accept a restriction – they do so indeed within the same agreement – but there is no question of mutuality, which would exist only if X too accepted a restriction. In his commentary on *Dyestuffs* Whish uses the concept of obligation to connect arrangements and CPs. He writes:

> The *Dyestuffs* formulation corresponds with the *Austin* position that an agreement must consist of mutual rights and obligations (since the knowing substitution of cooperation for competition would subject each of the parties at least to a moral obligation to refrain from resorting to competition).[70]

But it is no clearer how obligations are meant to flow from the knowing substitution of cooperation for competition than from the acceptance of a restriction.

I have argued elsewhere that CPs, modelled in the Gricean way, do not involve obligations.[71] Here, in summary form, is an argument that the same is true of CPs modelled as instances of joint action. The core of the argument is the thesis that there is no interesting relation of conditionality connecting reliance and moral obligation: more precisely, there is no such relation between the state of affairs (SR) that X in doing Ax relies on Y to do Ay and the state of affairs (SO) that Y is morally obliged to do Ay. The reasoning behind the thesis is given in the appendix to this chapter. It is plausible, if more controversial, to hold that the position remains the same if to SR there are added the facts that X has communicated SR to Y and that, because of this, Y knows that SR obtains; and from here it is a short step, via the assumption that 'involve' connotes an interesting general relation of conditionality, to the conclusion that joint action as modelled does not involve moral obligation. There seems no reason to think that the conclusion changes if some form of non-moral obligation is in question or if the joint action is a CP.

Appendix: reliance and obligation

In our ordinary moral thinking, the fact that one person relies on another to do something is often taken to be a relevant factor in judging that the latter is obliged to do that thing. 'I was *relying* on you to do it' we

[70] Whish (1993), 196. See also 483. [71] Black (1992), 203 ff.

reproachfully say to someone who has let us down, the implication often being that he was obliged to do it.

Reliance is likewise often relevant to judgments of legal obligation. Even though it is doubtful whether, as Lord Diplock claimed, there is 'a general principle of English law that injurious reliance on what another person did may be a source of legal rights against him',[72] there are many ways in which English law protects a person who has relied on another,[73] the most obvious being the various doctrines of estoppel.[74] Reliance is also important in the law of tort (for example in the rules on liability for statements[75]), in the law of contract[76] (for example in its concern with the objective appearance, rather than the subjective fact, of agreement[77]) and in the law of restitution[78] (for example in the controversial principle that relief may be available where services have been supplied under a failed contract[79]). It is widely recognised that, since the heyday of freedom of contract in the late nineteenth century, the boundaries between these three areas have become increasingly blurred, one of the main reasons for this being the courts' increased willingness to protect reliance that has not been the subject of a bargain.[80]

In the law of damages, one of the standard measures is the so-called 'reliance interest'.[81] This is a misnomer (a better name is 'the status quo interest'), as reliance by the claimant is neither necessary nor sufficient for damages to be awarded to him according to this measure;[82] nevertheless the claimant's reliance is often an important reason for the award of such damages. Reliance also underlies the equitable concept of a fiduciary relationship[83] and various principles of constitutional and administrative law, notably the principle of legal certainty[84] and its associated principles

[72] *The Hannah Blumenthal* [1983] 1 AC 834, 916.

[73] For a legal taxonomy of kinds of reliance, see Cooke and Oughton (1993), 75–9, 153–8.

[74] See Cane (1992), ch. 10; Cooke and Oughton (1993), 74–5; M. Thompson (1983); Treitel (1995), 100 ff, where it is noted that only some forms of estoppel presuppose detriment. *Wayling* v. *Jones* (1993) 69 P & CR has caused uncertainty as to the scope of the concept of reliance used in the law of proprietary estoppel: E. Cooke (1995); and Davis (1995).

[75] See Rogers (1994), ch. 11. [76] See Feinman (1984a). [77] See Treitel (1995), 1.

[78] See Beatson (1987). [79] See Cooke and Oughton (1993), 47.

[80] See note 61 above and note 5 of chapter 4. These developments have led some writers to contemplate the fusion of contract law and tort law into a general law of obligations: Rogers (1994), 15–16. For the view that this was broadly the position before the nineteenth century, see Atiyah (1979), especially part I and 461–2.

[81] There are various versions of this measure: Kelly (1992).

[82] See Cooke and Oughton (1993), 125. [83] See Martin (1985), 577 ff.

[84] See *Broome* v. *Cassell & Co. Ltd* [1972] 1 All ER 801, 809; and *Wright* v. *British Railways Board* [1983] 2 All ER 698, 705.

of non-retroactivity[85] and legitimate expectation.[86,87] At a higher level, reliance is central to the rule of law itself[88] and to the jurisprudential principles that follow from it.[89,90]

The prominence of reliance in the law is partly explained by considerations of public policy that arguably extend beyond the domain of morals; one such consideration is the need to protect and promote certain forms of commercial relationship (for example, credit) in a market economy.[91] But it seems that the law's concern for reliance is also explained, at least in part, by the widespread belief in reliance's moral significance.

In this appendix I investigate the relation between reliance and moral obligation. Specifically, the question is whether reliance and obligation (I shall omit the word 'moral' from now on) are connected by some relation of conditionality. I shall consider four such relations and argue that only one of them connects reliance and obligation, and that it does so only in a trivial way. On the assumption that no other conditional relation need be taken into account, this yields the main premiss of the argument that CPs do not involve obligation, namely that there is no interesting relation of conditionality between reliance and moral obligation. At the end I offer some justification for the fact that reliance is nevertheless prominent in morality and law.

Reliance

It will be helpful to repeat the model of reliance and the substitution-instances from MacCormick's example:

85 See *Phillips* v. *Eyre* (1870) LR 6 QB 1, 23; *Lewis* v. *Lewis* [1985] 2 All ER 449, HL; and Atiyah (1979), 721, (1986), 7.

86 It is doubtful that, in English law, detrimental reliance is necessary for a legitimate expectation. For contrasting views, see Cane (1992), 143, 229; Shah (1995), 1616; and Singh (1994), 1215–16. In *Teoh* (1995) 69 ALJR 423, an Australian case, a legitimate expectation was found in the absence of any reliance, detrimental or otherwise: Taggart (1996). On the difficult relation between legitimate expectation and estoppel, see P. Craig (1992); Ganz (1986); and Shah (1995).

87 The principles of legal certainty, non-retroactivity and legitimate expectation are more clearly articulated in EC law: Hartley (1994), 149 ff; and Schwarze (1992), ch. 6.

88 See Boardman (1987); compare Hayek (1982), vol. 1, 95 ff, vol. 2, 37.

89 Raz (1979), 214 ff, derives eight subsidiary principles. Compare Fuller (1969), especially ch. 2.

90 On the limitations of reliance in the law, see Morris (1991). Morris argues that to invoke reliance as a ground of legal judgment is usually circular or superfluous. See also Fuller and Perdue (1936), 420.

91 Atiyah (1979), 390; compare Feinman (1984b), 716. For the view that economic factors underlie moral judgments, see Posner (1979), (1994).

X, in doing Ax, relies on Y to do Ay where:
(I) X does Ax;
(II) X has the goal Gx;
(III) If X does Ax, Gx is achieved if and only if Y does Ay;
(IV) X believes (III);
(V) X believes that Y does Ay;
(VI) (I) is true because (II), (IV) and (V) are true.

The substitution-instances:

(I*) Jones waits for the rope.
(II*) Jones has the goal of avoiding drowning.
(III*) If Jones waits for the rope, he avoids drowning if and only if Macdonald holds the rope.
(IV*) Jones believes (III*).
(V*) Jones believes that Macdonald will hold the rope.
(VI*) Jones waits for the rope because he has the goal described in (II*) and the beliefs described in (IV*) and (V*).

Reliance as a necessary or sufficient condition of obligation

In the light of the model, the question can be reformulated thus: does some conditional relation connect the fact that X in doing Ax relies on Y to do Ay with Y's being obliged to do Ay? Take first the two simplest conditional relations, expressed respectively by sentences of the form 'S1 is a necessary condition of S2' and 'S1 is a sufficient condition of S2'.

Some ontology will be helpful here. I shall take it that S1 and S2 are states of affairs,[92] and that a state of affairs may or may not be actual and is canonically represented by a nominalisation of a declarative sentence. Such a sentence ('Jones waits for the rope') can be nominalised in more than one way, for example by using a gerundial phrase ('Jones's waiting for the rope') or by prefixing 'the fact that' ('the fact that Jones waits for the rope'; 'the fact that' is commonly used only in connection with states of affairs that are actual, but I shall use it broadly, to cover also non-actual states of affairs). For simplicity I shall pretend that (a) all nominalisations of a declarative sentence represent the same state of affairs if any (I can accordingly talk, for convenience, of a declarative sentence as itself representing a state of affairs), (b) every declarative sentence

[92] Compare J. Kim (1971), 71: 'the relations of necessity and sufficiency seem best suited for properties and for property-like entities such as generic states and events.'

represents one and only one state of affairs and (c) every state of affairs is represented by one and only one declarative sentence.

The concepts of a necessary condition and a sufficient condition can now be explained as follows. Let 'S1', 'S2', . . . be schematic names of states of affairs, and 'P1', 'P2', . . . be the corresponding schematic declarative sentences representing them. Then to say that S1 is a necessary condition of S2 is to say that P1 if P2, and to say that S1 is a sufficient condition of S2 is to say that P2 if P1.

Now consider this suggestion: the fact that X in doing Ax relies on Y to do Ay (call this state of affairs SR) is a necessary condition of Y's being obliged to do Ay (call this state of affairs SO). By the explanation of the concept of a necessary condition: if Y is obliged to do Ay, X in doing Ax relies on Y to do Ay. This conditional is clearly false, for SO has any number of sufficient conditions that have nothing to do with SR. Suppose that X has climbed on to the ledge of a high window in order to commit suicide. He does not have good reason to die (his desire to do so is due to temporary and treatable depression) and no one else has any reason to wish him dead. Y comes into the room behind X and can easily pull X back inside. X is not aware that Y is behind him, or even that Y exists. Absent outlandish circumstances, Y has an obligation – grounded in the harm that will otherwise result to X – to save X. But X is not relying on Y to save him: in particular, contrary to clauses (II) and (III) of the model, Y's intervention would thwart rather than promote the achievement of X's goal; and, since X is unaware of Y, he does not have the belief described in the relevant instance of (V), that Y will save him. It can be assumed that the example does not involve any other instance of reliance. So SR is not a necessary condition of SO.

Next consider the suggestion that SR is a sufficient condition of SO. By the explanation of the concept of a sufficient condition: if X in doing Ax relies on Y to do Ay, Y is obliged to do Ay. This conditional is also false. The standard counterexample is the story that Kant used to take his constitutional so regularly that the people of Königsberg used to set their watches by him.[93] Assume that these people relied on Kant to take his constitutional at the same time each day. It is highly implausible to claim that Kant was therefore obliged to do so. That claim only starts to become plausible if further assumptions are added, for example that Kant

[93] See Simmons (1981), where the example is used to refute Postow's 'principle of reasonable expectation': Postow (1980). Other examples are given in MacCormick (1982), 198, and Atiyah (1981), 36.

intended to, or could reasonably foresee that he would, cause these people to rely on him. The intuitive judgment that Kant had no such obligation is less confident in the case of pro-tanto obligation (the main topic here) than of on-balance obligation,[94] but it is nevertheless confident in both cases. Thus SR is not a sufficient condition of SO.

The appeal to considered intuitive judgments of obligation, here and elsewhere in the discussion, does not reduce the argument to a merely hypothetical one ('If these judgments are true, the relation between reliance and obligation is so-and-so'), for such judgments have independent force as reasons. It is not my purpose to provide a general account of obligation to back these judgments, but their rational force does not require that. This is not to say that intuitive judgments are sacrosanct; it is a point familiar from discussions of reflective equilibrium that they can be revised in the dialectical process of accommodation between intuition and theory (see the discussion of models in the Introduction).[95] Someone who believed strongly enough a theory implying the conditional relations that are rejected here could apply modus tollens[96] to the argument and reject the intuitive judgments. But it would be hard to find a rational source for that strength of belief.

Reliance as a necessary part of a sufficient condition of obligation

The trouble with the simple relations of necessity and sufficiency is that they make the problem too easy: there appears to be a more substantial issue at stake, so another relation needs to be identified to capture that substance. I propose the relation expressed by sentences of the form 'S1 is an independent necessary part of a sufficient condition [inpsc for short] of S2'. It will be helpful first to define the simpler concept of a necessary part of a sufficient condition (npsc). The intuitive idea can be explicated in more than one way; I shall use this definition:

(NPSC) 'S1 is an npsc of S2' means that for some state of affairs S3, first, if P1 and P3 then P2 and, second, it is not the case that if P3 then P2.[97]

Three comments: first, it follows from the ontology sketched above that a logically compound declarative sentence – for example, of the form

[94] On the distinction between the two, see note 30 in chapter 4 above.

[95] On reflective equilibrium generally, see Daniels (1979); Goodman (1973), 65–8; and Rawls (1972), 20.

[96] This is the rule of inference that 'Not-P' may be inferred from '(Q if P)' and 'Not-Q'.

[97] If Mackie's concept of an inus condition is recast in terms of the ontology proposed here, S1 is an npsc of S2 if but not only if S1 is an inus condition of S2: Mackie (1974), 62.

⌜P1 and P3⌝ – represents a state of affairs. Second, I shall for simplicity ignore the possibility of repeated conjuncts, for example 'P1 and P1 and P3', and of variations in the order of conjuncts, and can therefore talk of 'the' conjunction of specified declarative sentences. Third, an alternative definition of an npsc differs in the denied second conditional of the definiens, thus: it is not the case that if not-P1 and P3 then P2. The antecedent of that version of the conditional states that not-P1, whereas mine leaves the question whether P1 out of account. The argument that follows can be formulated, with variations of detail, in terms of either definition of an npsc.

It might now be proposed that the problem be formulated thus: is SR an npsc of SO? But, given the definition of an npsc, the answer is then a trivial yes. On this formulation, therefore, the problem is still too easy, although now – unlike the cases of simple necessity and sufficiency – the answer is affirmative rather than negative. The reason why the answer is trivially yes is that every state of affairs is an npsc of every other. Consider any S1 and S2. S1 is a necessary part of, for example, that sufficient condition of S2 which is represented by 'P1 and if P1 then P2'. For, first, if P1 and (if P1 then P2) then P2, but, second, it is not the case that if (if P1 then P2) then P2. S1 is likewise a necessary part of any sufficient condition of S2 represented by a conjunction of 'P1' and a sentence equivalent to a material conditional with 'P1' as antecedent and 'P2' as consequent.[98]

Reliance as an independent necessary part of a sufficient condition of obligation

These trivial cases need to be excluded from the discussion. They have in common the fact that, in each case, the sentence representing the sufficient condition of S2 conjoins 'P1' and a logically compound sentence of which 'P1' is a component. A simple solution, then, is to restrict the discussion to *independent* necessary parts of sufficient conditions, defined thus:

(INPSC) 'S1 is an inpsc of S2' means that S1 is a necessary part of some sufficient condition of S2 that is not represented by a sentence conjoining 'P1' and a logically compound sentence of which 'P1' is a component.

This solution may need refinement, particularly if the simplifying assumptions are dropped which make representation a one–one relation between

[98] 'P2 if P1', read as a material conditional, is equivalent e.g. to 'Not both P1 and not P2' and to 'Either not P1 or P2'.

declarative sentences and states of affairs, but it is accurate enough for present purposes.

The question is now this:

(Q) Is SR an inpsc of SO?

The declarative sentence corresponding to (Q) is:

(R) SR is an inpsc of SO,

which expands to:

(S) The fact that X in doing Ax relies on Y to do Ay is an inpsc of Y's being obliged to do Ay.

The answer to (Q) is yes if (S) is true and no if (S) is false. (Q) and (S) are schematic and thus implicitly general: (S) is false if at least one of its substitution-instances is false. I shall argue that one, and hence at least one, of (S)'s substitution-instances is false and that the answer to (Q) is accordingly no. The position therefore is the same as – only more interesting than – the position for the simple relations of necessity and sufficiency.

The substitution-instance in question is taken from MacCormick's example:

(SUB) The fact that Jones, in waiting for the rope, relies on Macdonald to hold the rope (call this state of affairs SR*) is an inpsc of Macdonald's being obliged to hold the rope (call this state of affairs SO*).

For reasons already considered, it is plausible to hold that SR* by itself is neither a necessary nor a sufficient condition of SO*. But the example is naturally conceived as implicitly containing further elements. These are the facts that it would be reasonable for Jones to believe that Macdonald will hold the rope; that Macdonald *can* hold the rope; that Jones will – and it would be reasonable for Macdonald to believe that Jones will[99] – be significantly harmed (drowned) if Macdonald does not hold the rope; and that either Macdonald intentionally causes Jones to rely on him or it would be reasonable for Macdonald to believe that he is causing Jones to do so.[100] The following sentences are true of the example as expanded:

[99] On the central role of the concept of foreseeability in the tort of negligence, see Rogers (1994), 78.

[100] On the relevance of causation to liability in tort, see Rogers (1994), ch. 6; and Thomson (1994).

(A) Jones, in waiting for the rope, relies on Macdonald to hold the rope.
(B) It would be reasonable for Jones to believe that Macdonald will hold the rope.
(C) Macdonald can hold the rope.
(D) Jones will be significantly harmed if Macdonald does not hold the rope.
(E) It would be reasonable for Macdonald to believe (D).
(F) Macdonald lowers the rope.
(G) Macdonald's lowering the rope causes (A) to be true.
(H) Either:
  (i) Macdonald, in lowering the rope, intends (G) to be true;
  or
  (ii) it would be reasonable for Macdonald to believe (G).

It appears that the conjunction of (A)–(H) represents a sufficient condition of Macdonald's being obliged to hold the rope (or to do something at least as good from Jones's point of view: for simplicity, I shall ignore this alternative). That is, if that conjunction is true, then:

(J)[101] Macdonald is obliged to hold the rope.

Against this it might be said that a further sentence needs to be added to the conjunction to exclude possible circumstances that would defeat the claim of sufficiency. Such a sentence would apply to MacCormick's example as naturally as do (A)–(H), but it is not clear what such circumstances would be, especially as pro-tanto rather than on-balance obligation is in question. There is no need to pursue this issue, for the claim of sufficiency is accurate enough for the argument.

Now SR* is represented by (A), and SO* by (J). By the definition of an inpsc: SR* is an independent necessary part of that sufficient condition of SO* which is represented by the conjunction of (A)–(H) if and only if:

(α) if the conjunction of (A)–(H) is true then (J) is true;
(β) it is not the case that if the conjunction of (B)–(H) is true then (J) is true; and
(γ) the conjunction of (B)–(H) is not a logically compound sentence of which (A) is a component.

(α) has already been granted. Whether (γ) is true may depend on how broad a concept of a logical compound is applied: the conjunction of (B)–(H) does not contain an explicit occurrence of (A) within the scope of any of the standard logical constants (not, and, or, if . . . then . . .), but it may be

[101] '(J)' rather than '(I)', to avoid confusion with the first clause of the model of reliance.

argued that (G) (Macdonald's lowering the rope causes (A) to be true), and hence the conjunction, is in a broader sense a logical compound of which (A) is a component. There is no need to dwell on this, for it seems clear (subject to any refinements to exclude defeating circumstances: see above) that (β) is false; that is, (J) *is* true if the conjunction of (B)–(H) is true. So SR* is not an independent necessary part of the sufficient condition of SO* represented by the conjunction of (A)–(H). Assume that, if SR* is not an independent necessary part of that sufficient condition, it is not an independent necessary part of *any* sufficient condition of SO* (this assumption, which I call 'the debatable assumption', will be defended below). In that case (SUB) is false. Hence (S) is false and the answer to (Q) is no.

The debatable assumption

It may be objected that the debatable assumption is implausible. The only reason why SR* is not an independent necessary part of the sufficient condition of SO* represented by the conjunction of (A)–(H), the objection runs, is that the conjunction of (B)–(H) amounts to such a strong claim: that is why (β) is false. But (B)–(H) can be weakened so that, although (J) is true if the conjunction of (A) and the weakened (B)–(H) is true, it is not the case that if the conjunction of the weakened sentences alone is true then (J) is true. Thus, given the truth of (γ) as correspondingly modified, SR* is an independent necessary part of that sufficient condition of SO* which is represented by the conjunction of (A) and the weakened sentences. Hence, contrary to the argument of the previous section, (SUB) is true.

For simplicity, I shall construe the objection to be making a claim about a proper subclass of (B)–(H); this disregards the possibility of weakening (B)–(H) by subtracting or amending *parts* of those sentences. Thus construed, the objection says this:

(δ) if the conjunction of (A) and the members of the subclass is true then (J) is true;

(ε) it is not the case that if the conjunction of the members of the subclass alone is true then (J) is true; and

(ζ) the conjunction of the members of the subclass is not a logically compound sentence of which (A) is a component.

The question now is which of the sentences (B)–(H) should be subtracted to yield a subclass of which (δ)–(ζ) are true. An obvious candidate is (G)

(Macdonald's lowering the rope causes (A) to be true), for two reasons. First, the removal of (G) supports (ζ): (G) was seen above to pose a threat to the corresponding clause of independence, (γ). Second, (G) entails (A): this entailment ensures that (β) is false if (α) is true. But it appears that the subtraction of (G) is not enough, for it seems clear (again, subject to any refinements to exclude defeating circumstances) that, if the subclass comprises the remaining sentences, (ε) is false; that is, (J) *is* true if the conjunction of (B)–(F) and (H) is true. Thus, if (G) alone is subtracted, the position with (ε) is the same as with (β).

The objector will therefore say that further sentences among (B)–(H) need to be subtracted to yield an appropriate subclass. One proposal is to subtract the three sentences that seem least closely connected in their content to SR*: (C), (D) and (E). But it appears that this now achieves too much, for it seems clear that, if the subclass comprises the remaining sentences, (δ) is false; that is, it is not the case that if the conjunction of (A), (B), (F) and (H) is true then (J) is true. We are surely not prepared to say that Macdonald is obliged to hold the rope even if the following claims – compatible with that conjunction – are all true: contrary to (C), Macdonald cannot hold the rope, as he is too weak (to contend that he is still obliged to hold it would violate the principle that 'is obliged to' entails 'can'); contrary to (D), Jones will not be significantly harmed if Macdonald does not hold the rope (a nearby boat is approaching to rescue him); contrary to (E), it would not be reasonable for Macdonald to believe (D) (he can see the boat approaching); and, contrary to (G), Macdonald's lowering the rope does not cause (A) to be true (Jones's reliance has some other cause, for example the fact that a third party previously told Jones that Macdonald would lower the rope). Thus the objection fails when developed in terms of either of the two suggested subclasses. But no other proper subclass of (B)–(H) is any more helpful to the objector's case. So no state of affairs represented by a conjunction of (A) and sentences among (B)–(H) is a sufficient condition of SO* of which SR* is an independent necessary part.

The objector may now broaden his attack by arguing as follows. In looking for such a sufficient condition, there is no good reason to limit the search to states of affairs represented by conjunctions of (A) and sentences among (B)–(H). The only reason for imposing such a limitation would be the thought that any state of affairs constituting such a sufficient condition must obtain in MacCormick's example. But that thought is mistaken, for a state of affairs can be a sufficient condition whether or not it obtains. Thus, to justify the debatable assumption, it is not enough to review states of affairs that obtain in the example: the assumption could only be justified by a review of *all* states of affairs. But such a review is impossible. Therefore the debatable assumption is unjustified and the argument of the previous section fails.

At this point, however, the burden of proof may legitimately be passed to the objector, for the states of affairs represented by conjunctions of (A) and sentences among (B)–(H) seem to be candidates as plausible as any for being a sufficient condition of SO* of which SR* is an independent necessary part. Given therefore that no such state of affairs is in fact such a sufficient condition, it is reasonable to think that no such sufficient condition will be found among other states of affairs. The objector can be left to try to identify one from among states of affairs not represented by conjunctions of those sentences, but, until a plausible candidate is produced, the debatable assumption can be accepted. The argument of the previous section therefore stands.

The result extended

The conclusion is that SR is not an inpsc of SO. The question now arises whether this result can be extended to moral concepts other than that of obligation. I shall only offer some preliminary thoughts.

There appears to be a hierarchy of moral concepts of roughly increasing strength, where to say that concept C1 is stronger than concept C2 (and conversely that C2 is weaker than C1) is to say that C2 applies if, but not only if, C1 does. Correspondingly, to say that a sentence applying C1 is stronger than one applying C2 (and conversely that the latter sentence is weaker than the former) is to say that the latter sentence is true if, but not only if, the former is. The hierarchy of moral concepts is most easily set out by means of sentences applying them:

(REA) There is a reason for Y to do Ay.
(SPT) Y should pro tanto do Ay.
(SOB) Y should on balance do Ay.
(OPT) Y ought pro tanto to do Ay.
(OOB) Y ought on balance to do Ay.
(LPT) Y is obliged pro tanto to do Ay.
(LOB) Y is obliged on balance to do Ay.
(DPT) Y has a duty pro tanto to do Ay.
(DOB) Y has a duty on balance to do Ay.

For example (LPT) appears to be stronger than (OPT), for it seems that to say that someone is obliged to do something is to say not only that he ought to do it, but that he is also bound to do it.[102] Similarly it is plausible to hold that (DPT) is stronger than (LPT), on the basis that the former implies that Y's obligation arises from some post, role or function of Y's. It does not seem true, however, that each sentence on the list is stronger than all its predecessors; the position appears rather to be that each pro-tanto sentence is stronger than its pro-tanto predecessors, and that each on-balance sentence is stronger than both its pro-tanto and its on-balance predecessors, but that a pro-tanto sentence is neither stronger nor weaker than its immediate on-balance predecessor if any. For example it is not the case either that (OOB) Y ought on balance to do Ay if, but not only if, (LPT) Y is obliged pro tanto to do Ay, or conversely.

I have argued that SR is not an inpsc of the state of affairs represented by (LPT). The question whether this result can be extended can be broken into a series of questions, one for each of the other sentences among (REA)–(DOB): in each case the question is whether SR is an inpsc of the state of affairs represented by the sentence at issue. There is no simple principle connecting the relations . . . is an inpsc of . . . and . . . is stronger than . . . that would make it possible to reason, from the case already settled, to the other cases. In particular, the following two forms of inference are invalid: (a) S1 is an inpsc of S2; P3 if, but not only if, P2; so S1 is an inpsc of S3; (b) S1 is an inpsc of S2; P2 if, but not only if, P3; so S1 is an inpsc of S3. Assuming transitivity of the conditional, (a) would be valid if 'is a sufficient condition', and (b) would be valid if 'is a necessary condition', were substituted for 'is an inpsc'; but the simple relations of sufficiency and necessity have already been rejected. The various cases therefore need to be considered individually.

The conclusion that SR is not an inpsc of the state of affairs represented by (LPT) is easily extended to (LOB): all that need be assumed is that in MacCormick's example, as expanded, Macdonald is subject to no other pro-tanto obligation that overrides his obligation to hold the rope.

As to (REA), it is highly plausible to say that, if X in doing Ax relies on Y to do Ay, there is a reason for Y to do Ay. In that case, SR is a sufficient

[102] See Warnock (1971), 94. Contrast Pietroski (1993), 490, 497: Pietroski reads 'Y ought prima facie to do Ay' as 'Y has a prima facie obligation to do Ay' and says that 'Y ought prima facie to do Ay' is true if and only if, ceteris paribus, Y has an actual obligation to do Ay. On the distinction between the prima-facie and the pro-tanto, see note 30 in chapter 4 above.

condition of the state of affairs represented by (REA). But then, trivially, SR is an independent necessary part of such a sufficient condition. Hence the result reached for (LPT) does not extend to (REA).

As to (OPT), Raz has argued that Y ought to do Ay if and only if there is a reason for Y to do Ay; he explains the difference between the two claims in pragmatic terms.[103] The equivalence is fairly plausible in the case of the pro-tanto 'ought' and can with equal plausibility be extended to the pro-tanto 'should'.[104] If the extended equivalence is true, the position in the case of (SPT) and (OPT) is the same as in the case of (REA), i.e. the result reached for (LPT) extends to neither (SPT) nor (OPT). If the extended equivalence is false, the position is unclear, but it can at least be said that the closer (SPT) or (OPT) is in meaning to (LPT), the more plausible it is to suppose that the result for (LPT) extends to (SPT) or (OPT).[105]

That leaves (SOB), (OOB), (DPT) and (DOB). My hypothesis is that the result for (LPT) extends to all of these, for again it appears that MacCormick's example, as expanded, can be further revised to establish that SR is not an inpsc of the state of affairs represented by any of them.

The prominence of reliance in morality and law

I have argued that SR is not an inpsc, let alone a necessary or sufficient condition, of SO; SR is an npsc of SO, but that is a trivial point. To this extent, reliance is less important morally than it may appear to be from the factors mentioned at the start of this appendix. Justification is therefore needed for the prominence given to reliance in morality and law. Its prominence in law is partly explained, as mentioned earlier, by considerations of public policy that may extend beyond morality, but there are two reasons for its prominence that apply equally to morality and law. First, there are the preliminary conclusions of the previous section, that SR is a sufficient condition of there being a reason for Y to do Ay and – if Raz's extended equivalence is true – of the facts that Y should pro tanto and that Y ought pro tanto to do Ay. The second point is that commonly, where SR is instantiated, additional elements are present which, with or without the instance of SR, constitute a sufficient

[103] Raz (1977), 210, (1990), 28–33.

[104] Raz says that his equivalence implies that '"ought" means "prima-facie ought"': Raz (1977), 210.

[105] Warnock would probably say that SR is an inpsc of the state of affairs represented by (OPT) but not of that represented by (LPT): Warnock (1971), 101.

condition of the corresponding instance of SO. This has been seen in MacCormick's example: it is naturally conceived as implicitly containing further elements which together constitute a sufficient condition of SO*. The reason why this is natural is that such elements are common in cases of reliance. Thus reliance is a fairly reliable *indicator* of obligation. This relation of indication is a useful guide in judgments of moral and legal obligation.

6

The spectrum from independent action to collusion

Overview

A persistent question for antitrust is how to deal with the spectrum that runs from independent action to collusion: conduct at any point on the spectrum can be anti-competitive, but different types of intervention are appropriate for different points. The collusive end is suited to provisions such as Article 81 EC, section 2 of the UK Competition Act 1998 and section 1 of the US Sherman Act, which deal with agreements, concerted practices and conspiracies. At the independent end various approaches may be effective: a market investigation, as under Part 4 of the Enterprise Act; regulation, as applied to utilities; where dominance is an issue, the application of provisions such as Article 82 EC, section 18 of the Competition Act and section 2 of the Sherman Act (with collective, rather than sole, dominance[1] we start to move along the spectrum towards collusion); and, where there is a concentration, the application of merger control.

The middle of the spectrum contains the hard cases, in particular the 'oligopoly problem': this, as explained in chapter 5, is the fact that in certain circumstances oligopolists will display parallel behaviour which is anti-competitive but results from decisions that are plausibly described as made on an individual basis.[2] One question is whether the types of intervention fitted to the collusive end can, without distorting the concepts they use, be extended to any such cases and, if so, to which.[3] There is a deeper issue here as to the relation between law and fact: legal distinctions are usually binary, whereas the facts to which they are applied tend to be matters of degree (a contrast that motivates the use of rules of reason in US antitrust: see chapter 3). For example the question whether a situation

[1] For the indicia of collective dominance, see Case T-342/99, *Airtours plc* v. *Commission* [2002] ECR II-2585, [2002] 5 CMLR 317, para. 62.

[2] See Posner (2001), ch. 3; Scherer and Ross (1990), chs. 6–9; and Whish (2003), ch. 14.

[3] The Court of First Instance laid down limits to the application of Article 81 to apparently unilateral conduct in Case T-41/96, *R. Bayer AG* v. *Commission* [2001] CMLR 176.

falls within Article 81 has a yes-or-no answer (and, given the potential consequences of breach, it is important to know what it is) but the facts with which practitioners have to deal range over various dimensions: degree of effect on inter-state trade, degree of restriction of competition and – the present question – the proximity of the facts to paradigm cases of agreement or concertation.

To form a principled view as to which types of intervention are fitted to which points on the spectrum, an understanding is needed of the spectrum itself. This is not provided by the authorities and the literature. Part of the trouble, as also noted in chapter 5, is the prevailing anarchy of terms: in particular, there is a cluster of words beginning with 'co' – concert, cooperate, coordinate, concord, correlate, collude, conspire, consensus – which are often used in antitrust, and more generally in economics and game theory, but without any clear indication of their meanings and relations to each other.[4] The aim of this short final chapter is to use materials from chapter 5 to model the spectrum in a way that shows where various kinds of conduct fall on it and how they are related to each other. I shall appropriate the thin term 'correlate' and describe the various kinds as grades of correlation: broadly, each grade is stronger than, in the sense of being sufficient but not necessary for, its predecessor (if any). I then apply the results to introduce some terminological order[5] and to illuminate both the oligopoly problem and the related concept of 'coordinated effects' as that concept is used in the European Commission's Guidelines on the assessment of horizontal mergers. The discussion of the Guidelines will also include some remarks on the *Airtours* judgment.

Grades of correlation

As before, the discussion will for simplicity be limited to situations involving two parties X and Y and their respective actions Ax and Ay. I shall also for the most part only consider cases of reciprocity, for example where X relies on Y and conversely.

The first grade of correlation is the limit case where there is no correlation:

[4] See e.g. Baird *et al.* (1994), ch. 5; Phlips (1995), 2, 15; and Soames (1996), criticised in Black (1996a).

[5] For other proposals to introduce order, see Faull and Nikpay (1999), para. 1.76; Ullmann-Margalit (1977), 129–33; and Whish (2003), 505, 508–9.

(1) X does Ax;
(2) Y does Ay;

and the actions are wholly independent of each other: for example, X neither expects Y to do Ay nor relies on him to do so. Call this *independent action.*

The next grade is *mutual belief*, where (1) and (2) are supplemented by:

(3) X believes that Y does Ay;
(4) Y believes that X does Ax.

(1)–(3) are thus the same as the first three clauses of the Gricean model of a concerted practice, in the previous chapter. As noted there, belief includes expectation. Mutual belief can be strengthened to various degrees, so that belief is replaced by justified belief – where justification might be conceived either actionally or statally (see chapter 1) – or by knowledge, or by iterations of these concepts – for example, X believes that Y believes – or by common versions of them, for example common knowledge. (As noted in that chapter, on some accounts of a common version it is the special case of iteration where the iteration continues to infinity.) Mutual belief can also be diluted, for example so that X and Y merely hope rather than believe.

The next grade is *mutual reliance*, where (1) and (2) are replaced by:

(5) X, in doing Ax, relies on Y to do Ay;
(6) Y, in doing Ay, relies on X to do Ax;

with reliance understood according to the model in chapter 5. (5) and (6) replace (1) and (2), rather than supplementing them as (3) and (4) did, because (5) entails (1) and (6) entails (2).

Mutual reliance is stronger than mutual belief (but not stronger than all the variants of the latter) because (3) means the same as just one clause, (V), of the model of reliance (see chapter 5.) Mutual reliance can likewise be strengthened or diluted in various ways, by modifying the model of reliance within the vague boundaries imposed by our intuitive understanding of the concept, as described in chapter 5.

It is strengthened to *mutual reliance with a common goal* by adding to (5) and (6) the clauses:

(7) X, in relying on Y to do Ay, has the goal Gx;
(8) Y, in relying on X to do Ax, has Gy;
(9) Gx = Gy.

As in chapter 5, I pass over the potential difficulties – described in chapter 1 – of deciding when goals are the same.

The next grade is *mutual reliance with a common goal and with knowledge*. Here another two clauses are added:

(10) X knows (5)–(9);
(11) Y knows (5)–(9).

As before, these can be strengthened or diluted by substituting for knowledge the other states already considered; certain dilutions are important for the treatment of the oligopoly problem, as will be shown later.

Joint action, as argued in chapter 5, comprises (5)–(11) and:

(12) (10) is true partly because Y communicates (6) and (8) to X;
(13) (11) is true partly because X communicates (5) and (7) to Y.

The concept of communication is also important in the oligopoly problem (see below). Introduction of that concept creates a spectrum within a spectrum, for, as previously shown, communication comes in various forms and degrees.

Chapter 5 argued that concerted practices, within the meaning of Article 81 EC, are instances of joint action. It is tempting to think that *agreement* is modelled by adding further clauses to the model of joint action; but, as chapter 5 also argued, joint action is neither necessary nor sufficient for an agreement. It is therefore misleading to view agreement as the highest grade of correlation, forming one end of the spectrum of which the other is independent action: agreement is better described as falling off the spectrum. (Compare the point, made in that chapter, that concerted practices should not be regarded as pale or diluted agreements.)

Applications

The European Commission's Guidelines on the assessment of horizontal mergers[6] distinguish coordinated from non-coordinated effects (paragraphs 24–57), but does not define coordination. Paragraph 40 identifies various forms of coordination, but does not explain what coordination is. Paragraph 42 introduces the idea of the 'terms' of coordination: talk of terms suggests that coordination is akin to agreement – a suggestion

[6] Guidelines on the assessment of horizontal mergers under the Council Regulation on the control of concentrations between undertakings, 2004/C 31/03, OJ C31/5, 5.2.2004.

supported by the phraseology of 'reaching' terms (para. 42) – but the suggestion is refuted by paragraph 39, which draws from *Airtours* and *Gencor*[7] the principle that coordination can exist in the absence of an agreement or concerted practice within the meaning of Article 81. Perhaps, then, the terms of coordination are supposed not to be undertakings which may constitute an agreement as modelled in chapter 4 above, but to be predictive conditionals along the lines of 'If one party does such-and-such, the others will do so-and-so'. This arguably chimes with the statement, in paragraph 44 of the Guidelines, that coordination may emerge where firms can 'arrive at a common perception as to how the coordination should work'. How the Commission conceives the relation between coordination and its terms is uncertain: the idea may be that coordination is behaviour in accordance with the terms.

Paragraph 41 sets out three conditions which it says are necessary for coordination to be sustainable; these are adopted, with adjustments, from paragraph 61 of *Airtours*, where they are said to be necessary for a finding of collective dominance. This raises, but does not answer, the question whether collective dominance and sustainable coordination are the same thing. In brief, the conditions are (a) the firms' ability to monitor each other's behaviour, (b) the existence of deterrents and (c) the inability of outsiders to jeopardise results. The divergence from *Airtours* is greatest in (b), for, whereas the Guidelines present (b) as a condition for sustainable coordination, in *Airtours* the condition is introduced by saying that the coordination must be sustainable: that is, in *Airtours* sustainable coordination is the condition and in the Guidelines it is the thing conditioned. The version in *Airtours* elides various concepts: in the following quotation they are italicised and the eliding phrases underlined:

> the situation of *tacit coordination* must be *sustainable* over time, <u>that is to say</u>, there must be an *incentive* not to depart from the common policy . . . The notion of *retaliation* in respect of conduct deviating from the common policy is <u>thus</u> inherent in this condition . . . [T]here must be adequate *deterrents* . . . <u>which means that</u> each member . . . must be aware that highly competitive action on its part . . . would *provoke identical action* by the others.

Although it may be that, in the situations with which merger control is concerned, these things normally go together, the formulation is

[7] *Airtours* (note 1 above), para. 61; Case T-102/96, *Gencor Ltd* v. *Commission* [1999] ECR II–753, [1999] 4 CMLR 971, para. 277.

confusing, for it is at least theoretically possible that each should exist without any of the others. That possibility might be foreclosed by stretching definitions: thus the Commission's published draft of the Guidelines used a very broad sense of 'deterrent':

> If firms expect coordination to break down for a sufficient time if anybody deviates, and thus revert to a non-coordinated outcome[,] this constitutes in itself a deterrent mechanism.[8]

The position is further obscured by the mention, in the passage from *Airtours*, of 'tacit' coordination. Is the distinction between explicit and tacit coordination the same as that between coordination that does (if any does) and coordination that does not amount to collusion – a concept that occurs in the draft Guidelines[9] but not in the final version; or is it a distinction that applies both to collusion and to non-collusive coordination; or does it apply only to the latter? And is tacit coordination a kind of coordination, or is it no more such a kind than a toy mouse is a kind of mouse? On this second reading, 'tacit' has an attributive, 'as if', sense, in which 'tacit coordination' means behaviour that appears to be, but is not, coordination. (Compare the point on tacit communication, in chapter 5.)

The three conditions are the closest the Guidelines come to explaining what coordination is, but they can be interpreted in various ways. It seems clear that they are presented as necessary, but are they intended also to be jointly sufficient? And what sort of conditions are they? Here there are four possibilities (corresponding to the fourfold classification of questions in the discussion of *Ghosh*, in chapter 4): that they define the meaning of 'coordination' or that they give an analysis or a test of, or are conditions of some other kind for, coordination. To interpret the conditions as giving a definition or analysis is unsatisfactory for two reasons. In the first place, their fulfilment is supposed to amount not to coordination simpliciter but to sustainable coordination: that leaves open the possibility of coordination, albeit unsustainable, where the conditions are not met. In the second place, the definition or analysis would be circular: thus the first condition is stated in the words 'the coordinating firms must be able to monitor . . . whether the terms of *coordination* are

[8] Draft Commission Notice on the appraisal of horizontal mergers under the Council Regulation on the control of concentrations between undertakings, OJ C331/18, 31.12.02, para. 61.

[9] Note 8 above, para. 61.

being adhered to' (emphasis added; compare the circularity objections to *Ghosh*).

The interpretation of the conditions as giving a test is supported by paragraph 62 of *Airtours*, which says, as already noted, that they are necessary for a 'finding' of collective dominance and also talks of proving and establishing; but, given that paragraph 41 of the Guidelines describes the conditions merely as ones that must be fulfilled for coordination to be sustainable, the Commission appears not to be thinking in terms of a test. The best interpretation is that the conditions in the Guidelines are causal: the claim in its crudest version is that their fulfilment causes coordination, but the relation of causal antecedence could be more complex than that. The problem remains, however, that to identify causal antecedents of coordination is not to explain what coordination is. It might be replied that this does not matter, as 'coordinate' has an established meaning; but its meaning in this context is too cloudy for the reply to be satisfying.

Clarity is achieved by drawing on the grades of correlation to make some stipulations of meaning. I suggest that the statement that X and Y collude means that X and Y have either an agreement or a concerted practice, as modelled in chapters 4 and 5. The same goes for the statement that they coordinate collusively. Non-collusive coordination – acknowledged in paragraph 39 of the Guidelines (see above) – is mutual reliance, or in some cases mutual belief, with a common goal and with knowledge (the clauses on a common goal and knowledge need to be modified to apply to mutual belief), or with some dilution of the knowledge condition, as described earlier. The draft Guidelines talked of 'mutual coordination':[10] this, if not a pleonasm, means coordination, collusive or not. 'Non-mutual coordination', if not a contradiction in terms, can be used to describe the situation where one party adjusts his conduct in the light of the other's, but not vice versa: on this use, non-mutual coordination is modelled just by the relevant clauses about X above. As to the distinction between explicit and tacit coordination, I suggest that it be abandoned: either it is the same as that between collusive and non-collusive coordination – in which case the additional terms cause confusion – or 'explicit' and 'tacit' have no clear meaning in this context.

How well do these proposals fit the Guidelines? Assume that paragraph 41 means that fulfilment of each of the three conditions is a necessary

[10] Note 8 above, para. 41.

causal antecedent of non-collusive coordination, i.e. – given the proposed stipulation – of mutual reliance (or belief) with a common goal and with knowledge or something weaker than knowledge. As to the first condition (monitoring), grant that X's doing Ax and Y's doing Ay constitute their adhering to the terms of coordination: given reasonable background assumptions, it is plausible to say that X's ability to monitor whether Y does Ay is a necessary causal antecedent of the truth of (10) (X knows (5)–(9)) – how else could X know (6) and (8) (which respectively say that Y, in doing Ay, relies on X to do Ax, and that Y's goal in thus relying on X is Gy)? – and correspondingly for Y and (11) (Y knows (5)–(9)). The more (10) and (11) are weakened to accommodate cases that fall short of knowledge, the stronger the background assumptions need to be for the claim of necessity to remain plausible: for example, stronger assumptions are needed to preclude the possibility that Y, without monitoring X's behaviour, merely believes (7) (X, in relying on Y to do Ay, has Gx). The model of mutual reliance with a common goal and with knowledge thus provides a qualified basis for the first condition.

As to the second, the model gives no grounds for the thesis that the existence of deterrents is a necessary causal antecedent of non-collusive coordination as such;[11] but that thesis is plausible – again, given reasonable background assumptions – for the specific instances of the model with which merger control is concerned, for in those instances X and Y would normally prefer to free-ride than respectively to do Ax and Ay: deterrents are likely to be needed to prevent free-riding. Similarly, although the third condition – on jeopardy from outsiders – is not implied by the model, it is plausibly applied to the relevant instances.

The claim – implied by the stipulation above – that non-collusive coordination does not meet the clauses on communication, (12) and (13), causes a difficulty, for the Guidelines appear to allow that such coordination may involve mutual communication: thus paragraph 47 says 'The more complex the market situation is, the more transparency or communication is likely to be needed to reach a common understanding on the

[11] Chapter 5 asserted a different thesis, that the model of concerted practices accommodates the view that they often involve mutual deterrents, in the sense that such deterrents provide a reason for X's belief – specified in the model of reliance – that Y does Ay. That thesis remains true when the model of concerted practices is weakened to one of non-collusive coordination, for the weakening does not remove the clauses about reliance, numbered (5) and (6) in the present chapter.

terms of coordination'.[12] Two responses are available. One is to distinguish a narrow sense of 'communication', used in (12) and (13), from a broad one used in the Guidelines. As explained in chapter 5, communication at its narrowest consists of a speaker's saying something to a hearer in words which they both understand in the words' normal sense, and at its broadest it ranges from that case to somewhere short of the case where one person simply causes another to believe something (or to have some other mental state). The senses at issue in clauses (12) and (13) on the one hand and in the Guidelines on the other may fall at different points between these extremes. A less charitable response is to conclude that the Commission is confused about the distinction between collusive and non-collusive coordination.

Non-collusive coordination is involved in at least some of the cases that pose the oligopoly problem: it is plausible to hold that some of these instantiate (5)–(11) but not (12) and (13) – if the parties communicated in the relevant respects, there would be a concerted practice[13] – while others only instantiate (5)–(9) and diluted variants of the clauses on knowledge, (10) and (11), because the parties' states fall short of knowledge: oligopolists often have to rely on fragile inferences about each other's behaviour. The definition of non-collusive coordination, as mutual reliance (or belief) with a common goal and with knowledge or something weaker than knowledge, thus helps to draw the boundaries of the class of problematic cases. It does not purport – and it is not a purpose of this chapter – to answer the question how, as a matter of law or policy, such cases should be treated. One difficulty raised by this question is that, given the variety of forms and degrees of communication, it will sometimes be hard in practice to distinguish these cases from concerted practices. That fact might be invoked to support the controversial view that at least some instances of non-collusive coordination should

[12] It is unclear whether 'transparency or communication' means 'either transparency or communication' or 'transparency, i.e. communication'. The former reading is supported by paragraph 53, which talks of transparency where firms can observe each other's actions – for mutual observation does not amount to communication – and by paragraph 51, which says of certain practices describable as forms of communication that they 'may increase transparency': it can be argued that the 'may' would be coy if communication and transparency were the same thing. On the other hand, the 'may' could be intended to signify that these practices, while increasing communication pro tanto, may decrease it on balance.

[13] On the importance of communication in cases of conspiracy by oligopolists under section 1 of the US Sherman Act, see Scherer and Ross (1990), 345.

be treated by types of intervention applicable to the collusive end of the spectrum.

Of the 'co' words listed earlier, there remain 'cooperate', 'concord', 'conspire' and 'consensus'. 'Cooperate' has become a term of art in game theory: a cooperative game is one in which the players have complete freedom of preplay communication to make binding agreements.[14] Cooperation in this sense does not match any of the grades of correlation and is in itself of little interest for antitrust (which is not to deny that game theory – specifically *non*-cooperative game theory – is a valuable tool in this area[15]). One option, drawing on the definition's mention of communication, is to identify cooperation with joint action,[16] another – likewise drawing on the words of the definition – is to identify it with agreement; but, since either of these proposals would merely duplicate terms, there is no point in adding to the game-theoretic definition. 'Concord' and 'consensus' have both been used to characterise the notion of a concerted practice, but, as they do little to illuminate it,[17] they are best abandoned in this context. 'Conspire' means the same as 'collude'.

[14] See chapter 5, note 29.

[15] See Faull and Nikpay (1999), paras. 1.77–1.104; and Phlips (1995).

[16] Given that concerted practices are instances of joint action, and depending on the intended force of 'explicit', this proposal may conflict with the statement in Phlips (1995), 2, that a concerted practice may exist without explicit cooperation between the parties.

[17] See the start of chapter 5. In passages quoted there, Phlips describes a concerted practice as a 'concordance of wills' and Faull and Nikpay say that for a concerted practice to exist there must be a 'consensus between the parties'.

REFERENCES

Achinstein, P. 1983. *The Concept of Evidence*. Oxford: Oxford University Press.

Acton, H. 1993. 'The Morals of Markets: An Ethical Exploration'. In H. Acton, *The Morals of Markets and Related Essays*. Indianapolis: Liberty Press.

Alexander, L. 1985. 'Pursuing the Good – Indirectly'. *Ethics* 95.

Allingham, M. 2002. *Choice Theory: A Very Short Introduction*. Oxford: Oxford University Press.

Alston, W. 1989. 'Varieties of Privileged Access'. In W. Alston, *Epistemic Justification: Essays in the Theory of Knowledge*. Ithaca: Cornell University Press.

Altham, J. 1985. 'Wicked Promises'. In I. Hacking (ed.), *Exercises in Analysis: Essays by Students of Casimir Lewy*. Cambridge: Cambridge University Press.

Anonymous. 1983. 'Fixing the Price Fixing Confusion: A Rule of Reason Approach'. *Yale Law Journal* 92.

Archard, D. 1993. 'Self-Justifying Paternalism'. *Journal of Value Inquiry* 27.

Ardal, P. 1976. 'Promises and Reliance'. *Dialogue* 15.

Areeda, P. 1985. 'The Changing Contours of the Per Se Rule'. *Antitrust Law Journal* 54.

1989. *Antitrust Law: An Analysis of Antitrust Principles and Their Application*. Boston: Little, Brown.

Arneson, R. 1998. 'Paternalism'. In E. Craig (1998), vol. 7.

2002. 'The End of Welfare As We Know It? Scanlon Versus Welfarist Consequentialism'. *Social Theory and Practice* 28.

Arrow, K. 1951. 'An Extension of the Basic Theorems of Classical Welfare Economics'. Proceedings of the Second Berkeley Symposium. Berkeley: University of California Press.

1963. *Social Choice and Individual Values* (2nd edition). New Haven: Yale University Press.

Atiyah, P. 1979. *The Rise and Fall of Freedom of Contract*. Oxford: Clarendon Press.

1981. *Promises, Morals, and Law*. Oxford: Clarendon Press.

1986. *Essays on Contract*. Oxford: Clarendon Press.

Audi, R. 1989. *Practical Reasoning*. London: Routledge.

Aumann, R. 1976. 'Agreeing to Disagree'. *Annals of Statistics* 4.

Austin, J. 1962. *Sense and Sensibilia*. London: Oxford University Press.

Bach, K. 1995. 'Terms of Agreement'. *Ethics* 105.

Baier, A. 1985. *Postures of the Mind.* Minneapolis: Minnesota University Press.

Baird, D., H. Gertner and R. Picker. 1994. *Game Theory and the Law.* Cambridge, MA: Harvard University Press.

Barry, B. 1973. *Political Argument.* London: Routledge and Kegan Paul.

1986. 'Lady Chatterley's Lover and Doctor Fischer's Bomb Party: Liberalism, Pareto Optimality, and the Problem of Objectionable Preferences'. In Elster and Hylland (1989a).

Beale, H., *et al.* (eds.). 1999. *Chitty on Contracts* (28th edition). vol. 1. London: Sweet & Maxwell.

Beals, A., and B. Siegel. 1966. *Divisiveness and Social Conflict.* Palo Alto: Stanford University Press.

Beard, D. 2003. 'The Cartel Criminal Offence'. *Competition Law Journal* 2.

Beatson, J. 1987. 'Benefit, Reliance and the Structure of Unjust Enrichment'. *Current Legal Problems* 40.

Benn, S. 1971. 'Freedom, Autonomy, and the Concept of a Person'. *Proceedings of the Aristotelian Society* 12.

Bennett, J. 1976. *Linguistic Behaviour.* Cambridge: Cambridge University Press.

Benson, P. (ed.). 2001a. *The Theory of Contract Law.* Cambridge: Cambridge University Press.

2001b. 'The Unity of Contract Law'. In Benson (2001a).

Bentham, J. 1948. *An Introduction to the Principles of Morals and Legislation.* Oxford: Blackwell.

Berkowitz, L. 1962. *Aggression: A Social Psychological Analysis.* New York: McGraw-Hill.

Bernstein, M. 1998. 'Well-Being'. *American Philosophical Quarterly* 35.

Beschle, R. 1987. '"What Never? Well, Hardly Ever": Strict Antitrust Scrutiny as an Alternative to Per Se Antitrust Illegality'. *Hastings Law Journal* 38.

Binmore, K. 1994. *Playing Fair.* Cambridge, MA: MIT Press.

1998. *Just Playing.* Cambridge, MA: MIT Press.

Binmore, K., and A. Brandenburger. 1990. 'Common Knowledge and Game Theory'. In K. Binmore (ed.), *Essays on Foundations of Game Theory.* Oxford: Blackwell.

Bishop, S., and M. Walker. 2002. *The Economics of EC Competition Law: Concepts, Application and Measurement.* London: Sweet & Maxwell.

Black, O. 1987a. 'Induction and Experience: An Alleged Infinite Regress'. *Fundamenta Scientiae* 7.

1987b. *The Infinite Regress of Justification.* PhD thesis, University of London.

1988. 'Infinite Regresses of Justification'. *International Philosophical Quarterly* 28.

1992. 'Communication and Obligation in Arrangements and Concerted Practices'. *European Competition Law Review* 13.

1993. 'Competition and Negative Obligation'. *European Competition Law Review* 14.

1994a. 'Ends, Desires and Rationality'. *International Philosophical Quarterly* 34.

1994b. '"Most Favoured Customer" Clauses: Application of the Restrictive Trade Practices Act 1976'. *European Competition Law Review* 15.

1995a. 'Accepting a Relevant Restriction by Accepting Something Else'. *European Competition Law Review* 16.

1995b. 'What Is the Difference Between a Term and a Restriction? – *Associated Dairies* and the Scope of Section 9(3) RTPA'. *European Competition Law Review* 16.

1996a. 'Concertation and Coordination: A Distinction without a Difference?' *European Competition Law Review* 17.

1996b. 'Legal Validity and the Infinite Regress'. *Law and Philosophy* 15.

1997. 'Per Se Rules and Rules of Reason: What Are They?' *European Competition Law Review* 18.

1998. 'The Relation Between Reliance and Obligation'. In P. Kampits *et al.* (eds.), *Applied Ethics*. Kirchberg am Wechsel: Austrian Ludwig Wittgenstein Society.

2002. 'What Makes Me the Person I Am'. *Dialegesthai*, November 2002.

2003a. 'Collusion and Coordination in EC Merger Control'. *European Competition Law Review* 24.

2003b. 'Concerted Practices, Joint Action and Reliance'. *European Competition Law Review* 24.

2003c. 'Grades of Correlation: The Spectrum from Independent Action to Collusion, and Its Implications for Antitrust'. *Competition Law Journal* 2.

2003d. 'Independent Promises and the Rescission of Contracts'. *Legal Studies* 23.

2003e. 'Infinite Regresses, Infinite Beliefs'. In W. Löffler and P. Weingartner (eds.), *Knowledge and Belief*. Kirchberg am Wechsel: Austrian Ludwig Wittgenstein Society.

2003f. 'Joint Action, Reliance and the Law'. *King's College Law Journal* 14.

2003g. 'What Is an Agreement?' *European Competition Law Review* 24.

2004a. 'Agreements, Undertakings and Practical Reason'. *Legal Theory* 10.

2004b. 'Reliance and Obligation'. *Ratio Juris* 17.

Boadway, R., and N. Bruce. 1984. *Welfare Economics*. Oxford: Blackwell.

Boardman, W. 1987. 'Coordination and the Moral Obligation to Obey the Law'. *Ethics* 97.

Bock, B. 1990. 'An Economist Considers Some Basic Issues of Antitrust Law in the United States'. *European Competition Law Review* 11.

Bork, R. 1965. 'The Rule of Reason and the Per Se Concept: Price Fixing and Market Division' (Part 1). *Yale Law Journal* 74.

1966. 'The Rule of Reason and the Per Se Concept: Price Fixing and Market Division' (Part 2). *Yale Law Journal* 75.

1978. *The Antitrust Paradox*. New York: The Free Press.

Boulding, K. 1962. *Conflict and Defense.* New York: Harper.
Brandt, R. 1979. *A Theory of the Good and the Right.* Oxford: Clarendon Press.
1982. 'Two Concepts of Utility'. In Miller and Williams (1982).
Bratman, M. 1999a. *Faces of Intention.* Cambridge: Cambridge University Press.
1999b. 'I Intend That We J'. In Bratman (1999a).
1999c. *Intentions, Plans, and Practical Reason.* Stanford: CSLI Publications.
1999d. 'Shared Cooperative Activity'. In Bratman (1999a).
1999e. 'Shared Intention'. In Bratman (1999a).
Brickman, P., and D. Campbell. 1971. 'Hedonic Relativism and Planning the Good Society'. In M. Appley (ed.), *Adaptation-Level Theory: A Symposium.* New York: Academic Press.
Brickman, P., *et al.* 1978. 'Lottery Winners and Accident Victims: Is Happiness Relative?' *Journal of Personality and Social Psychology* 36.
Bright, C. 1995. 'Deregulation of EC Competition Policy: Rethinking Article 85(1)'. New York: Fordham Corporate Law Institute.
Brock, D. 1993. 'Quality of Life Measures in Health Care and Medical Ethics'. In Nussbaum and Sen (1993).
Broome, J. 1979. 'Choice and Value in Economics'. *Oxford Economic Papers* 30.
1991a. 'Utility'. *Economics and Philosophy* 7.
1991b. *Weighing Goods: Equality, Uncertainty and Time.* Oxford: Blackwell.
2000. 'Normative Requirements'. In J. Dancy (ed.), *Normativity.* Oxford: Blackwell.
2001a. 'Are Intentions Reasons? And How Should We Cope With Incommensurable Values?' In C. Morris and A. Ripstein (eds.), *Practical Rationality and Preference: Essays for David Gauthier.* Cambridge: Cambridge University Press.
2001b. 'Normative Practical Reasoning'. *Proceedings of the Aristotelian Society,* Supplementary Volume 75.
2002. 'Practical Reasoning'. In J. Bermùdez and A. Millar (eds.), *Reason and Nature: Essays in the Theory of Rationality.* Oxford: Oxford University Press.
2004. 'Reasons'. In R. Wallace *et al.* (eds.), *Reason and Value: Essays on the Moral Philosophy of Joseph Raz.* Oxford: Oxford University Press.
Brownson, W. 1974. 'The Structure of Competition in the School and Its Consequences'. *Philosophy of Education* 30.
Brunet, E. 1984. 'Streamlining Antitrust Litigation by "Facial Examination" of Restraints: The Burger Court and the Per Se Rule of Reason Distinction'. *Washington Law Review* 60.
Buchanan, A. 1985. *Ethics, Efficiency, and the Market.* Totowa: Rowman & Allanheld.
Buchanan, A., and D. Brock. 1990. *Deciding for Others: The Ethics of Surrogate Decision Making.* Cambridge: Cambridge University Press.
Burrows, P. 1993. 'Patronising Paternalism'. *Oxford Economic Papers* 45.

1995. 'Analyzing Legal Paternalism'. *International Review of Law and Economics* 15.

Caillois, R. 2001. *Man, Play and Games.* Urbana: University of Illinois Press.

Campbell, A. 1981. *The Sense of Well-Being in America: Recent Patterns and Trends.* New York: McGraw-Hill.

Cane, P. 1992. *An Introduction to Administrative Law.* Oxford: Clarendon Press.

Cartwright, J. 1984. 'An Evidentiary Theory of Promises'. *Mind* 93.

Castañeda, H. 1999. *The Phenomeno-Logic of the I.* Bloomington: Indiana University Press.

Chang, R. (ed.). 1997. *Incommensurability, Incomparability, and Practical Reason.* Cambridge, MA: Harvard University Press.

Chisholm, R. 1976. *Person and Object.* Chicago: Open Court.

Christman, J. (ed.). 1989. *The Inner Citadel: Essays on Individual Autonomy.* New York: Oxford University Press.

Cohen, G. 1977. 'Labor, Leisure, and a Distinctive Contradiction of Advanced Capitalism'. In G. Dworkin *et al.* (eds.), *Markets and Morals.* Washington, DC: Hemisphere Publishing Co.

1993. 'Equality of What? On Welfare, Goods, and Capabilities'. In Nussbaum and Sen (1993).

Cohen, M. (ed.). 1984. *Ronald Dworkin and Contemporary Jurisprudence.* London: Duckworth.

Coleman, J. 1987. 'Competition and Cooperation'. *Ethics* 98.

Combs, A. 1979. *Myths in Education.* Boston: Allyn and Bacon.

Competition Commission. 1998. *Ladbroke Group Plc and the Coral Betting Business: A Report on the Merger Situation.* London: Competition Commission.

2003a. *Merger References: Competition Commission Guidelines.* London: Competition Commission.

2003b. *Market Investigation References: Competition Commission Guidelines.* London: Competition Commission.

Confederation of British Industry. 1995. *Loosening the Strait-Jacket: CBI Proposals for Reform of the Scope and Administration of Article 85.* London: Confederation of British Industry.

Cooke, E. 1995. 'Reliance and Estoppel'. *Law Quarterly Review* 111.

Cooke, P., and D. Oughton. 1993. *The Common Law of Obligations.* London: Butterworths.

Cooley, C. 1899. 'Personal Competition'. *American Economic Association Studies* 4.

Cooper, G. 1993. 'The Competition Controversy in Community Ecology'. *Biology and Philosophy* 8.

Craig, E. 1990. *Knowledge and the State of Nature.* Oxford: Clarendon Press.

(ed.). 1998. *Routledge Encyclopedia of Philosophy.* London: Routledge.

Craig, P. 1992. 'Legitimate Expectations: A Conceptual Analysis'. *Law Quarterly Review* 108.

Crampton, P. 1994. 'Alternative Approaches to Competition Law: Consumers' Surplus, Total Surplus, Total Welfare and Non-Efficiency Goals'. *World Competition* 17.

Criminal Law Revision Committee. 1966. *Eighth Report: Theft and Related Offences* (1966 Cmnd 2977). London: HMSO.

Crisp, R. 1998. 'Virtue Ethics'. In E. Craig (1998), vol. 9.

2000. 'Utilitarianism and Accomplishment'. *Analysis* 60.

2001. 'Utilitarianism and Accomplishment Revisited'. *Analysis* 61.

Crisp, R., and B. Hooker (eds.). 2000. *Well-Being and Morality: Essays in Honour of James Griffin*. Oxford: Clarendon Press.

Crisp, R., and M. Slote (eds.). 1997. *Virtue Ethics*. Oxford: Oxford University Press.

Dahlke, H. 1964. 'Cooperation'. In J. Gould and W. Kolb (eds.), *Dictionary of the Social Sciences*. London: Tavistock.

Daniels, N. 1979. 'Wide Reflective Equilibrium and Theory Acceptance in Ethics'. *Journal of Philosophy* 76.

Darwall, S. 2002. *Welfare and Rational Care*. Princeton: Princeton University Press.

Davidson, D. 1980a. 'Causal Relations'. In Davidson (1980b).

1980b. *Essays on Actions and Events*. Oxford: Clarendon Press.

1980c. 'How Is Weakness of the Will Possible?' In Davidson (1980b).

Davies, S. 1997. 'Two Conceptions of Welfare: Voluntarism and Incorporationism'. *Social Philosophy and Policy* 14.

Davis, C. 1995. 'Estoppel – Reliance and Remedy'. *Conveyancer and Property Lawyer* 59.

Dean, N. 2003. 'Creating a Stir'. *New Law Journal*, 13 June 2003.

Dearden, R. 1972. 'Competition in Education'. *Proceedings of the Philosophy of Education Society of Great Britain* 6.

Demarco, J., and R. Fox. 1992. 'Putting Pressure on Promises'. *Southern Journal of Philosophy* 30.

De Moor, A. 1986. 'Contract and Agreement in English and French Law'. *Oxford Journal of Legal Studies* 6.

1987. 'Are Contracts Promises?' In J. Eekelaar and J. Bell (eds.), *Oxford Essays in Jurisprudence*. Oxford: Oxford University Press.

Department of Trade and Industry. 2001. *Productivity and Enterprise: A World Class Competition Regime*. London: Department of Trade and Industry.

Deutsch, M. 1973. *The Resolution of Conflict: Constructive and Destructive Processes*. New Haven: Yale University Press.

Deutscher, I. 1952. 'Socialist Competition'. *Foreign Affairs* 30.

Diener, E. 1984. 'Subjective Well-Being'. *Psychological Bulletin* 95.

Diogenes Laertius. 1980. *Lives of Eminent Philosophers*. Cambridge, MA: Harvard University Press.

Dixit, A., and S. Skeath. 1999. *Games of Strategy*. New York: Norton.

Downie, R. 1985. 'Three Accounts of Promising'. *Philosophical Quarterly* 35.

Downie, R., and E. Telfer. 1971. 'Autonomy'. *Philosophy* 15.

Dummett, M. 1978. 'Truth'. In M. Dummett, *Truth and Other Enigmas*. London: Duckworth.

Duncan, O. 1975. 'Does Money Buy Satisfaction?' *Social Indicators Research* 2.

Dworkin, G. 1972. 'Paternalism'. *Monist* 56.

1988. *The Theory and Practice of Autonomy*. Cambridge: Cambridge University Press.

Dworkin, R. 1978. *Taking Rights Seriously*. London: Duckworth.

1986a. *Law's Empire*. London: Fontana.

1986b. *A Matter of Principle*. Oxford: Clarendon Press.

Easterbrook, F. 1984a. 'The Limits of Antitrust'. *Texas Law Review* 63.

1984b. 'Vertical Arrangements and the Rule of Reason'. *Antitrust Law Journal* 53.

Easterlin, R. 1974. 'Does Economic Growth Improve the Human Lot? Some Empirical Evidence'. In P. David and M. Reder (eds.), *Nations and Households in Economic Growth*. New York: Academic Press.

Ehrlich, I., and R. Posner. 1974. 'An Economic Analysis of Legal Rulemaking'. *Journal of Legal Studies* 3.

Elliott, D. 1982. 'Dishonesty in Theft: A Dispensable Concept'. *Criminal Law Review*.

Elster, J. 1985. *Sour Grapes: Studies in the Subversion of Rationality*. Cambridge: Cambridge University Press.

1989. 'The Market and the Forum: Three Varieties of Political Theory'. In Elster and Hylland (1989a).

Elster, J., and A. Hylland (eds.). 1989a. *Foundations of Social Choice Theory*. Cambridge: Cambridge University Press.

1989b. 'Introduction'. In Elster and Hylland (1989a).

Elster, J., and J. Roemer (eds.). 1993a. *Interpersonal Comparisons of Well-Being*. Cambridge: Cambridge University Press.

1993b. 'Introduction'. In Elster and Roemer (1993a).

Faull, J., and A. Nikpay. 1999. *The EC Law of Competition*. Oxford: Oxford University Press.

Feinberg, J. 1973. *Social Philosophy*. Upper Saddle River: Prentice Hall.

1984. *Harm to Others*. New York: Oxford University Press.

1986. *Harm to Self*. New York: Oxford University Press.

Feinman, J. 1984a. 'The Meaning of Reliance: A Historical Perspective'. *Wisconsin Law Review*.

1984b. 'Promissory Estoppel and Judicial Method'. *Harvard Law Review* 97.

Feltkamp, R. 2003. 'Some Reflections on the Structure of the State Aid Rules in the Treaty of Rome'. *EC Competition Policy Newsletter* 1.

Fielding, M. 1976. 'Against Competition: In Praise of Malleable Analysis and the Subversiveness of Philosophy'. *Proceedings of the Philosophy of Education Society of Great Britain* 10.

Finnis, J. 1980. *Natural Law and Natural Rights*. Oxford: Clarendon Press.

Flew, A. 1983. 'Competition and Cooperation, Equality and Elites'. *Journal of Philosophy of Education* 17.

Flynn, J. 1982. 'Rethinking Sherman Act Section 1 Analysis: Three Proposals for Reducing the Chaos'. *Antitrust Law Journal* 49.

Fogelin, R. 1983. 'Richard Price on Promising: A Limited Defence'. *Journal of the History of Philosophy* 21.

Foot, P. (ed.). 1967. *Theories of Ethics.* Oxford: Oxford University Press.

Foster, E., and H. Sonnenschein. 1970. 'Price Distortion and Economic Welfare'. *Econometrica* 38.

Fox, E. 1990. 'The Future of the Per Se Rule: Two Visions at War With One Another'. *Washburn Law Journal* 29.

Fox, E., and L. Sullivan. 1989. *Cases and Materials on Antitrust.* St Paul: West.

Fox, R., and J. Demarco. 1993. 'The Immorality of Promising'. *Journal of Value Inquiry* 27.

Frank, R. 2003. *Microeconomics and Behavior* (5th edition). New York: McGraw-Hill Irwin.

Frankfurt, H. 1999a. 'Autonomy, Necessity, and Love'. In Frankfurt (1999b).

1999b. *Necessity, Volition, and Love.* Cambridge: Cambridge University Press.

1999c. 'On the Necessity of Ideals'. In Frankfurt (1999b).

1999d. 'On the Usefulness of Final Ends'. In Frankfurt (1999b).

Franklin, D. Unpublished. 'Valuing Health, Healthcare and Health Equality'.

Freeman, P., and R. Whish (eds.). 2002. *Butterworths Competition Law.* London: Butterworths.

Freeman, S. 1998. 'Contractarianism'. In E. Craig (1998), vol. 2.

Frege, G. 1952. 'On Sense and Reference'. In P. Geach and M. Black (eds.), *Translations from the Philosophical Writings of Gottlob Frege.* Oxford: Blackwell.

Fried, C. 1981. *Contract as Promise.* Cambridge, MA: Harvard University Press.

Fuller, L. 1969. *The Morality of Law.* New Haven: Yale University Press.

Fuller, L., and W. Perdue. 1936. 'The Reliance Interest in Contract Damages'. *Yale Law Journal* 46.

Ganz, G. 1986. 'Legitimate Expectation'. In C. Harlow (ed.), *Public Law and Politics.* London, Sweet & Maxwell.

Gaus, G. 1998. 'Why All Welfare States (Including Laissez-Faire Ones) Are Unreasonable'. *Social Philosophy and Policy* 15.

Gauthier, D. 1978. 'The Social Contract as Ideology'. *Philosophy and Public Affairs* 6.

1986. *Morals By Agreement.* Oxford: Clarendon Press.

Geach, P. 1972. *Logic Matters.* Oxford: Blackwell.

Geanakoplos, J. 1992. 'Common Knowledge'. *Journal of Economic Perspectives* 6.

Gellhorn, E. 1986. *Antitrust Law and Economics.* St Paul: West.

Gellhorn, E., and T. Tatham. 1985. 'Making Sense Out of the Rule of Reason'. *Case Western Reserve Law Review* 35.

Gert, B., and C. Culver. 1976. 'Paternalistic Behavior'. *Philosophy and Public Affairs* 6.

Gibbard, A. 1986. 'Interpersonal Comparisons: Preference, Good, and the Intrinsic Reward of a Life'. In Elster and Hylland (1989a).

Giddens, A. 1984. *The Constitution of Society*. Cambridge: Polity Press.

Gilbert, M. 1989. *On Social Facts*. Princeton: Princeton University Press.

1996a. 'Agreements, Coercion, and Obligation'. In Gilbert (1996c).

1996b. 'Is an Agreement an Exchange of Promises?'. In Gilbert (1996c).

1996c. *Living Together*. Lanham: Rowman & Littlefield.

1996d. 'Notes on the Concept of a Social Convention'. In Gilbert (1996c).

1996e. 'On Language and Convention'. In Gilbert (1996c).

1996f. 'Rationality, Coordination, and Convention'. In Gilbert (1996c).

1996g. 'Walking Together: A Paradigmatic Social Phenomenon'. In Gilbert (1996c).

Gilmore, G. 1995. *The Death of Contract*. Columbus: Ohio State University Press.

Glover, J. 1990. *Causing Death and Saving Lives*. Harmondsworth: Penguin.

Goldman, A. 1995. 'Simulation and Interpersonal Utility'. *Ethics* 105.

Goodin, R. 1989. 'Laundering Preferences'. In Elster and Hylland (1989a).

1993. 'Democracy, Preferences and Paternalism'. *Policy Sciences* 26.

Goodman, N. 1973. *Fact, Fiction, and Forecast* (3rd edition). Indianapolis: Bobbs-Merrill.

Gordley, G. 1991. *The Philosophical Origins of Modern Contract Doctrine*. Oxford: Clarendon Press.

Goyder, D. 1998. *EC Competition Law* (3rd edition). Oxford: Oxford University Press.

Greenawalt, K. 1992. *Law and Objectivity*. New York: Oxford University Press.

Grice, H. 1957. 'Meaning'. *Philosophical Review* 67.

Griew, E. 1985. 'Dishonesty: The Objections to Feely and Ghosh'. *Criminal Law Review*.

Griffin, J. 1986. *Well-Being: Its Meaning, Measurement and Moral Importance*. Oxford: Clarendon Press.

1993. 'Against the Taste Model'. In Elster and Roemer (1993a).

2000. 'Welfare Rights'. *Journal of Ethics* 4.

Hahn, F., and M. Hollis. 1979. 'Introduction'. In F. Hahn and M. Hollis (eds.), *Philosophy and Economic Theory*. Oxford: Oxford University Press.

Hammond, A., and R. Penrose. 2001. *Proposed Criminalisation of Cartels in the UK*. London: Office of Fair Trading.

Hammond, P. 1995. 'The Moral Status of Profits and Other Rewards: A Perspective from Modern Welfare Economics'. In R. Cowan and M. Rizzo (eds.), *Profits and Morality*. Chicago: University of Chicago Press.

Hampton, J. 1998. 'Rationality, Practical'. In E. Craig (1998), vol. 8.

Handler, M. 1941. *A Study of the Construction and Enforcement of the Antitrust Laws.* Washington, DC: US GPO, Temporary National Economic Committee.
Hare, R. 1973. 'Principles'. *Proceedings of the Aristotelian Society* 73.
Hargreaves Heap, S., *et al.* 1992. *The Theory of Choice.* Oxford: Blackwell.
Harman, G. 1974. Review of Schiffer (1972). *Journal of Philosophy* 71.
1986. *Change in View.* Cambridge, MA: MIT Press.
Harsanyi, J. 1982. 'Morality and the Theory of Rational Behaviour'. In Sen and Williams (1982).
Hart, H. 1961. *The Concept of Law.* Oxford: Clarendon Press.
1963. *Law, Liberty, and Morality.* Oxford: Oxford University Press.
Hartley, T. 1994. *The Foundations of European Community Law.* Oxford: Clarendon Press.
Harvey, J., *et al.* 1917. *Competition: A Study in Human Motive.* London: Macmillan.
Harvey, P. 1990. *An Introduction to Buddhism.* Cambridge: Cambridge University Press.
2000. *An Introduction to Buddhist Ethics.* Cambridge: Cambridge University Press.
Hausman, D. 1995. 'The Impossibility of Interpersonal Utility Comparisons'. *Mind* 104.
1997. 'The Impossibility of Interpersonal Utility Comparisons – A Reply'. *Mind* 106.
Hausman, D., and M. McPherson. 1993. 'Taking Ethics Seriously: Economics and Contemporary Moral Philosophy'. *Journal of Economic Literature* 31.
1998. 'Economics and Ethics'. In E. Craig (1998), vol. 3.
Hawk, B. 1994. *United States, Common Market and International Antitrust: A Comparative Guide.* Englewood Cliffs: Prentice Hall.
Hayek, F. 1982. *Law, Legislation and Liberty.* London: Routledge & Kegan Paul.
Head, J. 1974a. 'Merit Goods Revisited'. In Head (1974c).
1974b. 'On Merit Goods'. In Head (1974c).
1974c. *Public Goods and Public Welfare.* Durham, NC: Duke University Press.
1978. 'Common Knowledge'. *Philosophical Quarterly* 28.
Hegel, G. 1952. *The Philosophy of Right.* Oxford: Clarendon Press.
Heiner, R. 1986. 'Imperfect Decisions and the Law: On the Evolution of Legal Precedent and Rules'. *Journal of Legal Studies* 15.
Hempel, C. 1983. 'Studies in the Logic of Confirmation'. In Achinstein (1983).
Hertzberg, L. 1988. 'On the Attitude of Trust'. *Inquiry* 31.
Hicks, J. 1981. 'A Manifesto'. In J. Hicks, *Wealth and Welfare.* Cambridge, MA: Harvard University Press.
Hill, T. 1991. *Autonomy and Self-Respect.* Cambridge: Cambridge University Press.
2002a. 'Happiness and Human Flourishing'. In Hill (2002b).
2002b. *Human Welfare and Moral Worth: Kantian Perspectives.* Oxford: Clarendon Press.
2002c. 'Kantian Analysis: From Duty to Autonomy'. In Hill (2000b).

Hobbes, T. 1968. *Leviathan*. Harmondsworth: Penguin Books.

Holton, R. 1994. 'Deciding to Trust, Coming to Believe'. *Australasian Journal of Philosophy* 72.

Hooker, B. 1995. 'Rule-Consequentialism, Incoherence, Fairness'. *Proceedings of the Aristotelian Society* 95.

Houston, B. 1991. 'Showoffs, Achievers, and Rivals'. *Philosophy of Education* 47.

Howerth, I. 1912. 'Competition, Natural and Industrial'. *International Journal of Ethics* 22.

Huizinga, J. 1949. *Homo Ludens*. London: Routledge & Kegan Paul.

Hume, D. 1963. 'Of the Original Contract'. In D. Hume, *Essays, Moral, Political and Literary*. Oxford: Oxford University Press.

Hurka, T. 1993. *Perfectionism*. New York: Oxford University Press.

Hurley, S. 1989. *Natural Reasons*. New York: Oxford University Press.

Hylland, A. 1989. 'The Purpose and Significance of Social Choice Theory: Some General Remarks and an Application to the "Lady Chatterley" Problem'. In Elster and Hylland (1989a).

Inglehart, R. 1996. 'The Diminishing Utility of Economic Growth: From Maximizing Security Toward Maximizing Subjective Well-Being'. *Critical Review* 10.

Johansson, P. 1991. *An Introduction to Modern Welfare Economics*. Cambridge: Cambridge University Press.

Joliet, R. 1967. *The Rule of Reason in Antitrust Law: American, German and Common Market Laws in Comparative Perspective*. The Hague: Nijhoff.

Joshua, J. 2003. 'The UK's New Cartel Offence and Its Implications for EC Competition Law: A Tangled Web'. *European Law Review* 28.

Kagan, S. 1998. *Normative Ethics*. Boulder: Westview Press.

Kahneman, D., and J. Snell. 1990. 'Predicting Utility'. In R. Hogarth (ed.), *Insights in Decision Making*. Chicago: University of Chicago Press.

Kahneman, D., and A. Tversky. 1990. 'Prospect Theory: An Analysis of Decision Under Risk'. In P. Moser (ed.), *Rationality in Action: Contemporary Approaches*. Cambridge: Cambridge University Press.

Kahneman, D., and C. Varey. 1993. 'Notes on the Psychology of Utility'. In Elster and Roemer (1993a).

Kane, R. 1974. *Through the Moral Maze: Searching for Absolute Values in a Pluralistic World*. New York: Paragon House.

Katz, A., and L. Teitelbaum. 1978. 'PINS Jurisdiction, the Vagueness Doctrine, and the Rule of Law'. *Indiana Law Journal* 53.

Kavka, G. 1986. *Hobbesian Moral and Political Theory*. Princeton: Princeton University Press.

Kawall, J. 1999. 'The Experience Machine and Mental-State Theories of Well-Being'. *Journal of Value Inquiry* 33.

Kay, J. 2003. *The Truth About Markets*. London: Penguin Books.

Keating, J. 1964. 'Sportsmanship as a Moral Category'. *Ethics* 75.

Keita, L. 1999. 'Welfare Economics and Positive Neoclassical Economics'. *Journal of Value Inquiry* 33.

Kelly, M. 1992. 'The Phantom Reliance Interest in Contract Damages'. *Wisconsin Law Review*.

Kelman, M. 1987. *A Guide to Critical Legal Studies*. Cambridge, MA: Harvard University Press.

Kelman, S. 1981. 'Regulation and Paternalism'. *Public Policy* 29.

Kemmerling, A. 1986. 'Utterer's Meaning Revisited'. In R. Grandy and R. Warner (eds.), *Philosophical Grounds of Rationality: Intentions, Categories, Ends*. Oxford: Oxford University Press.

Kennedy, D. 1973. 'Legal Formality'. *Journal of Legal Studies* 2.

1976. 'Form and Substance in Private Law Adjudication'. *Harvard Law Review* 89.

Kew, F. 1978. 'Values in Competitive Games'. *Quest* 29.

Kim, J. 1971. 'Causes and Events: Mackie on Causation'. *Journal of Philosophy* 68.

Kim, K. 1991. 'Does Competition Lead to Improved Quality in Education?' *Philosophy of Education* 47.

Klein, P. 1976. 'Knowledge, Causality, and Defeasibility'. *Journal of Philosophy* 73.

Kleinig, J. 1982. *Philosophical Issues in Education*. London: Croom Helm.

Kluge, E. 1991. 'Competition and Function: The Canada–US Free Trade Agreement and the Philosophy of Health Care'. *Business and Professional Ethics Journal* 10.

Knapp, C. 1984. 'The Promise of the Future – and Vice Versa: Some Reflections on the Metamorphosis of Contract Law'. *Michigan Law Review* 82.

Knight, F. 1956. *On the History and Method of Economics*. Chicago: Chicago University Press.

Kohn, A. 1992. *No Contest* (revised edition). Boston, MA: Houghton Mifflin.

Kolnai, A. 1965. 'Games and Aims'. *Proceedings of the Aristotelian Society* 66.

Korah, V. 1986. 'EEC Competition Policy – Legal Form or Economic Efficiency'. *Current Legal Problems* 39.

Korsgaard, C. 1996. *Creating the Kingdom of Ends*. Cambridge: Cambridge University Press.

Kymlicka, W. 2002. *Contemporary Political Philosophy: An Introduction* (2nd edition). Oxford: Oxford University Press.

Lagenspetz, O. 1992. 'Legitimacy and Trust'. *Philosophical Investigations* 15.

Lane, R. 1994. 'Quality of Life and Quality of Persons: A New Role for Government?' *Political Theory* 22.

Larmore, C. 1987. *Patterns of Moral Complexity*. Cambridge: Cambridge University Press.

Leibenstein, H. 1980. *Beyond Economic Man: A New Foundation for Microeconomics*. Cambridge, MA: Harvard University Press.

Leibniz, G. 1875–90. *Philosophische Schriften.* Leipzig: Gerhardt.

Lentz, T., and R. Cornelius. 1950. 'All Together: A Manual of Cooperative Games'. Photocopy. Attitude Research Laboratory, St Louis, MO.

Lever, J. 1969. 'Bipartite Arrangements and the Restrictive Trades Practices Acts 1956 and 1968'. *Law Quarterly Review* 85.

Levmore, S. (ed.). 1994. *Foundations of Tort Law.* New York: Oxford University Press.

Lewis, C., and C. Langford. 1959. *Symbolic Logic* (2nd edition). New York: Dover Publications.

Lewis, D. 1969. *Convention: A Philosophical Study.* Cambridge, MA: Harvard University Press.

1973. *Counterfactuals.* Oxford: Blackwell.

1989. 'Dispositional Theories of Value'. *Proceedings of the Aristotelian Society*, Supplementary Volume 63.

Lieberman, M. 1998. *Commitment, Value, and Moral Realism.* Cambridge: Cambridge University Press.

Lipsey, R. 1989. *An Introduction to Positive Economics* (7th edition). London: Weidenfeld and Nicolson.

Lipsey, R., and K. Lancaster. 1956. 'The General Theory of Second Best'. *Review of Economic Studies* 24.

Little, D. 1957. *A Critique of Welfare Economics* (2nd edition). Oxford: Oxford University Press.

Loar, B. 1981. *Mind and Meaning.* Cambridge: Cambridge University Press.

Lomasky, L. 1987. *Persons, Rights, and the Moral Community.* Oxford: Oxford University Press.

2000. 'Liberty and Welfare Goods: Reflections on Clashing Liberalisms'. *Journal of Ethics* 4.

Luce, R., and H. Raiffa. 1985. *Games and Decisions.* New York: Dover Publications.

Luschen, G. 1970. 'Cooperation, Association and Contest'. *Journal of Conflict Resolution* 14.

Lyon, L., *et al.* 1939. *Government and Economic Life.* Washington, DC: Brookings Institution.

Lyons, D. 1965. *Forms and Limits of Utilitarianism.* Oxford: Clarendon Press.

1994. 'Benevolence and Justice in Mill'. In D. Lyons, *Rights, Welfare, and Mill's Moral Theory.* New York: Oxford University Press.

MacCallum, G. 1993. 'Competition and Moral Philosophy'. In G. MacCallum, *Legislative Intent and Other Essays on Law, Politics, and Morality.* Madison: University of Wisconsin Press.

MacCormick, N. 1972. 'Voluntary Obligations and Normative Powers (I)'. *Proceedings of the Aristotelian Society*, Supplementary Volume 46.

1982. *Legal Right and Social Democracy.* Oxford: Clarendon Press.

MacCulloch, A. 2003. 'The Cartel Offence and the Criminalisation of United Kingdom Competition Law'. *Journal of Business Law*, November 2003.

MacDonald, K., and R. Thompson. 2003. 'Dishonest Agreements'. *Competition Law Journal* 2.

Mack, R. 1965. 'The Components of Social Conflict'. *Social Problems* 22.

Mackie, J. 1974. *The Cement of the Universe*. Oxford: Oxford University Press.

McMahon, C. 1989. 'Promising and Coordination'. *American Philosophical Quarterly* 26.

McMurtry, J. 1984. 'Free Enterprise, Rationality and Competition'. *Journal of Business Ethics* 3.

1991. 'How Competition Goes Wrong'. *Journal of Applied Philosophy* 8.

McNaughton, D. 1998. 'Consequentialism'. In E. Craig (1998), vol. 2.

McNaughton, D., and P. Rawling. 2001. 'Achievement, Welfare and Consequentialism'. *Analysis* 61.

Malina, M., and R. Steuer. 1991. 'Trial Lawyers and ARCO: Jurisprudentially Inconsistent Approaches to Per Se Illegality'. *Fordham Law Review* 59.

Martin, J. 1985. *Hanbury and Maudsley: Modern Equity* (12th edition). London: Stevens & Sons.

Mason, E. 1939. 'Price and Production Policies of Large-Scale Enterprise'. *American Economic Review* 29.

May, M., and L. Doob. 1937. *Cooperation and Competition*. New York: Social Science Research Council.

Mead, M. 2003. *Cooperation and Competition Among Primitive Peoples*. New Brunswick: Transaction Publishers.

Meakin, D. 1986. 'The Moral Status of Competition: An Issue of Concern for Physical Educators'. *Journal of Philosophy of Education* 20.

Michelman, J. 1983. 'Some Ethical Consequences of Economic Competition'. *Journal of Business Ethics* 2.

Milgrom, P. 1981. 'An Axiomatic Characterization of Common Knowledge'. *Econometrica* 49.

Mill, J. 1972a. *Utilitarianism*. London: Dent.

1972b. *On Liberty*. London: Dent.

Miller, D. 1976. *Social Justice*. Oxford: Clarendon Press.

Miller, H., and W. Williams (eds.). 1982. *The Limits of Utilitarianism*. Minneapolis: University of Minnesota Press.

Miller, S. 1992. 'Joint Action'. *Philosophical Papers* 21.

Millgram, E. 2000. 'What's the Use of Utility?' *Philosophy and Public Affairs* 29.

Moore, A. 2000. 'Objective Human Goods'. In Crisp and Hooker (2000).

Moore, A., and R. Crisp. 1996. 'Welfarism in Moral Theory'. *Australasian Journal of Philosophy* 74.

Moore, G. 1959. *Principia Ethica*. Cambridge: Cambridge University Press.

Morris, C. 1991. 'Some Notes on "Reliance"'. *Minnesota Law Review* 75.

1996. 'Well-Being, Reasons, and the Politics of Law'. *Ethics* 106.

Munzer, S. 1998. 'Property'. In E. Craig (1998), vol. 7.

Musgrave, R. 1959. *The Theory of Public Finance*. New York: McGraw-Hill.

Nash, J. 1950. 'The Bargaining Problem'. *Econometrica* 18.

Naylor, F. 1975. 'Comprehensive Mythology'. In D. Cox and R. Boyson (eds.), *Black Paper 1975*. London: Dent.

Neale, A., and D. Goyder. 1980. *The Antitrust Laws of the USA: A Study of Competition Enforced by Law*. Cambridge: Cambridge University Press.

New, B. 1999. 'Paternalism and Public Policy'. *Economics and Philosophy* 15.

Nielsen, L. 1984. 'Common Knowledge, Communication, and Convergence of Beliefs'. *Mathematical Social Sciences* 8.

Nove, A. 1983. *The Economics of Feasible Socialism*. London: George Allen & Unwin.

Nozick, R. 1974. *Anarchy, State, and Utopia*. Oxford: Blackwell.

Nussbaum, M., and A. Sen (eds.). 1993. *The Quality of Life*. Oxford: Clarendon Press.

Odudu, O. 2001a. 'Interpreting Article 81(1): Object as Subjective Intention'. *European Law Review* 26.

2001b. 'Interpreting Article 81(1): The Object Requirement Revisited'. *European Law Review* 26.

Office of Fair Trading. 2003a. *Market Investigation References (Guidance About the Making of References Under Part 4 of the Enterprise Act)*. London: Office of Fair Trading.

2003b. *Mergers: Substantive Assessment Guidance*. London: Office of Fair Trading.

Ong, W. 1981. *Fighting for Life*. Ithaca: Cornell University Press.

Oppenheim, C., G. Weston and T. McCarthy (eds.). 1981. *Federal Antitrust Laws: Cases, Text, and Commentary*. St Paul: West.

Overvold, M. 1980. 'Self-Interest and the Concept of Self-Sacrifice'. *Canadian Journal of Philosophy* 10.

1982. 'Self-Interest and Getting What You Want'. In Miller and Williams (1982).

Parfit, D. 1984. *Reasons and Persons*. Oxford: Clarendon Press.

1997. 'Reasons and Motivation'. *Proceedings of the Aristotelian Society*, Supplementary Volume 71.

Parikh, R., and P. Krasucki. 1990. 'Communication, Consensus and Knowledge'. *Journal of Economic Theory* 52.

Patterson, D. 1992. 'The Value of a Promise'. *Law and Philosophy* 11.

Peacocke, C. 1979. *Holistic Explanation*. Oxford: Clarendon Press.

Peretz, G., and J. Lewis. 2003. 'Go Directly to Jail: Losing Badly in "Monopoly"'. *New Law Journal*, 24 January 2003.

Perry, L. 1975. 'Competition and Cooperation'. *British Journal of Educational Studies* 23.

Pettit, P. 1998. 'Desire'. In E. Craig (1998), vol. 3.

Phlips, L. 1995. *Competition Policy: A Game-Theoretic Perspective.* Cambridge: Cambridge University Press.

Pietroski, P. 1993. 'Prima Facie Obligations, Ceteris Paribus Laws in Moral Theory'. *Ethics* 103.

Pigou, A. 2002. *The Economics of Welfare.* New Brunswick: Transaction Publishers.

Piraino, T. 1991. 'Reconciling the Per Se Rule and Rule of Reason Approaches to Antitrust Analysis'. *Southern California Law Review* 64.

1994. 'Making Sense of the Rule of Reason: A New Standard for Section 1 of the Sherman Act'. *Vanderbilt Law Review* 47.

Plant, R. 1991. *Modern Political Thought.* Malden, MA: Blackwell.

Posner, R. 1979. 'Utilitarianism, Economics, and Legal Theory'. *Journal of Legal Studies* 8.

1986. *Economic Analysis of Law.* Boston: Little, Brown.

1994. 'The Concept of Corrective Justice in Recent Theories of Tort Law'. In Levmore (1994).

2001. *Antitrust Law* (2nd edition). Chicago: University of Chicago Press.

Postow, B. 1980. 'A Possible Ground of Political Obligation'. *Southern Journal of Philosophy* 18.

Prichard, H. 1949a. 'Exchanging'. In Prichard (1949b).

1949b. *Moral Obligation.* Oxford: Clarendon Press.

1949c. 'The Obligation to Keep a Promise'. In Prichard (1949b).

1949d. 'The Time of an Obligation'. In Prichard (1949b).

Prvulovich, Z. 1982. 'In Defence of Competition'. *Journal of Philosophy of Education* 16.

Putnam, H. 1994. *Words and Life.* Cambridge, MA: Harvard University Press.

Qizilbash, M. 1997. 'Well-Being and Despair: Dante's Ugolino'. *Utilitas* 9.

1998. 'The Concept of Well-Being'. *Economics and Philosophy* 14.

Radford, C. 1966. 'Knowledge – By Examples'. *Analysis* 27.

1984. 'I Will, If You Will'. *Mind* 93.

Rappoport, A., and C. Orwant. 1964. 'Experimental Games: A Review'. In M. Shubik (ed.), *Game Theory and Related Approaches to Social Behavior.* New York: Wiley.

Rawls, J. 1967. 'Two Concepts of Rules'. In Foot (1967).

1972. *A Theory of Justice.* Oxford: Oxford University Press.

1982. 'Social Unity and Primary Goods'. In Sen and Williams (1982).

1993. *Political Liberalism.* New York: Columbia University Press.

Raz, J. 1972. 'Voluntary Obligations and Normative Powers (II)'. *Proceedings of the Aristotelian Society*, Supplementary Volume 46.

1977. 'Promises and Obligations'. In P. Hacker and J. Raz (eds.), *Law Morality, and Society.* Oxford: Clarendon Press.

1979. *The Authority of Law.* Oxford: Clarendon Press.

1984. 'On the Nature of Rights'. *Mind* 93.

1986. *The Morality of Freedom*. Oxford: Clarendon Press.
1994a. 'Duties of Well-Being'. In Raz (1994b).
1994b. *Ethics in the Public Domain: Essays in the Morality of Law and Politics*. Oxford: Clarendon Press.
1994c. 'Liberalism, Scepticism, and Democracy'. In Raz (1994b).
1994d. 'Liberating Duties'. In Raz (1994b).
1994e. 'Rights and Individual Well-Being'. In Raz (1994b).
Reath, A. 1998. 'Autonomy, Ethical'. In E. Craig (1998), vol. 1.
Rees, R. 1993. 'Tacit Collusion'. *Oxford Review of Economic Policy* 9.
Reeve, S. 1906. *The Cost of Competition*. New York: McClure, Phillips.
Regan, D. 1985. 'On Preferences and Promises: A Response to Harsanyi'. *Ethics* 96.
Rich, J. 1988. 'Competition in Education'. *Educational Theory* 38.
Robins, M. 1984. *Promising, Intending, and Moral Autonomy*. New York: Cambridge University Press.
Roemer, J. 1996. *Theories of Distributive Justice*. Cambridge, MA: Harvard University Press.
Rogers, W. 1994. *Winfield & Jolowicz on Tort* (14th edition). London: Sweet & Maxwell.
Rotenstreich, N. 1972. 'On Confidence'. *Philosophy* 47.
Roth, P. (ed.). 2001. *Bellamy and Child: European Community Law of Competition* (5th edition). London: Sweet & Maxwell.
Russell, B. 1951. *New Hopes for a Changing World*. London: George Allen & Unwin.
Sainsbury, M. 1990. *Concepts Without Boundaries*. London: King's College London.
Samuelson, P. 1970. *Foundations of Economic Analysis*. New York: Atheneum.
Sartorius, R. (ed.). 1983. *Paternalism*. St Paul: University of Minnesota Press.
Scanlan, G. 2002. 'Dishonesty in Corporate Offences: A Need for Reform'. *Company Lawyer* 23.
Scanlon, T. 1972. 'A Theory of Freedom of Expression'. *Philosophy and Public Affairs* 1.
1975. 'Preference and Urgency'. *Journal of Philosophy* 72.
1990. 'Promises and Practices'. *Philosophy and Public Affairs* 19.
1993a. 'The Moral Basis of Interpersonal Comparisons'. In Elster and Roemer (1993a).
1993b. 'Value, Desire, and Quality of Life'. In Nussbaum and Sen (1993).
1998. *What We Owe to Each Other*. Cambridge, MA: Belknap Press.
2001. 'Promises and Contracts'. In Benson (2001a).
Schauer, F. 1991a. 'Exceptions'. *University of Chicago Law Review* 58.
1991b. *Playing by the Rules*. Oxford: Clarendon Press.
Schechter, M. 1982. 'The Rule of Reason in European Competition Law'. *Legal Issues in European Integration* 1982.
Schelling, T. 1980. *The Strategy of Conflict* (2nd edition). Cambridge, MA: Harvard University Press.

Scherer, F., and D. Ross. 1990. *Industrial Market Structure and Economic Performance* (3rd edition). Boston: Houghton Mifflin.

Scherer, M. 1987. 'Making the Rule of Reason Analysis More Manageable'. *Antitrust Law Journal* 56.

Schiffer, S. 1972. *Meaning*. Oxford: Oxford University Press.

1987. *Remnants of Meaning*. Cambridge, MA: MIT Press.

Schneewind, J. 1986. 'The Use of Autonomy in Ethical Theory'. In T. Heller *et al.* (eds.), *Reconstructing Individualism: Autonomy, Individuality, and the Self in Western Thought*. Stanford: Stanford University Press.

Schneider, C. 1995. 'From Consumer Choice to Consumer Welfare'. *Hastings Center Report*, Special Supplement 25.

Schopenhauer, A. 1951. 'The Vanity of Existence'. In A. Schopenhauer, *Essays from the Parerga and Paralipomena*. London: George Allen & Unwin.

Schumacher, E. 1973. *Small Is Beautiful: A Study of Economics as if People Mattered*. London: Blond & Briggs.

Schumpeter, J. 1975. *Capitalism, Socialism and Democracy*. New York: HarperPerennial.

Schwarze, J. 1992. *European Administrative Law*. London: Sweet & Maxwell.

Scitovsky, T. 1981. 'The Desire for Excitement in Modern Society'. *Kyklos* 34.

1992. *The Joyless Economy: The Psychology of Human Satisfaction* (revised edition). New York: Oxford University Press.

Scoccia, D. 1987. 'Autonomy, Want Satisfaction, and the Justification of Liberal Freedoms'. *Canadian Journal of Philosophy* 17.

Searle, J. 1967. 'How to Derive "Ought" from "Is"'. In Foot (1967).

1968. 'Prima Facie Obligations'. In J. Raz (ed.), *Practical Reasoning*. Oxford: Oxford University Press.

Seel, M. 1997. 'Well-Being: On a Fundamental Concept of Practical Philosophy'. *European Journal of Philosophy* 5.

Sen, A. 1981. 'Plural Utility'. *Proceedings of the Aristotelian Society* 81.

1982a. 'Behaviour and the Concept of Preference'. In Sen (1982c).

1982b. 'Choice, Orderings and Morality'. In Sen (1982c).

1982c. *Choice, Welfare and Measurement*. Cambridge, MA: Harvard University Press.

1982d. 'Equality of What?' In Sen (1982c).

1982e. 'The Impossibility of a Paretian Liberal'. In Sen (1982c).

1982f. 'Interpersonal Aggregation and Partial Comparability'. In Sen (1982c).

1982g. 'Interpersonal Comparisons of Welfare'. In Sen (1982c).

1982h. 'Introduction'. In Sen (1982c).

1982i. 'Liberty, Unanimity and Rights'. In Sen (1982c).

1982j. 'Personal Utilities and Public Judgments: Or What's Wrong with Welfare Economics?' In Sen (1982c).

1982k. 'Rational Fools: A Critique of the Behavioural Foundations of Economic Theory'. In Sen (1982c).

1985. 'Well-Being, Agency and Freedom: The Dewey Lectures 1984'. *Journal of Philosophy* 82.

1993. 'Capability and Well-Being'. In Nussbaum and Sen (1993).

2002a. 'Freedom and Social Choice: The Arrow Lectures'. In Sen (2002i).

2002b. 'Individual Preference as the Basis of Social Choice'. In Sen (2002i).

2002c. 'Internal Consistency of Choice'. In Sen (2002i).

2002d. 'Introduction: Rationality and Freedom'. In Sen (2002i).

2002e. 'Markets and Freedoms'. In Sen (2002i).

2002f. 'Maximisation and the Act of Choice'. In Sen (2002i).

2002g. 'Non-Binary Choice and Preference'. In Sen (2002i).

2002h. 'The Possibility of Social Choice'. In Sen (2002i).

2002i. *Rationality and Freedom*. Cambridge, MA: Belknap Press.

2002j. 'Rationality and Uncertainty'. In Sen (2002i).

Sen, A., and B. Williams (eds.). 1982. *Utilitarianism and Beyond*. Cambridge: Cambridge University Press.

Shafer-Landau, R. 1995. 'Vagueness, Borderline Cases and Moral Realism'. *American Philosophical Quarterly* 32.

Shah, R. 1995. 'Estoppel and Legitimate Expectation'. *New Law Journal*, 3 November 1995.

Sidgwick, H. 1907. *The Methods of Ethics* (7th edition). London: Macmillan.

Simmel, G. 1955. *Conflict and the Web of Group-Affiliations*. New York: The Free Press.

Simmons, A. 1981. 'Reasonable Expectations and Obligations: A Reply to Postow'. *Southern Journal of Philosophy* 19.

Simon, H. 1982. *Models of Bounded Rationality*. Cambridge, MA: MIT Press.

Singer, P. 1972. 'Altruism and Commerce: A Defence of Titmuss Against Arrow'. *Philosophy and Public Affairs* 2.

Singh, R. 1994. 'Making Legitimate Use of Legitimate Expectation'. *New Law Journal*, 9 September 1994.

Skorupski, J. 2000. 'Quality of Well-Being: Quality of Being'. In Crisp and Hooker (2000).

Smart, J. 1973. 'An Outline of a System of Utilitarian Ethics'. In J. Smart and B. Williams, *Utilitarianism: For and Against*. Cambridge: Cambridge University Press.

Smith, J. 2002. *Smith & Hogan: Criminal Law* (10th edition). London: Butterworths.

Smith, M. 1994. *The Moral Problem*. Oxford: Blackwell.

Smith, N. (ed.). 1982. *Mutual Knowledge*. London: Academic Press.

Soames, T. 1996. 'An Analysis of the Principles of Concerted Practice and Collective Dominance: A Distinction without a Difference?' *European Competition Law Review* 17.

Sobel, D. 1994. 'Full Information Accounts of Well-Being'. Ethics 104.

1998. 'Well-Being as the Object of Moral Consideration'. *Economics and Philosophy* 14.
Stalnaker, R. 1991. 'A Theory of Conditionals'. In F. Jackson (ed.), *Conditionals*. Oxford: Oxford University Press.
Stocker, M. 1992. *Plural and Conflicting Values*. Oxford: Clarendon Press.
Stoljar, S. 1988. 'Promise, Expectation and Agreement'. *Cambridge Law Journal* 47.
Strasser, M. 1985. 'Dependence, Reliance and Abortion'. *Philosophical Quarterly* 35.
Strawson, P. 1971. 'Intention and Convention in Speech Acts'. In J. Searle (ed.), *The Philosophy of Language*. Oxford: Oxford University Press.
Sullivan, L. 1977. *Handbook of the Law of Antitrust*. St Paul: West.
1987. 'The Viability of the Current Law on Horizontal Restraints'. *California Law Review* 75.
Sumner, L. 1996. *Welfare, Happiness, and Ethics*. Oxford: Clarendon Press.
Taggart, M. 1996. 'Legitimate Expectation and Treaties in the High Court of Australia'. *Law Quarterly Review* 112.
Tännsjö, T. 1996. 'Classical Hedonistic Utilitarianism'. *Philosophical Studies* 81.
Taylor, S., and J. Mansell. 2003. 'White-Collar Crime – Caught in the Act'. *Legal Week* 5.
Thompson, G. 1972. 'Effects of Cooperation and Competition on Public Learning'. *Educational Research* (British) 15.
Thompson, M. 1983. 'From Representation to Expectation: Estoppel as a Cause of Action'. *Cambridge Law Journal* 42.
Thomson, J. 1994. 'Remarks on Causation and Liability'. In Levmore (1994).
Titmuss, R. 1971. *The Gift Relationship: From Human Blood to Social Policy*. London: Pantheon.
Treitel, G. 1995. *The Law of Contract* (9th edition). London: Sweet & Maxwell.
Tuomela, R. 1995. *The Importance of Us*. Stanford: Stanford University Press.
Tversky, A. 1981. 'Choice, Preference and Welfare: Some Psychological Observations'. Paper presented at a colloquium on 'Foundations of Social Choice Theory', Ustaoset (Norway).
Ullmann-Margalit, E. 1977. *The Emergence of Norms*. Oxford: Clarendon Press.
Unger, P. 1996. *Living High and Letting Die: Our Illusion of Innocence*. New York: Oxford University Press.
VanDeVeer, D. 1986. *Paternalistic Intervention: The Moral Bounds of Benevolence*. Princeton: Princeton University Press.
Van Praag, B. 1993. 'The Relativity of the Welfare Concept'. In Nussbaum and Sen (1993).
Varian, H. 1978. *Microeconomic Analysis*. New York: Norton.
Velleman, D. 2000a. 'Deciding How to Decide'. In Velleman (2000c).
2000b. 'How to Share an Intention'. In Velleman (2000c).
2000c. *The Possibility of Practical Reason*. Oxford: Clarendon Press.
Vickers, J. 1995. 'Concepts of Competition'. *Oxford Economic Papers* 47.

Warnock, G. 1971. *The Object of Morality.* London: Methuen.

Weale, A. 1978. 'Paternalism and Social Policy'. *Journal of Social Policy* 7.

1998. 'Welfare'. In E. Craig (1998), vol. 9.

Weinstein, N. 1982. 'Community Noise Problems: Evidence Against Adaptation'. *Journal of Environmental Psychology* 2.

Weintraub, R. 1996. 'The Impossibility of Interpersonal Utility Comparisons: A Critical Note'. *Mind* 105.

1998. 'Do Utility Comparisons Pose a Problem?' *Philosophical Studies* 92.

Wertheimer, B. 1984. 'Rethinking the Rule of Reason: From Professional Engineers to NCAA'. *Duke Law Journal.*

Whish, R. 1993. *Competition Law* (3rd edition). London, Butterworths.

2003. *Competition Law* (5th edition). London: LexisNexis UK.

Whish, R., and B. Sufrin. 1987. 'Article 85 and the Rule of Reason'. *Oxford Yearbook of European Law* 1987.

Williams, B. 1978. *Descartes: The Project of Pure Enquiry.* Harmondsworth: Penguin Books.

1985. *Ethics and the Limits of Philosophy.* London: Fontana.

2002. *Truth and Truthfulness.* Princeton: Princeton University Press.

Williams, G. 1983. *Textbook of Criminal Law* (2nd edition). London: Stevens & Sons.

Williamson, T. 1994. *Vagueness.* London: Routledge.

Wilson, J. 1989. 'Competition'. *Journal of Moral Education* 18.

Wolff, J. Unpublished. 'Libertarianism, Utility and Economic Competition'.

Wood Hutchinson, D. 1984. 'Antitrust 1984: Five Decisions in Search of a Theory'. *The Supreme Court Review* 1984.

Woozley, A. 1981. 'Promises, Promises'. *Mind* 90.

Young, R. 1980. 'Autonomy and the Inner Self'. *American Philosophical Quarterly* 17.

INDEX

For EU product safety concerns, contact us at Calle de José Abascal, 56–1°, 28003 Madrid, Spain or eugpsr@cambridge.org.

www.ingramcontent.com/pod-product-compliance
Lightning Source LLC
LaVergne TN
LVHW090355210926
848480LV00002B/351
* 9 7 8 0 5 2 1 1 4 2 0 7 6 *